ON PHILOSOPHY

ON PHILOSOPHY

NOTES FROM A CRISIS

JOHN McCUMBER

STANFORD UNIVERSITY PRESS

STANFORD, CALIFORNIA

6/11/13
WN
$ 25 –

Stanford University Press
Stanford, California

Printed in the United States of America on acid-free, archival-quality paper

Library of Congress Cataloging-in-Publication Data

McCumber, John, author.

On philosophy : notes from a crisis / John McCumber.
  pages cm
Includes bibliographical references and index.
ISBN 978-0-8047-8142-8 (cloth : alk. paper) — ISBN 978-0-8047-8143-5 (pbk. : alk. paper)
1. Philosophy, Modern—History. 2. Reason. 3. Metaphysics. I. Title.
B791.M44 2012
191—dc23

                    2012014037

Typeset by Bruce Lundquist in 10/14 Minion Pro

In memory of David Laflin McCumber 1947–1994

CONTENTS

ACKNOWLEDGMENTS

I am indebted to Emily-Jane Cohen for her guidance at Stanford University Press, and to Amy Allen for feedback on the manuscript. An anonymous reader for the press was also very helpful. Conversations with Jonathan McCumber taught me much about David Foster Wallace.

Parts of this book descend from lectures given at the American Catholic Philosophical Association, Boston University, California State University at Los Angeles, DePaul University, Emory University, Haverford College, John Carroll University, Pomona College, the Radical Philosophy Association, SPEP, Suffolk University, Swarthmore College, Texas A&M University, and the University of North Texas. I am grateful for the generous hearing and critical feedback I received in each case.

ABBREVIATIONS

APA American Philosophical Association

AA Immanuel Kant, *Werke*

BT Martin Heidegger, *Being and Time* (marginal pagination)

CJ Immanuel Kant, *Critique of Judgment*, cited after *AA*, vol. 5

CPR Immanuel Kant, *Critique of Pure Reason*, cited after *AA*

CPrR Immanuel Kant, *Critique of Practical Reason*, cited after AA, vol. 5

CW John McCumber, *The Company of Words: Hegel, Language, and Systematic Philosophy*

DOe René Descartes, *Oeuvres*

FFO Iris Marion Young, "Five Faces of Oppression"

FR Paul Rabinow, ed., *The Foucault Reader*

GM Friedrich Nietzsche, *On the Genealogy of Morality*

GT Judith Butler, *Gender Trouble*

HWe G. W. F. Hegel, *Werke*

IJ David Foster Wallace, *Infinite Jest*

IM Robert Pippin, *Idealism as Modernism*

IP Avner Cohen and Marcelo Dascal, eds., *The Institution of Philosophy: A Discipline in Crisis?*

MESM Cynthia Willett, *Maternal Ethics and Other Slave Moralities*

MO John McCumber, *Metaphysics and Oppression*

MR Genevieve Lloyd, *The Man of Reason*

NFD Frederick Douglass, *Narrative of the Life of Frederick Douglass, an American Slave*

NE Aristotle, *Nicomachean Ethics*; cited after Bekker edition

OWA Martin Heidegger, "The Origin of the Work of Art"

PF	John McCumber, *Philosophy and Freedom*
PhR	G. W. F. Hegel, *Elements of the Philosophy of Right*
PhS	G. W. F. Hegel, *Phenomenology of Spirit*
PI	John McCumber, *Poetic Interaction*
QT	Martin Heidegger, "The Question Concerning Technology"
R	Martin Heidegger, *Die Selbstbehauptung der deutschen Universität / Das Rektorat: 1933/34*
RC	Charles Mills, *The Racial Contract*
RR	John McCumber, *Reshaping Reason*
SC	Carole Pateman, *The Sexual Contract*
SG	Arthur Fine, *The Shaky Game: Einstein, Realism, and the Quantum Theory*
SL	G. W. F. Hegel, *Science of Logic*
SSI	Sandra Harding, *Science and Social Inequality*
TD	John McCumber, *Time in the Ditch*

Further Notes on the Texts

Works of Aristotle will be cited after *Aristotelis opera edidit Academia Regia Borussica*, ed. Immanuel Bekker (Berlin, 1831–1870) [Bekker edition].

Works of Descartes will be cited after *Oeuvres de Descartes*, ed. Charles Adam and Paul Tannery, 12 vols. (Paris: Cerf, 1897–1910).

Works of Kant will be cited by volume and page number of the Berlin Academy edition, *Werke*, 28 vols. (Berlin, 1902–) [hereinafter *AA*, except for the *Critique of Pure Reason* (*CPR*), which will be cited by page numbers to the "A" and "B" editions in the Academy edition. The *Critique of Judgment* (*CJ*) and the *Critique of Practical Reason* (*CPrR*) are in volume 5 of the Academy edition.

Works of Plato will be cited after *Platonis opera quae extante omnia*, ed. Henri Estienne (Paris, 1578) [Stephanus edition].

All translations unless otherwise noted are my own.

ON PHILOSOPHY

INTRODUCTION

A little over twenty years ago, according to a 1989 anthology edited by Avner Cohen and Marcelo Dascal, there may have been a crisis in philosophy. Such, they suggest, occurs when "dissidents question the accepted standards on all fronts" (*IP*, xiii), and at that time two main challenges appeared to be under-way. Globally, the rise of postmodernism was throwing into doubt both the meaning and the usefulness of such accepted normative terms as "truth," "reason," "freedom," and "progress." Within philosophy itself, at least within American philosophy, the "pluralist revolt" at the American Philosophical Association (APA) was challenging the clubby practices by which leadership roles were distributed among professors in leading departments of philosophy.

I will say more about postmodernism in the course of this book. As to the pluralists, I will simply note that their revolt was consciously modeled on the larger revolt of people of color, nonheterosexuals, and women which, by that time, had already been underway for about twenty-five years. The pluralists claimed, as A. J. Mandt shows in his essay in the anthology (Mandt 1989), that they were being adversely judged not on the basis of their philosophical merits as individuals but on the basis of philosophical groupings to which they belonged (e.g., phenomenologists, pragmatists, Catholics). The response of the philosophical establishment to the pluralists, as Mandt conveys it, was very like establishment responses to those earlier demands: a denial that anyone in a position of power was personally prejudiced against such groups, coupled with a self-reassuring insistence that philosophical rewards were in fact distributed solely in terms of philosophical merit. A paraphrase of Saul Bellow's famous remark on African writers captures the spirit: "When they produce [Quines and Davidsons], we will read them."[1]

The crisis died away, as crises tend to do in tenured professions. The pluralists began electing people to offices at the APA, and the postmodernists drifted off to other departments. Twenty years after, reports on philosophy are good.

Crisis as Separation: Scraps on the Wind

And yet, occasionally, there are things . . . scraps on the wind which land in your office and suggest that, on some levels and in some ways, some things may be missing from this picture. Permit me to mention a few that have come my way. The recital will be depressing, but it is necessary to the coming diagnosis.

Some scraps blow in from the Internet, which tells me that mainstream philosophers no longer win the most prestigious fellowships.[2] Philosopher Jason Stanley may thus be right when he says that "the great figures of American philosophy, lauded the world over, are passed over within the American academy." It may even be a matter not of neglect but of downright ostracism: Stanley has it that "we [philosophers] are ignored at dinner parties, and considered arrogant and perhaps uncouth."[3]

It has been a long time since I have seen a philosopher at a dinner party, so I am unable to confirm Stanley's point. I do know that other humanists are not very happy about the current crisis in the academic economy (or the general economy), and their problems are shared by philosophy. A visit to the web page of the APA recently yielded the news that there were not enough available jobs to justify printing the May 7, 2010, edition of *Jobs for Philosophers*; there were protests on that same site against the projected closing of philosophy departments at two universities in England.[4] A few months later (November 18, 2010), the APA reported that "only one NEH Summer Seminar for College and University teachers in Philosophy has been awarded for 2011." But how many were awarded in all fields that year?

So it seems that while philosophy shares the general problems inevitably encountered by the humanities in a science-based culture, its unique problems are restricted to social occasions. Away from the dinner parties, deep within the admittedly troubled academy, philosophy departments function as smoothly, or as bumpily, as ever. Philosophers (or their graduate assistants) teach basic argumentative writing to undergraduates, often to great numbers of them, and generally these students do well on GREs, LSATs, and the like. Philosophers also teach logical analysis, and sometimes deconstruction, to graduate students, and occasionally those graduate students get jobs. Disputes arise among philosophers, to be sure—philosophical, academic, personal, and otherwise. Some get resolved, others fester, and none of them matter very much to outsiders. But all in all, philosophy does its job. Twenty years after Cohen and Dascal, all's quiet on the philosophical front—or, to adapt Remarque's original German title, *In der Philosophie nichts neues.*

This sounds more like doldrums than a crisis; but what, exactly, is a crisis? According to legend, the Chinese character for "crisis" is composed of the character for "danger" plus the character for "opportunity." So understood, a crisis is a moment of indeterminacy, of decisively open future. This is the temporal sense conveyed by the medical heritage of the term in English, in which it denotes a sudden change of course, for better or worse, in the progress of a disease. But there is another, older sense of the term, connected with the root meaning of the associated Greek verb *krinō*—which means to separate or divide.[5] In this sense, I suggest, philosophy is in "crisis" because it is undergoing a number of separations at once: separations of philosophers from the wider culture, from each other, and from philosophy itself.

In an earlier work (*TD*) I suggested that philosophy's exit from the national conversation, now in the ill-remembered past, may have been a self-protective move during the tumult of the McCarthy Era. If so, the self-protection continues; indeed, it has moved to new heights. A couple of years ago, I needed to consult the main publication of the APA, *Proceedings and Addresses,* and so I went off to the Young Research Library at UCLA. The entire west end of the ground floor is a vast collection of recent issues of various periodicals, lying quietly on their sides on bookcases about twenty shelves high. But I couldn't find *Proceedings and Addresses* anywhere among the philosophy journals, so I went to a nearby computer terminal to get the exact call number. Armed with that I returned to the journal stacks, only to find that it was still not there. Returning to the computer, I noticed a small statement below the call number: "Library now has online subscription only."

Well and good, I thought; I'm happy to save trees. Only there was no evidence that trees were being saved, because the overall number of journals in the library had clearly not decreased. The shelves were packed and groaning. Why had the print edition of *Proceedings and Addresses* been cancelled at a major research library? I went to the electronic version of the journal, only to find that it was three years behind. As I write, any issue of *Proceedings and*

Addresses after 2007 is unavailable to me unless I had bought it at the meeting or obtained it through membership in the APA. What, one might ask, is so risky about *Proceedings and Addresses* that three years must pass before its contents are generally available to outsiders?

Other scraps arrive from the media. A few years ago, *Newsweek* published a lament by philosopher Eric Wielenberg claiming that philosophers get insufficient respect from the general public (Wielenberg 2006). I had heard this before, of course, and not only from Jason Stanley; the general public, after all, killed Socrates. But why today? Is contemporary America peopled by Anytuses and Meletuses?

Consider what it is, in Wielenberg's view, that a philosopher does:

> I find a question or puzzle that interests me. I try to figure out a solution, usually reading what others have had to say about it along the way. If I come up with anything good, I write it down and see if anyone is interested in publishing it.

If this is what philosophers do, one wonders why they would be entitled to any respect at all. Is it really true that the only thing that makes a philosophical problem or issue worth engaging with is that it "interests" some individual philosopher? When doctors are curing new diseases and physicists are inching closer to nature's deepest secrets, when literary and political theorists are giving voice and hope to untold millions of oppressed and excluded people, shouldn't philosophers be obliged to be more than "interesting" to themselves and each other? Shouldn't they have to think about whether the problems they are interested in are of any importance to other academics, or even to the public at large?[6] And if a philosopher doesn't take such people into account, why *should* they respect her? Who is disrespecting whom here?

The separation of philosophy from the larger culture goes along with an increasing separation of philosophers from other philosophers. This has long been the norm in the case of the infamous analytic-continental split. Far more revealing than the split itself is that a full sixty years after it began as a turf battle between phenomenologists and logical positivists, it remains inscrutable. This can be established by a simple experiment: Take any American philosopher and ask her whether she is continental or analytical. You will usually get an immediate and definite answer; no philosopher is ignorant of where she stands with regard to the split, and few can credibly claim to be in the middle. Then ask, Why? All too often, you will either get some simpleminded caricature of the other side (analysts are "symbol-pushing logic-choppers"; continentals are "woolly-minded irrationalists"), or a lot of hemming and hawing which eventually reduces to the fact that this was the only kind of philosophy your interlocutor was able to study; the other side was simply not taught where she went to grad school. Philosophers, whose raison d'être has always been the critical examination of basic values and beliefs, are thus separated into two contrasting camps but are unable to state the contrasts. Not having located the basic issues on which they disagree, they have not begun to resolve them. And if philosophers cannot successfully deal with such basic issues regarding their own discipline, why think that they are going to have much success elsewhere?

Separation is also evident within each side of the split. Scott Soames has described the contemporary situation of analytical philosophy in such terms:

> Gone are the days of large, central figures, whose work is accessible and relevant to, as well as read by, nearly all analytic philosophers. Philosophy has become a highly organized discipline, done by specialists primarily for other specialists. (Soames 2003, 2:463)

According to Soames, the fragmentation of analytical philosophy into a vast number of (sometimes) overlapping networks is motivated by a desire for progress, and progress is indeed being made—on the microlevel:

> It is, I think, a mistake to look for one big, unified picture of analytic philosophy [in the last twenty years]. What we need is a collection of more focused pictures, each giving a view of the major developments of related lines of work, and each drawn with an eye to illuminating the larger lessons for work in neighboring fields. (Soames 2003, 2:464)

Progress in philosophy thus requires philosophers to be specialists, which—to Soames—allows them to disregard the work of anyone outside their own microspecialty and its "neighbors." Such narrowness would not get you much funding at the National Institutes of Health or the Large Hadron Collider—if philosophy had analogues to such things. That philosophy does not points to the main problem with Soames's portrait, which concerns not its content but its optimism. As the chronic underfunding of philosophy becomes acute, it is naïve to expect that the mutually ignorant fiefdoms Soames portrays will not turn on one another.[7]

There is also evidence, moreover, that philosophers are alienated from even their own microfields. Consider the implications of Zurich philosopher Hans-Johann Glock's acerbic description of the current fate of non-Anglophone analytical philosophy in his *What Is Analytical Philosophy?* (2008). Glock points out that analytical philosophy is now being done quite well by philosophers who write in languages other than English and who teach in universities outside the English-speaking world. But these philosophers, according to Glock, get no hearing at all from their Anglophone colleagues:

> There is no excuse, however, for the notable failure of many analytic philosophers to pay due attention to figures and ideas that hail from beyond their philosophical, their linguistic, or their national horizons. . . . This holds not just of those contemporaries who indulge in hackneyed jibes at the "continentals." It also afflicts some (first time) visitors to the continent who note, with genuine surprise, that some of the natives are neither Hegelians, nor Heideggerians, nor postmodernists, and may even be capable of intelligent questions and objections. (Glock 2008, 253–254)

On Glock's account, progress in any sense or on any level is no longer the point. For what he is saying is that contemporary philosophers do not care about good work that is being done *even in their own fields*, unless the work is done by people in their own (Anglophone) milieu—which means that they do not really care about those fields at all: philosophers are separating, apparently, from philosophy itself.

If this is so, then behind all the rhetoric about progress-through-specialization, all that is left for philosophers to care about is palling around with the right people. As with so much else, this approach was pioneered by W. V. O. Quine. Asked about John McDermott's observation that it was ironic that the new edition of William James was being edited by McDermott himself at Texas A&M rather than at James's own Harvard, "Professor Quine looked somewhat quizzical and said, 'I don't believe I know McDermott'" (Fiske 1981).

Just what "palling around" means was evidenced in an Open Letter written in 1992 by nineteen philosophers to protest Cambridge University's plan to award an honorary degree to Jacques Derrida. Earlier analytical philosophers would have based their opposition to Derrida on invocations of science and appeals to the logical rules of rational inquiry, but there is little of that here (though philosophy is at one point compared to physics). Rather, the letter's entire argument is based on the opinion of "philosophers, and certainly those . . . working in leading departments of philosophy throughout the world."[8]

Just why such well-employed philosophers were so concerned about Derrida's laurel is not clear. The proposed degree was not to be in philosophy but in "letters," and the Open Letter itself conceded that Derrida had been influential in the lettered fields of literature and film studies. But the deeper and more revealing problem with the Open Letter is that its appeal to the opinion of well-placed professionals is a case of the argument to authority. This used to be a fallacy;[9] that it should be so openly and exclusively appealed to as a principle of exclusion suggests that by 1992 philosophy's intellectual vision of itself had dimmed to the point that much of the field had been overwhelmed by what is called its "sociology." In particular, what mattered most in philosophy at the close of the millennium was, apparently, who had jobs in "leading departments."

Scraps, of course, are merely scraps; an inspiring list of exceptions to the trends noted above could easily fill the rest of this book. But these scraps converge: they come together to suggest that to many philosophers, what makes a problem philosophically important is that it is "interesting" (Wielenberg) to a small group of people (Soames) who are linked, not by the quality of their work (Glock) but by their employment in major departments of philosophy (the Open Letter). What is here being converged on is Richard Rorty's observation that in philosophy today, "the institutional tale [wags] the scientific dog" (Rorty 1982, 217). Which issues come to be discussed philosophically is decided merely by the sociological constraint that the philosophers who want to discuss them should belong to a "good" philosophy department.

But Rorty's observation was made thirty years ago; "today" was 1982. Have things really stayed basically the same since then? Such stasis, if real, would be unique to philosophy. Physics and mathematics have recently been transformed by new technologies in the forms of computerized proof techniques and the Large Hadron Collider; literary theory by the rise of postcolonial studies and the new historicism; and so on. Philosophy, in contrast, soldiers on alone without basic change.

Maybe, it will be said, this holds among the "analysts." But while prestigious employment has not been much of an issue for continental philosophers, they too have their microfields. Continental philosophy used to center on arguments between Husserlian phenomenologists and Sartrean or Heideggerian existentialists, which is why the name of its umbrella group, "SPEP," was an abbreviation for "Society for Phenomenological and Existential Philosophy." Now "SPEP" abbreviates nothing at all, and its members too often flock separately around European superstars whose latest thought they eagerly expound.[10] In the tumult, Habermasians rarely intersect with postmodernists, Hegelians can't make themselves understood to anyone, and speculative realists excoriate anyone they consider to be a "correlationist."[11] Again, there are many exceptions; but much American continental philosophy remains what Reiner Schürmann called it just three years after Rorty's quote above: "reportage" (Schürmann 1985).

The danger here is that philosophy's widening separations will become "critical" in the temporal sense: that philosophy will reach a point where its future becomes decisively open. What do philosophers think, then, about philosophy's future?

As far as I can tell, very little. I have in recent years attended, as a member, the annual meetings of both the Modern Language Association (MLA) and the American Political Science Association (APSA). I found that both groups allocate serious resources to informed reflection on their respective disciplines. They devote major sessions at those meeting to scholars, senior and not, who debate issues of where the profession is and where it should go. The MLA even publishes an annual, *Profession*, with essays on such issues.

Neither the APA nor the SPEP has a habit of this; in fact, I cannot remember the last time either group scheduled such a session. As far as publications are concerned, in philosophy we find *Metaphilosophy*, which publishes some articles reflecting on the discipline but by no means only those, and the letters column of the APA's *Proceedings and Addresses*—if it still exists, for I am of course three years behind in my reading of it. As far as private conversations are concerned, the philosophers I know seem to be of two opinions: either the future of philosophy will be very like the present, or it will be very different.

Which sounds "decisively open" to me.

Philosophy and the Wider Crisis

In asking whether the two senses of "crisis" are converging—whether the multiple separations philosophers are undergoing from the nonphilosophical world, from each other, and from philosophy itself are approaching a point at which they cannot continue—it is well to remember another sense in which philosophy can be "in crisis": it can be *in the midst of* a crisis in its wider social environment. If the society or culture of which philosophers are a part is at a critical state, then philosophy, as a component of that culture, is also "in crisis." Indeed, in this sense, philosophy is usually, if not always, in (the midst of a) crisis, for the critical examination of our basic values and beliefs is a sufficiently unnatural way of thinking that people normally engage in it only when things are going seriously wrong—only when we are in or approaching a state of crisis.

Crises in the wider society do not always, of course, affect philosophers. The crisis of the Greek polis in the fourth century BCE was roundly ignored by Aristotle, who apparently believed that his account of the good life was unaffected by Alexander's incorporation of its political horizon into a larger imperial order. In the United States, the main crisis-inducing event of the twenty-first century has been treated similarly. A glance at the programs for the various meetings of the APA shows that, as of 2007, American philosophers were still conducting business as before—worrying about arcane topics such as the context sensitivity of language, obscure conundrums in the history of philosophy such as the proper formulation of Kant's categorical imperative, and highly general issues such as whether events are as real as objects. Though 9/11 and its aftermath have been taken up as objects of reflection by a number of prominent philosophers,[12] these are exceptions, not the rule.

But such isolation may have become a luxury that philosophers can no longer afford. The death of the polis at the hands of the Alexandrian Empire might not have mattered much to Aristotle—but he was not its target. The same cannot be said of contemporary philosophers with respect to terrorism. There are many things about the West that terrorists clearly abhor—political and sexual freedom, modern versions of Christianity and/or Judaism, Middle East policy, science, capitalism. All of them, however, have one important thing in common: their current forms have largely been shaped by philosophers. It is hard to imagine what political and sexual freedom might be without Locke and Nietzsche, modern religion without Feuerbach and Kierkegaard, recent Middle East policy without Strauss, science without Descartes, democracy without Rousseau, colonialism without the British Empiricists[13]—or capitalism without Marx. And where would any of these things be without Kant?

We should not assume that religious terrorists the world over do not know this, or that they are not smart enough to figure it out. Philosophy is not only one combatant among others in the struggle with terrorism, then; it is, or may become, a primary target of the terrorists. This means that what many have called the "war of ideas" is not, in fact, an option for philosophers, but a struggle for their own self-preservation.

We must also, here, cast a wider net than 9/11, for we all know that terrorism is only part of a wider phenomenon. Garry Wills made this crystal clear in an op-ed piece in the *New York Times* on November 4, 2004:

Where [besides America] do we find fundamentalist zeal, a rage at secularity, religious intolerance, fear of and hatred for modernity? Not in France or Britain or Germany or Italy or Spain. We find it in the Muslim world, in Al Qaeda, in Saddam Hussein's Sunni loyalists. . . . It is often observed that enemies come to resemble each other. We torture the torturers, we call our God better than theirs—as one American general put it, in words that the President has not repudiated. (Wills 2004)

Wills is arguing two things here. One is that what the terrorists hate is Enlightenment itself—the ongoing commitment to reason in private and public affairs that defines modernity at its best. Wills's other point is that when we see 9/11 as an attack on Enlightenment values, we see that those values are under serious attack here at home as well as out there in the "Muslim world."

What 9/11 forced into the open is a global backlash, not merely against philosophy but against the Enlightenment itself. This backlash is a complex historical development with many different branches, but it can be seen to stretch from the mountains of Pakistan to the American Bible Belt and beyond— for example, into the mind of an American general. It may even extend into philosophy, for since Foucault it has become commonplace for postmodern thinkers to attack, or at least question, the Enlightenment. Does this not ally postmodern thinkers such as Foucault with the anti-Enlightenment backlash, as Habermas has suggested (Habermas 1981)?

Let me sum this up. If we restrict our vision to the day-to-day activities of the philosophers in our circle—those in our own department or microfield—things seem to be going smoothly enough. If we look a little farther, however, there are indications that philosophy has lost its way: that those microfields are not components of some larger and successful enterprise but are merely adrift on separate intellectual oceans, held together by little more than reportage and "palling around." And if we look beyond philosophy itself to the larger societies in which philosophers work, we find looming threats directed both specifically against philosophy and against the broader set of Enlightenment values to which philosophy has long been committed. Philosophy's crisis yawns wide indeed. On the gloomy side, philosophy's future looks like a combination of growing internal incoherence and external menace. On the optimistic side, we see—what? There are a number of promising new programs in philosophy, but whether they promise renewal of the whole field is open to doubt. Consider two of the most vigorous: experimental philosophy and speculative realism. Both are motivated by the kind of disillusion expressed in the preceding pages: a feeling that philosophy is not merely in need of refinement or furthering but that it has gone seriously off the rails.[14] Hans Reichenbach, of course, thought the same thing

(Reichenbach 1951); and these approaches, like his, assimilate philosophy to science—the "experimentalists" to psychology and the "realists" to mathematics (see Meillassoux, Badiou, and Brassier 2008). Neither, then, can supply what we most need to see today: a defense of philosophy as philosophy.

Such defense, in turn, is rightly identified with a defense of the Enlightenment itself. But here, Foucault and the postmodernists are right—with a twist: in order to defend the Enlightenment, philosophy must turn against it, at least long enough to ask this question: Is there something in Enlightenment itself which has provoked this vehement, worldwide rejection?

The Paradoxes of Enlightenment

I think there is—that philosophical Enlightenment, in the main forms it has assumed since Kant, has turned all too many people into its enemies. Indeed, I suggest that philosophy's *sociological* crisis—the fact that philosophers find themselves increasingly separated from their larger communities, from each other, and from philosophy itself—has its roots in a *philosophical* crisis of Enlightenment.

But the roots are deeper still; the real problem lies not with Enlightenment values but behind them. Kant's 1784 essay "What Is Enlightenment?" (*AA*, 8:35–42) is not only philosophy's most lucid and condensed statement of Enlightenment principles but the ultimate reformulation of one of philosophy's oldest dreams. For Socrates, life should be guided by a form of dialogue which was egalitarian (since even Socrates did not have the knowledge needed to control it), honest, and critically supreme. Plato, traumatized by his teacher's death, relocated such speech from the agora, where Socrates conducted it and made his fatal enemies, to more secluded circumstances: various gymnasia (as in the *Charmides*), the house of Cephalus (in the *Republic*), the country stream where Socrates and Phaedrus while away an afternoon. As further protection, Plato devised his theory of Platonic love: for if you argue only against a background of disinterested affection, those with whom you argue will probably be less likely to put you to death.

Kant's vision, two millennia later, of the public use of reason, in which individuals speak their minds without direction from others, echoes the egalitarian honesty of Platonic dialogue. As he puts it toward the end of 1781's *Critique of Pure Reason*:

> In matters of concern to all human beings, without distinction, nature cannot be accused of partiality in the distribution of its gifts; and . . . with regard to the essential purposes of human nature, the highest philosophy cannot get fur-

ther than can the guidance that nature has bestowed even upon the commonest understanding. (*CPR* B, 859)

Kant's work thus stands, as Charles Mills has written, as "the best articulation of the moral egalitarianism associated with the Enlightenment, the American and French revolutions, and the rise of modernist individualism" (Mills 1998, 68).

When we couple the passage above with the *Critique*'s opening invocation of the "tribunal of reason" (*CPR* A, 11–12; cf. B, 779), we see that Kant's egalitarian dialogue takes place not merely *in* but *as* the agora. Three years later, in "What Is Enlightenment?," we see (as Peter Gay has written) the optimistic hope that the philosophers can become "the potential masters of Europe"—and eventually, Kant suggests elsewhere, of the world.[15] Platonic love and seclusion are now unnecessary. The philosopher-king is back, in the form of Frederick the Great, and this time he has an army. How could philosophers not rush to swear allegiance to this newly glorious version of their ancient dream?

But the new hope was paradoxical in two senses, both of which become evident when we put Enlightenment into time—when we view it not as a state but as a process. Doing that was essential to Kant, who opens "What Is Enlightenment?" with the formula that we live not in an "Enlightened age" but in an ongoing "age of Enlightenment." It proved crucial as well to Enlightenment thought in general, for which the revolutionary force of history, guided by *la déesse de la raison*, proved to be a far more important ally than Frederick the Great.[16] Viewing Enlightenment as a process wreaks havoc, however, with the principle of human equality, to which Kant has given such brilliant formulation. For human equality will come about only at the end of the process of Enlightenment, when everyone is enlightened and therefore actively rational. The current state of affairs is far from that, and before we are through the second paragraph of "What Is Enlightenment?" Kant has excluded "the entire fair sex" from his Prussian agora. He also excludes, and with equal brutality, those of other races. As he put it in 1764, in words from which his thought never recovered, "this fellow was quite black from head to foot, a clear proof that what he said was stupid."[17]

These comments do not merely express bachelor spleen or white ressentiment. Nor do they merely reflect Kant's unique personal psychology, or the mind-set of a culture with strong economic incentives for the exploitation of women and people of color, or the heritage of a long cultural tradition of excluding such people. They express all those things and more: they lead us to a problem intrinsic to philosophy itself, which produces paradoxical effects in Kant's very conception of Enlightenment.

The problem is with time. I have noted that human equality, if it is to be achieved by an historical process, cannot exist at the beginning of that process. Kant's proclamation of Enlightenment as a process thus *requires* an initial state in which humanity is divided not merely into male and female, European and non-European, but—and, for him, far more importantly—into those who are participating in the grand process of Enlightenment and those who are not. This division goes deep: if Enlightenment is the fulfillment of reason, and reason is the nature of humanity, then those who have not entered into the process of becoming enlightened, whether for reasons of nature or of culture, are not fully human. *Extra ecclesiam nihil salus*, we may say: there is no salvation outside the Church of Enlightenment—as Kant himself implies, through a small word of just three letters, in the concluding sentence to "What Is Enlightenment?" As a result of the process of Enlightenment, he tells us, government "finds it profitable to treat the human being, which is *now* [*nun*] more than a machine, in keeping with its dignity" (emphasis added). "Now" here means "then": only once Enlightenment is established can we be more than machines. In short, as Kant puts it in "On Pedagogy," "the human being can only become human through upbringing [*Erziehung*]. He is nothing but what upbringing makes him" (*AA*, 9:443).

Kant's effort to validate human equality, valiant in the *Critique of Pure Reason*, thus reverses itself and ends in the opposite: in a division within humanity so radical that those on the wrong side of it are not really within humanity at all. Here we have the conceptual groundwork not of Enlightenment but of a general theory of oppression. It is not simply that, as Lucius Outlaw has shown with particular elegance, Enlightenment's overly abstract view of human nature excluded from it particularities of race and gender, allowing the struggles of people stamped with those particularities to drop from view.[18] It is also the case that Enlightenment thought (and not only Kant's formulation of it) establishes, in spite of its abstraction, one pair of particularities which, though not itself aimed directly against women, people of color, and nonheterosexuals, can be filled in so as to apply invidiously to them: the dichotomy between those who are on the way to Enlightenment and those who are not. Both tactics, then, contributed to what Outlaw calls a situation in which "a circumscribed dehumanizing, dominated subworld was constructed and institutionalized, into which Africans were herded and confined as slaves" (Outlaw 1996e, 163).

The joint themes of oppression and confinement will occupy us later; for the moment, I wish to point out, with Outlaw here, that they are nothing new. Since

Aristotle, as we will see in Chapter 3, philosophy has been associated with a theory of rightful oppression, according to which some people *should* let others think for them. Kant tells us that this happens not simply because of supposedly natural groups to which such people are consigned but because members of those groups are not on the road to Enlightenment. Kant's racism and sexism are not blemishes on his philosophy; they are specifications of some of its most basic and ancient views.

This makes oppression integral to philosophy. It has long been known, for example, that one of the basic ways in which philosophers, Kantian or other, justify the oppression of women and people of color is by assimilating them in one way or another to nature and the categories we use to describe it—passive, irrational, unthinking, unfree. What has not received sufficient attention, I think, is the strictly philosophical side of this: where did the category of "nature" come from? What philosophical exigencies shaped it, and how did they get to be exigencies? Such questions, which cannot be reduced to personal psychology or sociocultural conditioning, are central to understanding how these exigencies operate. For once the category of "nature" is there, something has to occupy it; and once philosophers ask who in the human world is to play the role of "natural being," their personal psychology, cultural biases, and economic interests provide them, all too easily, with answers. But whence the category of "natural being" itself?

That placing Enlightenment into time ratifies human inequality is the first paradox of Enlightenment. The second begins when we consider that the public use of reason, for Kant, has to proceed under the guidance of philosophy (for details, see the "Doctrine of Method" at the end of the *Critique of Pure Reason*). For it is philosophy, now reformed as Kantian critique, which tells us how reason functions. Without it, reason falls into unresolvable metaphysical disputes.

Critique, however, has limits. On the one hand, Kant was very happy to be criticized as to whether he had properly carried out his philosophical project, that is to say, whether he had correctly stated the "transcendental" principles of the mind's various basic functions. His willingness to subject himself to critique is not mere philosophical congeniality. It is an application of one of the basic principles of modernity, that of the rule of law. The idea that the person who wields the law—who formulates it and enforces it—is also subject to it can be found, to be sure, in premodern political theory. But not often, and not consistently. In Plato's *Republic*, for example, everybody had to tell the truth—except the rulers.

Hence Kant, though he formulates the critical philosophy, is subject to it himself—for it is a statement of the basic principles of the human mind, and he has a human mind. The basic principles and findings of his own project, once he has articulated them, are *not*, however, subject to criticism. Consider his reaction to Fichte.[19] Fichte, almost forty years younger than Kant, considered himself to be a good Kantian. But he thought there were some loose ends that the Great Man had left untied, and so he undertook to clean them up. This catapulted him into an entirely different philosophy—but Fichte did not know it. He thought he was still a Kantian. So he sent his book off to Kant, hoping to receive the Master's blessing.

He got the reverse. Kant was horrified and wrote an "Open Letter on Fichte's *Wissenschaftslehre*" in which he said:

> The critical philosophy must remain . . . confident that no change of opinion, no touching up or reconstruction into some other form, is in store for it; the system of the *Critique* rests on fully secured foundations, established forever; it will be indispensable too for the noblest ends of mankind in all future ages.[20]

This goes far beyond correcting Fichte and indeed is as pure a statement of philosophical foundationalism as you are ever likely to find. What it reveals is the distance between being able to criticize the way you use your basic critical categories and being able to bring those categories themselves under critical fire.

Fast-forward to the early twenty-first century and imagine that philosophy has not moved beyond these two Kantian paradoxes. What would we find? On the one hand, growing numbers of people whom Kant would classify as less than human: women and people of color, certainly, and presumably also those whose gender he would consider (in his word) unmentionable.[21] These people are not on the way to Enlightenment, and their discourse therefore does not follow its rules. Indeed, even if they were on that path, their discourse would not follow the rules with exactitude, for they would not yet be rational enough for that. There being no other rules to follow, their discourse is unregulated: *Wildheit ist die Unabhängigkeit von Gesetzen* (AA, 9:442)—savagery is independence from laws. On the other hand, we would find philosophers still believing themselves to be in possession of an unchangeable architectonic of rules and procedures, "established forever" by critique and increasingly unable to hear, let alone understand and evaluate, members of that growing group of people.

Some of these expectations are fulfilled in the Open Letter mentioned previously, when it characterizes Derrida's work as "little more than semi-intelligible attacks upon the values of reason, truth, and scholarship" (Derrida 1995, 420–421). But if the letter writers expectably view Derrida as an unregulated thinker, and so as what Kant might call a philosophical savage, they do not see themselves as critical philosophers. By their own clear testimony, they are armed not with rules and procedures "resting on fully secured foundations" but merely with well-paid jobs. No matter; their foundations are assumed to be no less absolute. As W. V. O. Quine, one of the signers of the letter, put it in his "Speaking of Objects" (Quine 1969b, 24–25), "I philosophize from the vantage point of our own provincial conceptual scheme and scientific epoch, but I know no better." Full stop, end of essay.

Quine's refusal to ask if his "provincial conceptual scheme," even if the best one around, could be made still better means that his adherence to foundationalism is no less resolute than Kant's. One way in which they differ is that, where for Kant philosophy was to be set on "the secure path of a science" (*CPR* B, vii), it has for Quine been on that path for some time:

> But if one pursues philosophy in a scientific spirit as a quest for truth, then tolerance of wrong-headed philosophy is as unreasonable as tolerance of astrology would be on the part of the astrophysicist, and as unethical as tolerance of Unitarianism would be on the part of hell-fire fundamentalists.[22]

It is not my task here to trace the ways in which egalitarianism and elitism, critique and dogma, coil and intersect through the work of these two great philosophers.[23] I do pause to note, however, that this dichotomy has not just captured philosophers but has shaped the university itself. Consider this statement from Franklin D. Murphy, an early chancellor of UCLA (1960–1968) and then, even more influentially, head of the Times-Mirror Corporation in Los Angeles (1968–1980):

> I had, and I still have, very grave questions as to these black studies programs, Indian study programs, Chicano studies programs. I think they're devoid of much intellectual content. I think it was psychotherapy rather than intellectual activity. But I'm not going to second-guess anybody, because maybe some psychotherapy was needed to quiet people down. I think it's a miscarriage of space and everything else, on a campus that's very short on space, to provide a sort of social meeting room for these people. . . . The history of the blacks in this country and the history of the Chicano in this country ought to be an integral part of history. And any department of history with integrity will put it in. And they'd

even have a separate course. But to create these so-called centers is, I think, really quite absurd. (Murphy 1976, 249–250)

The problem with the centers, of course, is that they do not meet accepted standards of "reason, truth, and scholarship." Outside these, we find psychotherapy, a kind of pacifier for the mind.

The Winds of Paradox

Certain scraps of evidence suggest that philosophy today is fragmented and lacking in self-respect. This Introduction has suggested that in virtue of the paradoxes of Enlightenment, it is rigid and elitist. The next question is how these are connected. Are contemporary philosophy's multiple separations somehow produced by its rigidity and elitism?

The paradoxes tell us, in a nutshell, that philosophy's ancient and unexceptionable allegiance to egalitarianism and reason have assumed forms which are ill equipped to deal with the temporal nature of Enlightenment. The results are that the egalitarianism of the first paradox unexpectedly drives an elitist wedge into humanity, while the rigid reason of the second loses its comprehensive power and becomes dismissive. Philosophers thus find themselves, professionally speaking, on the wrong side of history; for the most important intellectual development of the last half century, at least as important as the rise of science in preceding centuries, is the global uprising of the very people whom Kant dismissed as philosophical savages. However sympathetic to this philosophers may be as human beings, the only way its Kantian heritage gives philosophy itself to understand this uprising is, to be blunt, as a return to intellectual savagery.

The first, entirely predictable result of this is the kind of isolation lamented by Stanley and Wielenberg. The new paradigms in the humanities and social sciences, many of which see themselves as opposed to Enlightenment, pass philosophy by, leaving philosophers with less and less to talk about—until what they have is only what is "interesting" to one or a few of them. The philosophical groups united by such interests are small, transient, and both unwilling and unable to lay claim to the kind of critical apparatus Kant thought he had established "on secured foundations." The thinness of their repertoire of rules, laudable when we compare them to Kant's overblown transcendentality, renders those rules inadequate to deal with the real problems of the age, and so the rules lose respect, even among those who—often grumpily—adhere to them.

The paradoxes of Enlightenment thus come to spell out the tragedy of philosophy: what should have saved it is what has destroyed it. Its adherence to reason, admirable in itself, became, like the probity of Antigone or the cleverness of Oedipus, fatally strong.[24]

But was it adherence to reason which did this, or adherence to a specific form of reason? Sally Sedgwick has argued that with Hegel, a new concept of reason comes on the scene: a concept according to which reason has no fixed principles but gains all its content from shared human experience—from history.[25] Adopting this Hegelian view allows us to undo reason's rigidity, making it malleable; then, and only then, we can reshape it to meet current needs—a reshaping which, by the end of this book, will not only render reason malleable (in an Hegelian sense) but fragile (in a Heideggerian sense). But if reason is malleable, then it is historical: it is what it is because it has *come to be* what it is. In order to reshape it, we must know its history, and we must, in particular, know two things about that history. First, that it is what produced us; there is nothing in today's philosophy which is not, one way or another, a product of its history. Second, that it does not stop with us; indeed, we have an obligation to transcend it. But we cannot transcend it unless we understand both it and ourselves as its current outcome. The "crisis" in philosophy thus turns out to be, in the first instance, its separation from its own history.

It is to the recovery and transcendence of that history that the rest of this book will be devoted. The aim is to be able not merely to adhere to the Enlightenment as we have it (largely from Kant), or to abjure it altogether, but to reshape it into a critical practice more adequate to the times.

Prefatory Synopsis

When humanity withers, philosophy blossoms—or so implied Hegel, at the end of the "Preface" to the *Philosophy of Right*. For it is the fact that "a shape of life has grown old" (*PhR*, 21) which allows Hegel to get his philosophy underway; only what has no future can be philosophically comprehended, for to have a future means to be capable of surprising us. If Hegel could not assert in his "Preface" that Germanic modernity had already withered, he would be unable to say anything at all in the rest of the book. The Owl of Minerva would be grounded.

Hegel was, in this respect, neither an observer nor a prophet. Germanic modernity had not withered when he wrote, and we can only wish that it had withered later on rather than exploding in a cataclysm of hatred. As we move beyond Germany and into the twenty-first century, however, his words start to ring true. It takes no special acuity to see that the human race today is not withering but burgeoning—its problems worldwide, while serious, are largely those of material and intellectual growth. So we don't know what is going to happen and Minerva's owl must delay takeoff. I shall not, therefore, write an Hegelian book; right now I shall, rather, give a preliminary account of one thing that is yet to come: this book.

In the second half of the twentieth century, philosophers devoted themselves to reflection on the rise of modern empirical science, which had by then been going on for about a century. They mined it for epistemological, ontological, and ethical insights, adapted philosophical method to it, and in so doing shaped much of the intellectual culture of their time. But if the "rise of scientific philosophy" (Reichenbach 1951) was an inspiration to philosophers, the "rise of the formerly oppressed of the world" is less so. Reflection on the identities and experiences of women, people of color, and the wholly disparate groups I can only, and apologetically, call "nonheterosexuals"[26] remains far too ghettoized today. Indeed, as I write, David Hilbert is pointing out that the newly released National Research Council rankings of philosophy departments show that the mere presence of women and minorities in a philosophy department, whatever their field, goes with a lowering of its reputation.[27] It is as if philosophers fear that opening out to such things will be the withering of philosophy: that the discipline will lose its core, whatever that is, and find its own death just as global humanity comes alive. In other words, the relationship of philosophy to the species which conducts it is wholly inverse: when humanity withers, philosophy thrives; when humanity thrives, philosophy withers.

The thesis of this book is that philosophy can lose its traditional "core" and still be philosophy. To ground this, I will turn to the only place where we can hope to discover the core of philosophy: to its history. My aim will be to show that philosophy has always had a set of core presuppositions and tactics; that those presuppositions must now be definitively abandoned; and that doing so will enable philosophy to thrive in tandem with humanity, rather than inversely to it.

If the problems of Enlightenment thought have to do with the relation of what is in time to what is not, then they are much older than Kant. Philosophy's *real* crisis has been building, I claim, since Parmenides. I will explore it, and the resources philosophers have now developed for coping with it, in four pairs of chapters.

The first two chapters will develop two correlative notions. One concerns the kind of humanness to which philosophy must open itself, which I call the "speaking of matter"; the other concerns a general principle of philosophical closure which I call "ousia." Both notions can be understood in terms of philosophy's core binary, that of form and matter. They are correlative in that it is from the point of view of ousia that what must be repressed in humanity appears as the speaking of matter, and it is from the point of view of the speaking of matter that its philosophical *re*pression via ousia can be identified as *op*pressive.

Chapters 1 and 2 thus presuppose each other. Chapter 1 will seek to free the speaking of matter from its dispersal among a variety of human pursuits. I will adduce examples and treatments of it in the philosophy of science and in literature, finally focusing on David Foster Wallace's detailed account of Boston AA in his *Infinite Jest*. Chapter 2 will seek to lay bare the longstanding role of ousia as philosophy's core principle by questioning philosophy's equally longstanding view of itself as a search for truth.

Not that philosophy is *not* such a search; matters here are too complex for sudden either/or's. What we find, when we get beyond the view that philosophy is *simply* a search for truth, is what I will call an "ontological schema." A "schema" for Kant is a sort of a priori image, formed from the pure conditions of sensibility and too general to be given in an intuition (*CPR* B, 179). The structure I shall explore is not a priori in any Kantian transcendental sense, but it is not directly derived from sensory experience, either—even if we construe that broadly enough to include social conditions. It is formulated and argued for by Aristotle as an ontological doctrine, that is, as an account of what it is to be; and the exigencies which lead him to adopt it are the failures of Plato's Theory of Forms and of Aristotle's own earlier metaphysics of substance to do the jobs that ontology is supposed to do. The result of this is a structure which, though originally derived through conceptual considerations, is a clear model for, and ingredient in, much real world oppression.

As Foucault has shown, we cannot speak responsibly about historical structures without tracing them to specific origins, and after Chapter 2 has given a general account of ousia, I will consider its history more specifically in Chapters 3 and 4. Chapter 3 will be a more detailed account of its role in Aristotle, culminating in a double view of how philosophers close themselves off from the speaking of matter: by "tolerating" it, in what Aristotle calls *karteria*, as long as no one pays attention to it (as with the speech of women); and by responding with anger when it gains a hearing. Chapter 4 will continue the story into some stage setting with Descartes, after which it will examine how ousia begins to be subverted, as a general schema, in Kant's account of reflective judgment.

Such judgment has two sides—that of the beautiful and that of the sublime—and Chapters 5 and 6 will look at Hegel and Heidegger, respectively, as developing each. This will mean disinterring Hegel from the myths that he is either a throwback to pre-Kantian metaphysics or a continuation of Kant's critique of that. It will also mean cutting Heidegger partially free from the reality of his Nazi engagement. The result will be a view of reason itself as "malleable" in Hegel, with Aristotelian *karteria* replaced by what Hegel calls "reconciliation." In Heidegger, reason becomes "fragile," and reconciliation is supplemented by "letting-be."

The final two chapters, Chapters 7 and 8, will show how these two aspects of Hegel's and Heidegger's thought can be incorporated into a "postcritical" or "situating" practice which opens philosophy out to one aspect of the speaking of matter, what I call public language. I will consider examples from Hegel and Frederick Douglass to show how this can work, focusing on Abraham Lincoln's "House Divided" speech.

CHAPTER I

FROM SCIENTIFIC REVOLUTIONS TO BOSTON AA

PHILOSOPHY AND THE SPEAKING OF MATTER

To begin formulating a less problematic, less Kantian version of Enlightenment requires formulating an alternative to its temporal beginning. This is, for Kant, the state of "self-incurred tutelage" (*AA*, 8:35), that is, an inability (*Unvermögen*) to think and act for oneself for which one is oneself responsible (*verschuldet*). *Vermögen* is one of Kant's standard terms for a faculty or power of the mind, the set of which is the object of critique itself. His use of this word, plus his characterization of the tutelage as something for which one is "responsible," brings the unsurprising insight that Kant is, from the outset, thinking of Enlightenment in the terms of his own moral theory. When he goes on, as he immediately does, to say that "self-incurred" means not due to lack of mental capacity (*Verstand*), he has (as we saw in the Introduction) excluded women and people of color from the process. Their incapacity is not self-incurred but due to nature.

We are looking, by contrast, for an "unenlightened" state to which issues of mental capacity and incapacity, and of responsibility and its absence, do not apply. In sketching this, I will draw, briefly, on some recent developments in the philosophy of science, some not-so-recent developments in feminism, and the account of "Boston AA" in David Foster Wallace's *Infinite Jest*.

Philosophy of Science: From Discovery to Shakiness
The best-known part of my story tells how Thomas Kuhn's *The Structure of Scientific Revolutions* put paid to the tidy distinction, associated with Hans Reichenbach, between the contexts of discovery and justification (Reichenbach

1938, 7–8). The "context of discovery" for Reichenbach concerns how scientists obtain data and come up with hypotheses to explain it. These matters vary from scientist to scientist and from case to case and so are ineluctably subjective. The context of discovery is therefore excluded from philosophical reflection on science, which is restricted to the context of justification: the ways in which scientific objectivity is established for a theory or an hypothesis after someone has advanced it. These center, for Reichenbach, on the use of a fixed set of logical rules to guide the inferences, usually probabilistic, made from the data.

For Kuhn, what philosophers of science needed to do was not to approach science in terms of preestablished dichotomies like this one but to understand the ways in which it actually develops. The facts of history, he argues, teach that scientific change includes components of both contexts; indeed, they are often so intertwined that the very distinction between the two becomes questionable.[1] In particular, for Kuhn, justification itself has historically variable components: what counts as justification to one group of scientists may not do so for another.

The practices of justification accepted in a particular scientific community are an important part of what Kuhn calls its "paradigm," the sum of its governing doctrines, principles, and practices. The history of science then appears as a succession of paradigms in which the shift from one paradigm to a newer one, because it involves the acceptance of new and different practices of justification, cannot proceed in accordance with the rules of either the older or the newer paradigm. It therefore appears as "irrational"; and indeed, any new paradigm must appear as irrational to a scientific community defined by an older one.

At the moment of a paradigm shift, then, the rules and procedures of science itself become unstable—or, as Arthur Fine has put it, "shaky":

> Without firm foundations or rigid superstructures, their outcome is uncertain. Indeed not even the rules of play are fixed. It follows that at every step we have to be guided by judgment calls. (SG, 2)

These judgment calls, for Fine, can be decidedly unscientific in character; Einstein's rhetorical dismissals of the quantum theory are an example (SG, 2). Nor are they always made with a view to objective truth—for that would constitute a fixed rule of play (SG, 9). Moreover, in a decisive move beyond Kuhn, Fine argues that the shakiness involved in paradigm shifts is not restricted to certain "revolutionary" moments but is an ingredient in "all the constructive work of science" (SG, 2).

Shakiness can be generalized not only to science as such, as Fine does, but beyond it altogether. A first step in this is provided by Steven Shapin and Simon Schaffer's account of Robert Boyle's scientific method. The heart of this is experimentation, and at the heart of a scientific experiment stands a machine (classically, for Boyle, the air pump). When an experiment is performed, "the machine constitutes a resource that may be used to filter out human agency . . . as if it were said, 'It is not I who says this; it is the machine'" (Shapin and Shaffer 1985, 56).

Human agency needs to be "filtered out" because it brings with it prejudices, prepossessions, and interests which could bias the observation (see Shapin and Shaffer 1985, 218). In that it eliminates these things, the machine seems to have the role of eliminating subjectivity in general, including everything belonging to the context of discovery. In fact, as Shapin and Schaffer argue at length, this is not the case. The machine filters out *individual* idiosyncracy, but such issues as what a machine is, how its movements are to be interpreted, and who gets to interpret them are variable matters within the experiment and are, if not individually "subjective," socially constructed.

Important here is that the machine operates as the only "actor" in the experimental space. The humans are present merely as witnesses to its functioning (Shapin and Shaffer 1985, 56). What Shapin and Schaffer locate in Boyle's theory of experimentation is thus, as Bruno Latour puts it, an attempt to allow "mute objects to speak through the intermediary of loyal and disciplined scientific spokespersons" (Latour 1993, 30), that is, through the witnesses to the experiment who communicate it to the learned public at large. Even though natural objects are mere matter, they can send us messages which need to be listened to and learned from.

This is perhaps the major claim, at once cognitive and moral, of early modern science. We can relate it to Fine's account of shakiness when we realize that paradigm shifts can be empirically provoked. For this to happen, some phenomenon must arise that is anomalous not only to the current theories in its domain but to the very principles by which those theories are formulated and justified. At such a point, all rules are suspended and the situation becomes shaky indeed.[2]

In seeing shakiness as originating in materiality, we are focusing not on science itself but on a kind of experience scientists sometimes have: the kind in which a material object, or arrangement of such objects, unexpectedly sends us a message. Scientists also have this kind of experience outside experimental contexts, as witness Charles Darwin's description of domestic pigeons in the first chapter of *On the Origin of Species*. The shared physical traits of the different breeds of domestic pigeon are all found, he writes, in the rock pigeon; aspects in which the different breeds differ from the rock pigeon are also aspects in which they differ from each other (Darwin 2008, 21–22). The pigeons are thus sending him a message: that they are all descended from the rock pigeon.

Such scientific experiences, experimental and nonexperimental, present cases of what I will call the "speaking of matter." That matter itself can speak to us sounds bizarre, and indeed it contravenes what we will see to be one of the most basic claims of the philosophical tradition: that matter, in and of itself, is inert and cannot do anything, let alone speak. I claim, by contrast, that it can, that its messages are endemic, and that the reception of them is hardly limited to scientists. I will argue later that it is with the speaking of matter, rather than Kantian "self-incurred tutelage," that critically emancipatory thought must begin.

To claim that matter itself can speak leads immediately to the question of what it means to "speak."[3] I will begin with a definition at once broad and restricted: to speak is to produce intelligible sounds—sounds to which those who hear them know, or can figure out, how to respond. This definition is broad in that it does not view speaking as the expression of a preestablished meaning, whether one psychologically resident in the speaker or one made available through his language. It is restricted, however, to verbal speech: the kind of message conveyed by Darwin's pigeons is, for the moment, out of order.

The reason for this is that concentrating on speaking—on the sending of messages by sound rather than vision—highlights the key role played in the speaking of matter by the phenomenon of sympathetic vibration.[4] On the least intellectual and so most material level of the propagation of sound, we find that if you hit an "A" tuning fork, every other "A" fork in the vicinity starts to vibrate. The first fork instigates vibrations in the atmosphere which, when they hit the other forks, cause them to vibrate as well. That, indeed, is what "sound" is: the resonance in one body of vibrations originating in another. Unpropagated sound, we may say, is an oxymoron. When our eardrums reverberate to sudden changes in air pressure, we hear a noise, and hearing itself is an obvious case of sympathetic vibration. But it is not only the eardrums which reverberate; one does not have to inhabit a human body for very long to know that something similar holds for all of its tissues and even its bones: coughs, laughs, sobs, and yawns all spread around rooms without anyone's conscious intervention, and these together constitute one form of what I call the speaking of matter.

Such "speaking" is to be contrasted with sympathy, which has been basic to much of ethical thought since David Hume and Adam Smith and is generally viewed as a psychological phenomenon. Hume and Smith take it to be such, I suggest, because they assimilate it to the intangibility of vision. Thus Hume, in the *Treatise of Human Nature*, grounds sympathy on resemblance: when I experience a being who resembles me undergoing a strong emotion, I automatically feel a similar emotion. That Hume conceives the resemblance in play as visual is evident from his restriction of it to human beings, for while we do not look much like other animals, we sound like them. We scream, bark, and roar like our simian, canine, feline, and ursine cousins, and the howl of a cat in particular sounds much like that of a baby. Since we do not feel the vibrations of light the way we do vibrations of sound, when Hume assimilates our understanding of what another person is feeling to vision he bestows upon such understanding the obscure status of a psychological or mental process:

> When any affection is induced by sympathy, it is at first known only by its effects, and by those external signs in the countenance and conversation which convey an idea of it. This idea is presently converted into an impression, and acquires such a degree of force and vivacity, as to become the very passion itself, and produce an equal emotion, as any original affection.[5]

For Smith, too, what primarily arouses our sympathy—misery—must be either seen or conceived. To see another's misery is not to experience it directly, and sympathy thus, as for Hume, is basically a psychological matter requiring an inference. Smith expresses the inference, and the need for it, as follows:

> As we have no immediate experience of what other men feel, we can form no idea of the manner in which they are affected, but by conceiving what we ourselves should feel in the like situation. (Smith 2000, 3)

My claim, by contrast, is that while we have no immediate *visual* experience of what others feel, we do have an *auditory* experience of it: when the anguish or the joy in someone else's body sets up vibrations in the atmosphere, the tissues in my body resonate to it. Sympathy is therefore a physical phenomenon, founded on the materiality of sound, and it is one to which we are consigned by our material being. In sympathetic vibration, a message is sent from matter to matter; our bodies can receive and respond to such messages without our knowing even that a message has been sent, still less what that message is. This, to be sure, holds (though more mysteriously) for visual messages as well; Darwin's observation that he was "much struck," on his youthful visit, by the "distribution of the inhabitants" of the Galápagos is testimony (Darwin 2008, 5).

Clear from the case of auditory messages but also generalizable to visual ones is that some bodily vibrations are culturally styled: an American who hits her thumb with a hammer is likely to yell "ouch!" while a French Creole might yell "ai-yo!" Wittgenstein argued that statements such as "I have a headache" are best construed not as reports of a headache but as such pain-behavior, more highly refined (Wittgenstein 1958, § 244, 89). Linguistic habits themselves are, like other habits, corporeal; they are generated as bodies are trained to respond in consistent ways to similar stimuli. Once formed, they can be triggered without the conscious intervention of the speaker, as in pain-behavior. When this happens, we can say that matter itself has sent us a message.

Such messages, originating in the materiality of a living body, may come forth in words, but they can hardly be expected to exhibit the conceptual precision and preestablished logical forms of enlightened discourse; the situation is far too shaky for that. They are more likely to sound, at first, like sighs and groans—the emissions of a body in pain or ecstasy. Then, perhaps, comes an unrelenting and frustrated struggle to give pattern to the groans, to gain articulation for what is provoking them.

In the speaking of matter, then, nature sends us a nonconceptual message through the functioning of a machine or the moaning (etc.) of a body. It is up to us to conceptualize this message: to explain the movements of the machine or to interpret the sounds of the body. It is important here to see that this conceptualizing is not optional: it is something we have to do, because a drive to conceptuality is implicit in the very concept of a nonconceptual message. To see this, we need a philosophical framework for understanding the speaking of matter. Before arguing that Kant's account of reflective judgment provides the basis for such a framework, I will attempt to deprive the notion of the speaking of matter of the strangeness which first attaches to it by looking at examples from a variety of fields.

How Does Matter Speak?

Shakiness occurs in science at that moment in which a scientist, "much struck" like Darwin, discovers a pattern in her data but has as yet no explicit generalization under which to bring it. The only way she can be sure the pattern is there at all is to present her data to another individual and to ask if that other person sees it there as well. If agreement is forthcoming, the perceived pattern can be considered the fruit of more than just idiosyncratic observation—and the scientist is warranted, in view of the general principles of reflective judgment, to go on and attempt to devise an explanation for the pattern in terms of general laws.

When scientists move on from their originally shaky experiences to formulate explanations and theories, they seek to obtain universal validity for them. Whether they ever achieve this is, in the wake of Kuhn if not before, open to doubt. The doubts are not relevant here, however, because the move from shakiness to conceptuality covers far more than science itself and does not always seek scientific universality. It is not only scientists who notice empirical patterns and attempt to devise general categories in terms of which to understand them. We all have bodies that have things to say—indeed, as Nietzsche observed, we spend a lot of time ignoring those messages, for if we attended to even a portion of them we could hardly become conscious of the world outside (*GM*, 38). But sometimes—in moments of great pain or joy, for example—our body's messages get through.

Such struggles to articulate, in fact, are all around us and may take any of a vast variety of paths in addition to those of science. Often, for example, matter speaks by means of the "loyal and disciplined spokespersons" we call artists. The poems of Sappho have always been held to furnish particularly clear examples:

> Let me see thee, but a glimpse—and straightaway
> Utterance of word
> Fails me; no voice comes; my tongue is palsied;
> Thrilling fire through all my flesh hath run;
> Mine eyes cannot see, mine ears make dinning noises that stun;
> The sweat streameth down,—my whole frame seized with
> Shivering—and wan paleness o'er me spreads,
> Greener than the grass; I seem with faintness
> Almost as dead. (Sappho 1938)

The words of the poem, to be sure, are Sappho's; but the wordless physical manifestations of desire which she describes with such painful exactitude are her body's. We find something similar, conveyed via imagery rather than words, in Cézanne's paintings or Michelangelo's statues.

Sometimes, indeed, matter has no spokesperson but speaks to us directly. Many people, standing at the edge of the Grand Canyon, have remarked on the baffling interplay of colors tumbling into its depths and on how unconceptual-izable the whole enormous thing is. But equally eerie is the canyon's sound—a sort of barely audible rushing somewhere within you, as if you were holding your ear to an impossibly immense seashell. Listen to someone crying for a loved one or a mother cooing to her child, and you will hear the same thing on a smaller scale. In none of these cases does the message come from what we call the human mind; it originates in the body and its sensations. Michelangelo captured the situation in his famous response to someone who asked him how he managed to put the magnificent shape of the Pietà into cold marble: "I didn't put it in, it was already there. I merely chipped away the excess." The matter sent the message; the artist merely "channeled" it.[6]

"Normative reflection," writes Iris Marion Young, "arises from hearing a cry of suffering or distress, or feeling distress oneself" (Young 1990b, 5). It is my thesis that in order to overcome the paradoxes of Enlightenment, and with them its own crisis, philosophy's normative reflection must not merely at-tend to the speaking of matter; it must incorporate such speaking into its own procedures.

Infinite Jest and the Speaking of Matter

That the speaking of matter can furnish methodological principles is shown by what is perhaps the most sustained and informative account of it in recent American literature—the one to be found in David Foster Wallace's novel *Infinite Jest*. I will consider two treatments of it there. One is "negative" in that it shows what the speaking of matter is not; this account serves as an intermedi-ate account between Boyle's air pump and the second, more positive account Wallace gives. That positive account is for its part couched as a reflection on the aims and procedures of Boston Alcoholics Anonymous ("Boston AA").

The negative account presents a men's consciousness-raising group into which one of the book's two protagonists, Hal Incandenza, stumbles by ac-cident. The meeting takes place behind a closed door in a windowless room, in which—as with Boyle's air pump experiments—a number of men are sit-ting, watching something from different angles (*IJ*, 799, 804). What they are watching in this "experimental space" is not (quite) a machine, however, but a middle-aged man named Kevin Bain, who as the scene begins is crying (*IJ*, 799–809). Like the air pump, Kevin utters no words but moves in certain ways: clutching a teddy bear as do all the men, he rocks back and forth on his hams. His nose is running and the back of his neck is turning red.

But these material messages are not what the spectators are looking for. At the center of the circle of chairs, several deep, is the group leader, Harv; and Harv already has an interpretation of what is going on: "I'd like to suggest that we men all hold our bears tight and let our Inner Infants nonjudgmentally listen to Kevin's Inner Infant expressing his grief and loss" (*IJ*, 800). One step up from the sheer materiality of the machine (or of a human body) is, apparently, what Harv calls the "Inner Infant," whose needs are primordial and need to be named: "name the feeling" is one of Harv's repeated injunctions to the group (*IJ*, 801, 802, 803, 804).

Harv is not only at the center of the room but is equipped with a blackboard and CD player; he is in control of the space and assumes the role of experimenter. The ensuing "experiment" does not, however, filter out Harv's agency; rather, he progressively orchestrates the entire sequence of events by evoking a series of responses from Kevin until the "experiment" reaches the conclusion Harv wants.

To Harv's first injunction to "name his feeling," Kevin responds jargonistically: "I'm feeling my Inner Infant's abandonment and deep-depression issues" (*IJ*, 802). Kevin then fleshes this out by saying that his Inner Infant is standing in his crib crying for his parents; Kevin believes their absence to be the reason for his current pain (*IJ*, 805). Harv's next statement to Kevin is couched as a request, but it is one which in fact *informs* Kevin of what he is supposed to be feeling: "We're asking you to name what your Inner Infant wants right now more than anything in the world" (*IJ*, 803). Kevin responds that his Inner Infant wants "to be loved and held." Harv has already appropriated this, however, with some jargon of his own: "The work we're here to do . . . is to work on our dysfunctional passivity and tendency to wait silently for our Inner Infant's needs to be magically met" (*IJ*, 802). Kevin's real problem is not what he thinks it is—the absence of his parents. It is his need to take action. Kevin is thus trapped between what he himself feels—the loneliness he traces back to the absence of his parents—and what Harv and the group insist that he be feeling: the need to take action.

Harv's first step in getting Kevin to take action is to repeat what Kevin has named as the Inner Infant's need, but in slightly different words which emphasize Kevin's passivity: "Please, Mommy and Daddy, come and hold me." When Kevin accepts this wording, his Inner Infant recedes and his voice takes on "an edge of good old adult mortified embarrassment." As Kevin distances himself further from his Inner Infant, his voice becomes a "monotone of pathos" and also takes on a lisp, in a more or less conscious "performative invocation" of the Infant (*IJ*, 804).

Harv then takes the next step in the encounter: since Kevin's parents are not going to come (they died when he was eight [*IJ*, 803]), Harv tells Kevin to ask one of the other men in the group to love and hold him (*IJ*, 805). After scanning the room Kevin points the arm of his teddy bear at Jim, who is seated toward the back of the room eating yogurt (*IJ*, 806). Harv, still in control, urges Kevin to ask Jim explicitly to come up and hold him and love him; Kevin makes a "mortified sound," puts his hand over his face, and begins "projectile weeping" (*IJ*, 806). He then asks Jim eleven times to come and hold him, but the other man remains impassive. Kevin's mortification reaches the point that he falls back to his "Infant persona" (*IJ*, 807).

The whole group now stop being witnesses and start calling out to Kevin to do something. Kevin appeals to Harv, who merely smiles (*IJ*, 807). Kevin then decides that he must get up and go over to Jim and ask him yet again (*IJ*, 806). He starts walking toward Jim, but Harv is still not satisfied: "Is this how an Infant moves toward its needs, Kevin?" he asks. So Kevin gets down, still holding his teddy bear, and crawls on three limbs toward Jim, his face "unspeakable." The scene ends (*IJ*, 808).

As with the air pump, we have here a closed room, a material object (Kevin), witnesses, and an experimenter (Harv). Yet the whole thing miscarries, because its real purpose is not to allow Kevin's matter to speak but to reinforce the power of Harv and his theories. From Harv's point of view the "experiment" has been successful: Kevin has given the expected responses as reliably as any machine. But Kevin has been trapped from the beginning in a conceptual vocabulary of "Inner Infant" and primordial needs, and what has been engaged with is not his matter but his adult ego—the one that is being mortified.

The more detailed, positive account of the speaking of matter contrasts with this on virtually every point. Such speech is exemplified at various points in the book, most notably in Mickey's speech (*IJ*, 958–960) and John L's speech (*IJ*, 345–347). It is reflected upon at length by the book's second protagonist, Don Gately (*IJ*, 343–379).

Boston AA as Wallace depicts it may or may not be fictional; the issue, in fact, is irrelevant here. More important is that its meetings are not held in closely bounded rooms but in the open cafeteria of a nursing home whose "indecisive green" walls are broken up by AA banners which have been brought in (*IJ*, 344); the group also meets, informally, in the public space of a diner

(*IJ*, 354). There is no leader: Boston AA is a "benign anarchy" whose officer presides only to open the meeting by drawing the name of the evening's first speaker (*IJ*, 345). Each speaker, at the end of his talk, then chooses the next (see *IJ*, 960). There is thus no one to direct the proceedings or keep order in any way (*IJ*, 357–358).

The audience is not composed of experts or of adherents to any theory but of members of a different AA group and so of strangers to the speaker (*IJ*, 343). The speakers, from one group, thus know each other but do not know the audience; members of the audience know each other but do not know the speakers. Each talk is thus given, essentially, to a roomful of strangers.

What keeps order in the room is outside the room. Indeed, it is the very fact that there *is* an outside:

> AA's patient enforcer was always and everywhere Out There: it stood casually checking its cuticles in the astringent fluorescence of pharmacies that took forged Talwin scrips for a hefty surcharge, in the onionlight through paper shades in the furnished rooms of strung out nurses who financed their own cages' maintenance with stolen pharmaceutical samples. (etc.; *IJ*, 359)

Everyone in the room is confronted with the same alternative—AA or death—and those who stay know it (*IJ*, 348). If they leave, that will be their doing: you cannot be expelled from AA. You can even bring a flask and drink from it during the meeting (IJ, 352, 356–357): "If you don't obey, no one will kick you out. They won't have to. You will kick yourself out" (*IJ*, 357).

The audience's job is simply to listen to the speaker (*IJ*, 353) and—at the end—to applaud and call out encouragement (*IJ*, 368). In private conversations (in the diner or after the main meeting) a few "suggestions" may be offered, but only if based on personal experience or on what one has personally found out, and only if presented in a "casual but positive and encouraging way" (*IJ*, 365). Unlike the case with Kevin Bain, then, no one tells you what you are feeling or what you must do.

The point of these arrangements is what Wallace calls "surrender"; and what must be surrendered is what, for modern philosophers since Descartes, is the most basic component of the human self: the individual will (*IJ*, 357).[7] This seems to accord poorly with the absolute license given by the fact that no one can be expelled, but the purpose of that is to make sure that the surrender is free:

> If you don't *want* to do as you're told—I mean as it's suggested you do—it means your personal will is still in control and . . . your personal will is the web your

Disease sits and spins in, still. The will you call your own ceased to be yours as of who knows how many Substance-drenched years ago. It's now shot through with the spidered fibrosis of your Disease. . . . You have to Starve the Spider: you have to surrender your will. . . . You have to want to surrender your will to people who know how to Starve the Spider. You have to want to take the suggestions, want to abide by the traditions of anonymity, humility, surrender to the Group conscience. (*IJ*, 357)

Just Do It, they say, and like a shock-trained organism without any kind of independent human will you do exactly like you're told. (*IJ*, 350)

The situation, in spite of its absence of rules and its "benign anarchy," is thus tightly controlled:

Check your head at the door. Though it can't be conventionally enforced, this, Boston AA's real root axiom, is almost classically authoritarian, maybe even proto-Fascist. (*IJ*, 374; emphasis added)

As with the air pump, and as did *not* happen with Kevin Bain, human agency is filtered out of the speaker by the root axiom, which is augmented by three corollaries. Each of these has to do with one aspect of time.

With regard to the past, causal attributions are frowned upon:

The why of the Disease is a labyrinth it is strongly suggested that all AA's boycott, inhabited as the maze is by the twin minotaurs of *why me?* and *why not?*, a.k.a. Self-Pity and Denial. . . . The Boston AA "In Here" that protects against a return to the "Out There" is not about explaining what caused your Disease. (*IJ*, 374)

The etiology of the addiction, a "labyrinth" in which causes are unclear at best, is merely a way to escape from responsibility (*IJ*, 370–376)—a way taken, we saw, by Kevin Bain. In Boston AA, you are free to talk about what you have suffered, but not about why. In Kant's terms, shortly to be explained more fully, you can recapitulate what you have been through, but you cannot apply the category of causality to it.

With regard to the future, the danger is more immediate. It lies in one's expectations of how the audience will react:

Speakers who are accustomed to figuring out what an audience wants to hear and then supplying it find out quickly that this particular audience does not want to be supplied with what someone else thinks it wants. (*IJ*, 367–368)

Keeping people from talking with their minds, in the sense of predicting what the audience will want to hear, is also promoted by having the audience be a roomful of strangers.

Finally, the sin of the present tense is irony—separating oneself from what one is saying and thereby elevating oneself above one's situation. As Wallace puts it elsewhere, "all U.S. irony is based on an implicit 'I don't really mean what I am saying'" (Wallace 1997, 67). To be an ironist is to raise yourself above your own words and therefore above the circumstances in which they (and you) come forth; it is to refuse to be present in your speech. Harv, who continually dissimulates his actions and intentions, is a case of this; Boston AA, by contrast, is an "irony free zone" (*IJ*, 369; see also *IJ*, 367).

These three "sins" are ways of avoiding surrender: by finding causes on which to blame our pasts, attempting to meet the expectations of our audiences, and raising ourselves above what we say. The opposite of them all, and therefore intrinsic to the speaking of matter, is spontaneous sincerity; and the content of such speech, whatever that content may be, is the "truth, unslanted and unfortified" (*IJ*, 369).

The speech of someone who has "checked his (or her) head at the door"—the speaking of matter—then comes about as follows. First, it operates, as we have seen, under specific regimes of space and time. The space is open, without determinate boundaries and without a "Harvish" leader at its center. Impulses also do not come at the speaker from the peripheries: no one in the audience urges this action or that. Rather, the audience, composed of strangers, remains impassive until the end. The space is thus entirely open, to allow the matter to come forth.

The temporal regime, consisting of the three corollaries I have noted above, is (unlike the spatial regime) up to the speaker: it is a set of rules by which she must abide in her speech. Since the rules are negative ones—no causality, no expectations, and no irony—they are ways for the brain to step aside, again allowing matter to come forth.

Bound by no expectations, the speaking of matter does not address anyone in particular and is not dialogical. Nor is it a soliloquy, for it does not match or express the speaker's thoughts. It begins, rather, with words which are empty—with formulas which are spoken no matter what the speaker is thinking: "Hi, I'm [first name], and I'm an alcoholic," followed by various hollow statements of how great it is to be sober today and to be here (*IJ*, 369). The point of these formulas is twofold. First, it shows the speaker's desire to surrender to the group by mouthing its platitudes. Second, if you repeat them often enough you will come to believe them (*IJ*, 350, 369). As with Derrida in *The Post Card*, then, we put ourselves together out of what we say.[8]

Third, the speech becomes egocentric, as the speaker recapitulates her own experiences with the Disease. This recital is structured not by causality but by free association (*IJ*, 352). Speech at Boston AA is thus anything but a smooth development or conscious argument. Like *Infinite Jest* itself, it is "full of blank cunctations and dissociated leaps" (*IJ*, 368). Though it is supposed to be limited to one's personal experiences, since no one can be expelled it can in fact be about anything whatsoever; pages 351–352 have a long paragraph presenting someone talking about his bowel movements. Nor is any affect forbidden: Gately himself, in early days, delivered many angry speeches against AA, "sitting there spraying vitriol, wet-lipped and red-eared, trying to get kicked out" (*IJ*, 353).

The lack of expectations thus does not apply only to the audience: the speaker has no expectations about what she herself is going to say next. The speaker in fact does not know what is going to work, not only for the audience but for herself. This is because no one knows how AA itself works; the entire experience is unfathomable:

> Part of getting comfortable in Boston AA is just finally running out of steam in terms of trying to figure stuff like this out. Because it literally makes no sense. (*IJ*, 368)

The unfathomability of AA is in fact a "binding commonality" of the group (*IJ*, 349); "the whole thing is so improbable and impossible that you're so flummoxed you're concerned you're maybe brain-damaged" (*IJ*, 351).

The speech—and the speaking of matter generally—is thus unified by the fact that the recapitulation of the speaker's experiences with the Disease always ends in the same place: with the speaker at the "same cliff's edge," confronting the alternatives of stay or die. This is what Boston AA calls the Bottom, and the ultimate job of the audience is to realize and accept that they are at the same Bottom (*IJ*, 348): "*Hearing* the speaker means like all of a sudden hearing how fucking similar the way he felt and the way I felt were" (*IJ*, 365).

The Bottom is not a turning point destined to be transcended: it "emerges" recurrently no matter how long someone has been sober (*IJ*, 349). The audience's acceptance of it as their own ongoing situation is an empathetic "Identification" (*IJ*, 345). This Identification, (which could be read as Wallace's equivalent of Platonic eros),[9] is the only expectation the audience has at the beginning of the speech. The speaker, speaking to strangers, does not even have that expectation but only a willingness to surrender.

The speaking of matter as conveyed in *Infinite Jest* is therefore a very complex discourse, requiring with equal stringency rules and the absence of rules. As Wallace puts it:

> It's about a goofily simple practical recipe for remembering that you've got the Disease day by day and how to treat that disease day by day. (*IJ*, 374)

> When you forget about the Disease, you forget who and what you are. (*IJ*, 355)

In its more extended versions, in science and art, the speaking of matter is precisely such a reminder of who and what we are.

The speaking of matter as presented by David Foster Wallace has obvious affinities, which I will not explore here, with meditation techniques and with psychoanalysis.[10] Its main point—as with Boyle's air pump—is to allow matter to speak in such a way as to be witnessed (but not interfered with). In this, the speaker recapitulates her experiences with the Disease without subjecting them to conceptual discipline.

The Speaking of Matter and Reflective Judgment

The speaking of matter as conveyed in all these ways—scientific investigation, artistic inspiration, and Boston AA—is not something that we can bring about; it happens, or does not happen, of its own accord. But as Wallace shows, even in its rawest forms it is something we can encourage or stymie, depending on whether we operate along the lines of Harv, on the one hand, or of Boston AA, on the other.

In order to incorporate the speaking of matter into philosophy, we must understand how the rules and nonrules for its encouragement relate to the rules and procedures that have been characteristic of philosophy for millennia—and, importantly perhaps, how they relate to the tacit agreements and exclusions which those rules and procedures presuppose. Any such comprehension will have to be general enough to cover such diverse things as artistic inspiration, scientific creativity, and the practices of Boston AA. It will thus be relatively empty; the many and marvelous ways in which matter speaks can hardly be comprehensively forced into a single set of categories.

The prospects for drawing from philosophy even a limited framework for understanding the speaking of matter seem dim indeed. The idea that matter itself can speak, that it can send us more or less coherent messages, is, as

I noted previously, about as foreign to the metaphysical tradition as anything could be. When we turn to the most implacable critics of metaphysics to date, the postmodernists, we find them to be generally inimical to two important traits of the examples brought forth so far. First, as I will argue in more detail below, motifs like Derridean *différance* and Foucaldian power, true to their origins in Husserl's passive time synthesis, resist conceptualization—a resistance that philosophy must recover as such.[11] The examples of the speaking of matter adduced above, by contrast, show an implacable drive *toward*, rather than away from, conceptualization. Second, and related, is that the speaking of matter is not "other" then we; as Wallace shows, its end is nothing less than "Identification" by the audience with the speaker—the audience's acceptance of what I have called, on the purely material level, sympathetic vibrations.

Nonetheless, philosophy does offer some resources for the task at hand, in the form of Kant's doctrine, advanced in the third and last of his *Critiques*, of reflective judgment.[12] In the *Critique of Judgment*, judgment is "reflective" when it begins without any predetermined concept under which the sensory manifold is to be brought. Since a concept for Kant is basically a rule (*CPR* A, 106; B, 198, 219), this means that there are no rules: the situation is "shaky."

But there is a *demand* for a concept, which Kant expresses at the very moment he first introduces the concept of reflective judgment:

> If the universal (the rule, principle, law) is given then judgment, which subsumes the particular under it, is *determining*. . . . But if only the particular is given and judgment *has to find* the universal for it, then this power is merely *reflective*. (*CJ*, 179; emphasis added)

Why does judgment "have to find" a concept? Why not merely leave things with an unconceptualized particular? The reason, expressed in Kant's language of mental faculties, is that in order to be brought under a determinate concept of the understanding, the sensory manifold must first be rendered accessible to the understanding in general: it must be recapitulated by the imagination as having a harmonious form (*CJ*, 191, 204–207, 251–252). In terms of Boston AA, such recapitulation occurs as the spontaneous recital of the speaker's experiences with the Disease—a recital which was unified by the way the recital homed in on the Bottom. In such recapitulation for Kant, the object presented must be sufficiently organized that it seems possible that the understanding could say something about it—could form a concept of it. This requires more than simply that the object be perceived as disposed in space and time; it must be given as having some sort of structure which, in the absence of a definite concept, is determinable only as a harmonious form.[13] Such harmonious form is not originally given in raw sensation but comes to be only in the imagination's recapitulation of it. So recapitulated, it is in Kant's language purposive; but since it lacks a concept, its purposiveness is without a definite purpose—as the Bottom, in Boston AA, is not a defined situation but a suspension between AA and death.

The coming-to-be of harmonious form as an indeterminate unity presupposes that it is possible for a more determinate unity to be found, for if the imagination knew at the outset that such further unity was impossible—that there was no common feature to the sensory givens which could be expressed in a concept—the recapitulation would not even begin; there would be no point to it. Thus, the drive to conceptual articulation is for Kant what inspires my imaginative recapitulation of the sensory givens; when I perceive a set of such givens as in any way coherent, I am already underway to a concept. That, I suggest, is why judgment "*has* to find" the universal.

Imaginative recapitulation, we may say, shows us Kant's version of the "filtering out" of human agency which, for Boyle, allowed matter to speak. For Kant, it is not all human agency which gets filtered out—his account of aesthetic experience is far too resolutely subjective for that—but the activity of the more "determinate" faculties, reason and the understanding. These must be placed in complete abeyance (you must "check your brain at the door") to allow the imagination to do its work of presenting the object as having a harmonious but entirely nonconceptualized form. This abeyance is presented by Kant as uncontroversial; he simply assumes that we can experience a thing without applying to it any concept at all of what it is. This assumption depends on the radical separability of the faculties of the mind and is (to me, anyway) one of the least persuasive parts of Kant's entire account of aesthetic experience; such abeyance, to the extent that it happens at all, is something which needs to be encouraged. Just such encouragement, we saw, was the point of the three corollaries of Boston AA—the demands to avoid causality, expectations, and irony.

Since reflective judgment is supposed to be without a concept, there can be no determinate criteria for what a "harmonious form" is. My perception of such a form on a given occasion may thus, for all I know, be entirely idiosyncratic. Thus, in a reflective judgment (or judgment of taste), agreement from others is only "imputed," not "postulated."[14] Others are free to disagree with my aesthetic judgments, and if they do, agreement cannot be logically forced on them. It will be forthcoming only if they have perceived the same object in the same way I have, a possibility which Kant calls "common sense" (*CJ*, 238–239, 293–296). In Boston AA, the common sense of a speech is validated by the audience's reaction at its end.

The validity of an aesthetic judgment can, then, be decided only dialogically: by discussing the matter with other people who have experienced that object, rather than by reasoning it out on one's own as in a mathematical proof (see *CJ*, 210).[15] We may say that reflective judgments have not the actual universality of mathematics but a drive to universality: their validity consists in the way that making them pushes us into dialogue with others and enlarges our thought (*CJ*, 293–296).

The scope of this account of reflective judgment is wider, even in Kant, than first appears. Since empirical concepts are formed from experience, it follows for him—though he does not actually say so—that all empirical judging first begins without a concept: the first human being to see a horse, for example, had no concept of the "equine" under which to bring it (see *CJ*, 286–287). Reflective judgment is therefore simply empirical judgment in its pristine form as an activity of the subject (*CJ*, 286–287). To put the matter in the broadest terms, the movement of reflective judgment is essential to language itself. This is shown not by Kant but by Wittgenstein, when he argued that private languages are impossible. If a word makes sense to one person, there are already rules for its use, and those rules can be followed by others as well.[16] The same argument can be made on the level of communities: if a word makes sense to one group of people, the rules of its use can also be followed in other groups—if only because we are, as Aristotle noted, the "most imitative of all animals" (*Poetics*, 2.1448b7). Unless human beings shared the capacity for imaginative recapitulation, they would never be able to formulate mutually intelligible cognitive judgments. It is this capacity, rather than any determinate concepts, which from an aesthetic point of view indicates something universally human.

Politics, Universality, and the Speaking of Matter

In the global uprising of the last half century, large numbers of human beings, formerly relegated in one way or another to the status of mere matter—people of color, women, gay men, lesbians, groups formerly colonized in a variety of ways—have stood up and started to talk. Some of the discourses they have produced can be viewed, philosophically speaking, as examples of the speaking of matter, that is, as phases of a giant search for new concepts.[17] The political valences of the speaking of matter reinforce and undo some of the by-now-familiar concerns of postmodernity.

When it assumes the form of a *search* for concepts, the discourse of the oppressed necessarily begins without them, that is, on shaky ground: in pains and joys felt by people whose experiences are not captured by the concepts currently available. The search has a drive to move beyond these because (like reflective judgment) it requires other people to validate it. Betty Friedan captured this in the first chapter of her world-changing *The Feminine Mystique*, originally published in 1963, which is titled "The Problem That Has No Name":

> The problem lay buried, unspoken, for many years in the minds of American women. It was a strange stirring, a sense of dissatisfaction, a yearning that women suffered in the middle of the twentieth century in the United States. Each suburban wife struggled with it alone. As she made the beds, shopped for groceries, matched slipcover material, ate peanut butter sandwiches with her children, chauffeured Cub Scouts and Brownies, lay beside her husband at night—she was afraid to ask even of herself the silent question—"Is this all? . . ."
>
> But on an April morning in 1959, I heard a mother of four, having coffee with four other mothers in a suburban development fifteen miles from New York, say in a tone of quiet desperation, "the problem." And the others knew, without words, that she was not talking about a problem with her husband, or her children, or her home. Suddenly they realized they all shared the same problem, the problem that has no name. They began, hesitantly, to talk about it. Later, after they had picked up their children at nursery school and taken them home to nap, two of the women cried, in sheer relief, just to know they were not alone.
>
> Gradually I came to realize that the problem that has no name was shared by countless women in America. . . .
>
> If I am right, the problem that has no name stirring in the minds of so many American women today is not a matter of loss of femininity or too much education, or the demands of domesticity. It is far more important than anyone recognizes. It is the key to these other new and old problems which have been torturing women and their husbands and children, and puzzling their doctors and educators for years. It may well be the key to our future as a nation and a culture. We can no longer ignore that voice within women that says: "I want something more than my husband and my children and my home." (Friedan 2001, 57, 62, 77)

Insofar as it is captured by the conceptual resources of Kant's account of reflective judgment, the speaking of matter contains a drive which pushes beyond feelings, not merely toward concepts but toward words, and so toward communities. This leads to an odd sort of human universality, for while no general definition or characterization can be given for what constitutes "the human," it is also true that no limits can be set on who is going to belong to such a verbalizing community. To return to Wittgenstein, the rules of use for any words used by members of one group to communicate with each other can also be understood by outsiders to both groups, and potentially by all "humans."

Not, however, in the same way. Hate speech is understood very differently if you belong to the hated group,[18] and even outside that very broad context some words ineluctably retain different sorts of meaning for different sorts of people. Men can learn how to use the word "menstruation," for example, but no man knows how it feels to menstruate. Situations like this are difficult to capture with traditional philosophical semantics, according to which the two main means of definition—verbal (dictionary) and ostensive (by pointing)—can be grasped by all. But when a woman talks about menstruation, it is not as something she learned about from a dictionary, and it is not as something she can point to. For her (that is, apparently[19]) it is a complex of sensations which is unified enough to call for words. Kant might call such a complex a "free play"; we might deem it a "semantically provocative feeling." A man, who cannot have the sensations in question, can learn how to use the words which have come to articulate it in social situations or language games; but he cannot learn the bodily feelings from which the words arose.

Even these limits do not, however, align precisely with the boundaries of specific groups. Inherent in the nature of language itself, Hegel argued at the beginning of the *Phenomenology of Spirit*, is that experiences are never wholly captured by language: each experience is to some degree unique, while the meanings of words are general (*PhS*, ¶¶ 90–110, 58–66). Thus, while no man can understand what it feels like for a woman to menstruate, no woman can fully understand how it feels for another woman to menstruate, either; while men are definitely outside the range of semantically significant feelings in this case, women are not exactly inside it. Whether one is understanding the feelings that a word captures or the rules for its use, in other words, is a matter of degree—to a degree.[20]

The speaking of matter points to a view of humanity not as a universal essence but as a ferment of communities, many of them temporary. It does not "reduce the Other to the Same" or deny the all-important differences between the oppressor and the oppressed. There are in fact two sorts of otherness sustained in the peculiar universalism of the speaking of matter. The first of these concerns the obvious difference between what we may call original and sympathetic vibration. In order for all the tuning forks to vibrate, one of them must be struck; its vibrations are more intense and come first. Similarly, just as there are obvious differences between a woman's understanding of "menstruation" and a man's, there is an obvious difference between churnings in my gut—sobs—caused by my sudden loss of a loved one and churnings in my gut caused by the sobs of someone else who has suddenly lost *his* loved one. The primal anguish evoked by Betty Friedan in the passage quoted above is not the same anguish that wells up in a male reader of her text, and for that reader to have even a minimal understanding of his own feelings he must appreciate that fact. The speaking of matter is shared but in only one direction: like all sound, it propagates.

Thus, to say that women, people of color, or people of unconventional gender incorporate the speaking of matter is not to place them somewhere outside the more privileged segments of humanity; still less is it to denigrate them in the traditional ways, by positioning them close to matter or nature and farther from the "men of reason." It is to allocate to them the primary role in an instigation of vibration: it is they who set others in motion. The susceptibility to such motion is something that all humans share, not only with each other but with matter itself. If this commonality is denied, the hearer steps into what we saw Wallace call "irony": she tries to raise herself above the speech, and so above the matter which speaks. The same happens in all identification with metaphysics, that is, with any "closed system" of mutually reinforcing words, concepts, rules, and propositions. The idea that "we" are metaphysical through and through, that we are trapped in it or are defined by our obliviousness to power, is another way of saying, to use Wallace's word, that we are at bottom ironical and cannot escape that status. Such irony is a commonplace in the wake of Heidegger's discussion of the inevitability of inauthenticity in *Being and Time* (*BT*, 129, 131, 179), which is perhaps why one of Wallace's favorite adjectives for "irony" is "postmodern."[21]

This kind of otherness shows us a couple of ways in which the speaking of matter departs from postmodern themes such as Derridean *différance* and Foucauldian power. Like these, it escapes the categorial grid of Western philosophy, for in that tradition matter is precisely what cannot speak—if it could speak, it would be able to think and would not be matter but mind. But there is more to the speaking of matter than its escape from conceptual totalization; it does not merely, in Derrida's words, instigate "the subversion of every realm" (Derrida

1973, 153). Nor does it exhibit the purely accidental productivity of Foucaldian power, which operates in accordance with "the secret that [things] have no essence or their essence was fabricated by a piecemeal fashioning from alien forms" (*FR*, 78). Rather, since even a single sob or laugh is a set of coherent bodily movements, the speaking of matter can be recapitulated as what Kant called a "harmonious form." As such, it calls for words from a position outside them. The forming of these words, over time, thus has the retrospective unity of something not entirely accidental. Indeed, as we will see, it is in a peculiar sense "teleological."

Derridean *différance* and Foucaldian power, because in themselves they flee determinacy and produce it, when they do, as external and accidental to themselves, are both ahistorical: not in the sense that they have some sort of transhistorical, atemporal presence, but in that the different ways in which they operate at different times do not ground or condition each other in any intelligible way. Such is not the case with the speaking of matter. The speeches given at Boston AA, for example, are not independent "epistemes" or "regimes" connected only tangentially with such large-scale historical contexts as American attitudes to alcohol and religion. They not only prolong these and subvert them; they develop out of them.

The speaking of matter is thus a developmental process. In that respect it has more to do with what Heidegger calls the "way to language" than with power and *différance* (Heidegger 1971c). But for Heidegger, Being, though it originates beyond language, always speaks in a particular language (preeminently, as we know, German). The speaking of matter, by contrast, comes from and brings with it something that all humans share: their material condition. When you hear matter speak, it is never from a place unequivocally outside you. Wherever the vibrations originate, they pass through your body too.

This brings us to the second kind of otherness involved in the speaking of matter, which is that between "metaphysics," our developed system of words and concepts, propositions and rules, taken as closed and thus as independent of what is outside it, and speaking matter itself. It is only when we identify ourselves with the former that the speaking of matter can be viewed as "other." Derrida tends to view such identification as inescapable—as a kind of entrapment within metaphysics:

> We have no language—no syntax and no lexicon—which is foreign to this history: we cannot enunciate any destructuring proposition that has not already had to slip itself into the form, the logic, and the implicit postulates of the very thing which it wishes to challenge. (Derrida 1978b, 280)

From the point of view I am currently formulating, the speaking of matter is indeed wholly other; but it is other to metaphysics—not to us. The resulting standpoint is close to the reverse of Derrida's position: insofar as our words come from the speaking of matter, we have none that are *not* foreign to metaphysics. If that were not the case, the kind of "Identification" between speaker and hearer produced at Boston AA would not be possible; for that "Identification" is achieved not by reason and argument but by "blank cunctations and dissociative leaps," by the spewing of vitriol and the description of bowel movements. The first kind of otherness is also necessary for the "Identification," because part of seeing how "fucking similar" my situation is to that of the speaker is recognizing the primacy of his.

The final contrast between the speaking of matter and more familiar postmodern themes concerns its peculiar kind of *telos*. In the philosophical tradition, a *telos* is something specific; indeed, for Aristotle it is often the form or essence of a thing.[22] A speech at Boston AA enables "Identification" and reaches its final stage, its *telos*, when it is summed up in the Bottom. The *telos* in question, however, is of an untraditional type. Such a speech is "purposive" (or teleological) in that its end gives a degree of retrospective unity to the discourse which led to it; but it is without specific "purpose" (or *telos*) in that this end leaves open the widest of all alternatives: life (in AA) or death. The Bottom thus has the peculiar teleological structure of Kantian "purposiveness without purpose," and now we can see that its universality is of the kind that Kant claims for reflective judgments. This is because "Identification" can only by *imputed* by the speech. The Bottom is not *your* situation until you admit that fact; and while not everyone does admit this, everyone can—to some degree. For the basic formula of the Bottom is, as we saw, "AA or death"; and while the "AA" part of that does not hold for everyone, the "or death" part does. To that extent, all our situations are "fucking similar."

To identify the Bottom as the *telos* of a speech at Boston AA is thus not to attribute anything specific to it. In particular, attributing to scientists, or to humans generally, an unbounded drive to community does not mean instating a particular form of such community—even an Enlightened form—as its *telos*. That is what Kant tried to do at the end of the *Critique of Judgment*, defining the relevant community as "humanity under the moral law" (*CJ*, 425–434). I have discussed his catastrophic failure elsewhere,[23] and will here merely remark that the paradoxes of Enlightenment I discussed in the Introduction render Kant's view of the resulting community rather defective.

On the present model, what people are homing in on throughout the many forms of the speaking of matter is a vocabulary which, even when aimed in the first instance at their own groups, will enable their individual experiences to be communicated to others at large. The drive for such a language is evident in Sandra Harding's recent discussions, in her *Science and Social Inequality*, of truly pluralistic science. At the core of Harding's treatment is the view that scientific separatism—what she calls the "delinking" of diverse epistemic traditions—is simply not an option: "We live in a continually shrinking world where policies and practices of one country inevitably have effects on their neighbors and on distant countries" (*SSI*, 56).

As for countries, so for communities: their boundaries are increasingly porous. Given this, the question for Harding is one of whether the integration of what were formerly free-standing scientific traditions will go forward under the hegemony of just one of them—what Harding calls "northern" or "western" science—or will proceed in a more democratic fashion, with borrowings and influences going in all directions, leading to a situation in which "there would be many culturally distinctive scientific traditions that share some common elements with other modern western science and, no doubt, each other" (*SSI*, 58).

True integration will not take place around the Western ideal of a single "unified science" in the form of a single set of sentences viewed as true by everyone—the aim, of course, of Kant and the Enlightenment in general. But there will eventually be—there will have to be—a set of sciences which exhibit partially discordant views (*SSI*, 153), all of which are couched in words which enable the disagreements, as well as the agreements, to be stated clearly.

That Harding's view of science can be transposed into a view of language highlights a final characteristic of the speaking of matter: it is not always entirely without concepts or words. Though it can begin in the "cries of suffering" which instigate normative reflection for Young, as a drive for articulation it acquires words and concepts as it goes along. There is thus a continuum between the alinguistic and the conceptual, and the speaking of matter may be found anywhere along that continuum; indeed, a given text or utterance may contain a variety of such levels within itself.

Slave narratives, for example, often move among such multiple levels. Frederick Douglass's 1855 *My Bondage and My Freedom* not only reworks his 1845 *Narrative of the Life of Frederick Douglass, an American Slave* but is reworked again in the 1895 *Life and Times of Frederick Douglass*; each version is in part, inevitably, a reflection on the earlier ones, and as Cynthia Willett has noted, *My Bondage and My Freedom* adds explicit comments on the central event of the *Narrative*, Douglass's encounter with the "slave breaker" Edward Covey. When Willett comes to read Douglass's autobiographies in terms of how they do and do not square with traditional Western concepts of freedom (a reading I will discuss a bit more in Chapter 8), she is thus in a sense collaborating with Douglass—reflecting on his reflections on his recapitulation of his life (*MESM*, 134).

Constructing a language which will capture the common elements of culturally distinctive traditions is a gradual process and, I suggest, a job for philosophers, at least in part; indeed, as I will argue in Chapter 2, they have been at it for millennia. It requires, as I put it earlier, that philosophers see reason itself as "malleable." Now we have a clue—if no more than that—as to what this malleability means: seeing reason not as the employment of a canonically fixed set of argument forms (as in the context of justification) but as the articulation and development of new rules, that is, of new words—a social process of discovery. The "laws of logic" are then to be seen as Quine saw them: as the most general outcomes of that overall process. Since generality is what the process itself is driven toward, logical generalizations are what Robert Brandom calls them: "late-coming" (Brandom 1994, 134). Seen this way, the aim of philosophy is to abet not merely the growth of science but the larger process of which science is part: the speaking of matter.

CHAPTER 2

WHAT IS THE
HISTORY OF PHILOSOPHY?

The History of Philosophy: Irrelevance or Contamination?

In the Introduction I traced philosophy's current problems to its Enlightenment heritage. They are actually much older, for the paradoxes of Enlightenment that I discussed there arise from failures in the relation of philosophy to time itself. To get at those failures—and, more importantly, to get at their remedies—will require the incorporation into philosophy of what I called, in Chapter 1, the "speaking of matter." And this will require in turn the restoration of certain relationships between philosophy and its history. This runs counter to current views that the history of philosophy is irrelevant to philosophy (and so, a fortiori, to everything else). Note Quine's remark (reported at Rorty 1982, 211) that those who are good at philosophy tend not to be good at the history of philosophy, and vice versa. Never the twain should meet, except over drinks at the faculty club—and then only if the historians are buying.

It is not that the history of philosophy is unimportant; we philosophers are (usually) proud of the long history of our discipline and (usually) require that every undergraduate major study at least some of it. Some philosophers even hold that the history of philosophy forms an essential background to contemporary debates. Even on this view, however, we must at some point put the history aside and start dealing with contemporary issues and figures—unless, of course, we want to be historians. The history thus remains separate from the philosophy.

And so it is understandable that "history of philosophy," as I conceive it—as what Jacques Derrida called "one great discourse" (Derrida 1982c, 177), a single train of critical thought that has run for millennia and has produced, among many other things, us—is not practiced in America. What we call "history of philosophy," as I will argue presently, is history which has been diced into a set of separate specializations—separate from each other and so from us. This is very different from the situation, for example, in Germany, where thinkers such as Dieter Henrich, Otto Pöggeler, Manfred Riedl, and Josef Simon have all focused not on individual thinkers but on the ongoing development of philosophical paradigms—paradigms which they also undertake to advance critically. And it differs from the situation in France, where Jacques Derrida was a "professor of the history of philosophy" at the École normale supérieure, and where Michel Foucault, on joining the Collège de France, defined his field as "the history of systems of thought."[1]

History, perhaps, is something Europeans want to be freed from and so must understand. We Americans think that we are already free of it and fear that any serious study of it risks trapping us in it again. Hence, to my knowledge, the United States contains not a single professor of the "history of philosophy" or of "systems of thought." In an academic climate where organizations proliferate and research centers burgeon, there is no society or center for the study of the history of philosophy (such a center is nascent at Emory University at the time of my writing). An outstanding American philosopher, John Searle, guilelessly begins a book on intentionality by lamenting that he is not sufficiently ignorant of what previous philosophers wrote on the topic and promising to do his best to ignore it (Searle 1983, ix–x).

Philosophy's detachment from its history has many motivations other than fear, and one of these must surely be its allegiance to the Enlightenment. Recall Kant's refusal, noted in the Introduction, to move from criticisms of the way he carried out his program to a critique of the basic principles of that program itself. The main rationale for that, we saw, lay in Kant's faith that something could be rationally established for all time, so that it never needed to be revisited. Such a view dismisses history, for on its basis what can history be but the repository of questions closed? Once you think you know that you have gotten something right—and only then—you can dismiss its history; the dismissal of history thus brings exemption from criticism, and to dismiss history is, all too often, to dismiss criticism of oneself. The spirit is rather like that conveyed in Constantine's supposed words on closing Plato's Academy: "Either the ancients agree with us, in which case we do not need to read them; or they disagree with us, in which case they are wrong." Of course, Constantine was not a philosopher but an emperor; yet his views are still around. When an Ivy League philosophy department hired a Plato scholar not so long ago, one of its senior figures was alleged to complain that there was no need to hire someone to "teach the mistakes."

The study of history often leads to uncomfortable levels and kinds of criticism; but the brute historical fact is that precisely such unbridled self-criticism has been the core of philosophy since Socrates. Getting philosophy to take history seriously is thus necessary for getting it to take itself seriously. To do this, philosophers must be able not only to tolerate the critics of our own most basic positions but to join them. We must adopt the humble and realistic Rortian position that was once paraphrased by Michael Williams to the effect that "we can never say that we know we have gotten anything right."[2]

Certainly the history of philosophy can be taught in ways that *make* it irrelevant to us. The very structure of the university, with "departments" offering "courses," conduces to two of them. One, provoked I suspect by precisely the fear I have mentioned, is what I will call the "Jurassic Park" style of history of philosophy: the giants of the past are kept safely locked away from one another in separate pens, lest they band together and destroy us in horrible ways. This separation produces Kant scholars who know a bit about Leibniz and suspect, at times, the existence of Fichte; Plato scholars who are dimly aware of Parmenides and know just enough Aristotle to think he perverted Plato; Derrida scholars who know nothing of Husserl; and so on.

The other unhappy kind of history of philosophy which we come upon in America is the "supermarket shelf" variety, in which purified flakes of past wisdom, not dangerous but not very nutritious either, are boxed up together and presented to the student as he rolls his intellectual shopping cart down the syllabus. The philosophers are not separated from one another—they are all right there on the shelf—but they are presented as coexisting in a sort of virtual intellectual present. That there is a dynamic, critical development from earlier thinkers to later ones—that philosophy is not simply a shelf of surpassed doctrines but an ongoing "learning process"—is once again lost, in the pabulum. The loss leads to topical anthologies in which philosophies separated from one another by centuries or even millennia are taken off the shelf, opened, and shaken for whatever they can contribute. That Plato came before Fichte, and Fichte before Husserl, is evident, at most, in the table of contents.

The Jurassic Park view sees the thinkers of the past as great, threatening individuals—but then, great individuals, like Achilles, are always threatening. The Supermarket Shelf view sees them as indistinguishably happy flakes, nestled together on a shelf. If either of these ways of packaging it is valid, there is in fact no such thing as the history of philosophy at all. There is merely a variety of thinkers and groups of thinkers, all of whom happen to be dead. But this raises two questions: (1) Is this view accurate? (2) Should it be? The first question leads us to ask: What is it that might escape these packages? Is there something about the history of philosophy which the pens and boxes of the standard philosophy curriculum fail to capture? The second question leads us to ask: Should we try and capture it? Or should we maintain that not doing so is salutary?

I have already suggested that common to both views is a denial of the way philosophy is structured over time: as a learning process such that later philosophers have benefited from earlier ones. There is thus an ongoing critical development, first written down in Greece, of which we are the latest result. So much is in fact empirically evident and gives us the answer to question (1). To avoid prejudicing question (2), let us not suppose that this development is a good thing. Let us even suppose, à la Searle, that it really amounts to an undesirable sort of "contamination" of later thinkers by older and less able ones. There is a lot of evidence that such contamination is real—so real that even those philosophers who advocate the most radically individualistic views of philosophy succumb to it. Rorty, for example, might never have come up with his view of philosophers as "ironists" radically independent of previous thought if he had not read Kuhn, who had read Bachelard, who was reacting against Émile Meyerson's attempt to give an Hegelian reading of Einstein's theory of relativity.[3]

Searle is not the first philosopher to fear his forebears. Modern philosophers in general are prone to nervous dismissals of previous thought as mere twaddle. Thus, Descartes's method of doubt was explicitly designed to put out of operation all that philosophers had achieved up to him (*DOe*, 7:17). Hume wanted their books burned (Hume 1894, 165). Kant charitably classified previous thought into "obsolete, worm-eaten dogmatism," skeptics who "loathe all steady cultivation," and indifferentism, "mother of chaos and night" (*CPR* A, ix–x). Hobbes's condemnation of Aristotle is, unlike his spelling, classic:

> And I belieeve that scarce any thing can be more absurdly said in naturall Philosophy, than that which is now called *Aristotle's Metaphysiques*; nor more repugnant to Government, than much of what hee hath said in his *Politiques*; nor more ignorantly, than a great part of his *Ethiques*.[4]

And yet, and yet. A few pages after Descartes doubts everything, he is appealing to the notion that there is no thought without a thinker—a clear relapse into Aristotelian substantialism.[5] Hobbes's anti-Aristotle quote is from *Leviathan*. Yet the subtitle of *Leviathan* is: "the Matter, Forme, & Power of a Common-Wealth Ecclesiasticall and Civill," and each of those first three terms is subsequently used in its Aristotelian sense (see *MO*, 128–144). When Hume says that "reason has no power whatever to move us; only passion can do that, and reason is, and ought to be, the slave of the passions, and can never pretend to any other office than to serve and obey them,"[6] he is taking those terms over from Aristotle, for whom reason also had no "power to move us" (see *PI*, 222–225). Kant's account of the faculty of understanding can be seen as a rethinking of Locke, just as his views on the faculty of reason are a reconceptualizing of Leibniz.[7] However critically, and however acutely, these thinkers engage previous thought, they also turn out to be committed to certain categories and formulas for no better reason than that some older thinker, or group of thinkers, also used them. The fact of such contamination shows that even when we aim at universal or necessary truth, we are shooting at it from the moving decks of culture and psychology—both of which are themselves the results of histories, of course, though of very different sorts.

So far we have it that the history of philosophy exists, and exists as relevant, at least in the recurrent failures of philosophers to break free of it. If this view is accurate, then the answer to question (2) above is no. What the Jurassic Park and Supermarket Shelf views of the history of philosophy fail to grasp is something that shouldn't be there in the first place.

Defining the History of Philosophy

It is a fine thing for a reasonable person, said Plato, to know everything; but a good second best is at least not to remain ignorant of oneself (*Philebus* 19c). If one's thought is contaminated by the thought of one's forebears, if there are formulas one is committed to for no better reason than that one's teachers, or one's teachers' teachers, were committed to them, then this is a fact about ourselves which philosophical integrity demands we recognize. Unacknowledged contamination is surely a bad thing for philosophers. But when contamination is recognized and sustained, is it even contamination? Isn't it, rather, loyalty to a tradition?

To begin answering this question, I must raise another one. I have claimed that the history of philosophy is not an intellectual Jurassic Park or supermarket shelf (and more evidence for that is to come); but is it *merely* a set of contaminations? Or is there something more to it? Intellectual honesty, as well as our Socratic descent as philosophers, bids us not to pass judgments, pro or con, until we know what it is that we are judging. And so, before pronouncing the history of philosophy to be good, bad, or irrelevant, we should ask what it is. It seems reasonable to look at the phrase componentially. The question "What is the history of philosophy?" then resolves into "What is history?" and "What is philosophy?"

But here we have a problem. "History" is already difficult to define, in part because of its ambiguity: it can refer to the actual facts of the past—"history" as what actually happened—or to what historians write, which usually requires the ordering of those facts into a coherent story. The situation with "philosophy" is even worse, for 2,500 years of effort have not produced an agreed-upon definition for the term. It is therefore tempting to say that philosophy is *essentially* indefinable, that indefinability is inherent in the nature of the thing—as is the case with "human being" for Sartre in "Existentialism Is a Humanism" (Sartre 2001, 45). Perhaps, in fact, the indefinability is the same in both cases: maybe philosophy is so direct an expression of humanness that it partakes of the open-ended nature of human existence.

Since Sartre believed that the human being has no fixed nature, the indefinability of the word matched the openness, the *néantité*, of the thing. This left in place the traditional demand that language capture reality "as it is." But in "Existentialism Is a Humanism," Sartre goes further: any attempt to define "human being" is not merely wrong-headed but a step toward fascism, because assigning a specific nature to humanity means denying its general capacity to transcend itself, thereby denying human freedom. Similarly, I suspect, for "philosophy." Even if philosophy had a distinct and determinate nature, it would be wrong—morally wrong, if not exactly a step toward fascism—to try to capture that nature in a definition. For all attempts to define philosophy—so far, anyway—have inevitably tended to define certain people *out* of philosophy. And I do not think anybody should be in the business of defining people out of philosophy. Anyone who wants to call himself a philosopher should be free to do so. The nature of philosophy, like that of "human being" for Sartre, should forever be "yet to be determined."

So I am going in fact to sidestep the whole project of defining philosophy, by adopting a strategy—really, more of a dodge—of Saul Kripke's. After discussing his view, adopted in accordance with the exigencies of modal logic, that if x is identical with itself it is necessarily identical with itself, Kripke confronts the question of whether this holds for our everyday notion of identity. Why should English obey the legislations of modal logicians?

Kripke's dodge is to say that even if the inference in question does not hold for the English word "identical," he, Kripke, is free to invent the word "schmidentical" for which it does hold. Schmidentity then turns out for Kripke to be the philosophically interesting version of what we ordinarily call "identity" (Kripke 1980, 108).

This device, though it seems frivolous, is actually (as Kripke says) of wide application and great potential for philosophy. It can identify where philosophers are pulling one of the oldest of bait and switches: giving us an account of some notion they have in fact invented while pretending it is an account of something we have been thinking about all our lives. This goes back, Heidegger has claimed, to Plato's accounts of truth and related notions (Heidegger 1998f, 155–181). Is it anything but honest to admit that Donald Davidson gives us a theory of *schmeaning*, instead of meaning? That John Rawls wrote *A Theory of* Schmustice, not of *Justice*? That Hegel and Heidegger have theories of *Schmahrheit*, not *Wahrheit*? That Aristotle replaced Plato's *schmeidē* (for they were not really *eidē*, or visible forms) with a theory of *schmousia*?

Philosophy as a Search for Truth

And so, on the way to understanding what the history of philosophy is, I am going to abandon the great and serious task of defining "philosophy" and take upon myself the rather more humble one of defining "schmilosophy," a task which has the added advantage of not being immoral because it doesn't hurt anyone to be told he is not really a "schmilosopher." Before beginning this, however, I want to think about—and, I hope, dispose of—a common way of defining, or at least characterizing, good old "philosophy."

The main criterion for a good definition, traditionally anyway, is that it should pick out all the objects that we want to pick out with the term we are defining, and no others. In the case of philosophy (as in that of schmilosophy), the objects are what we might call the "Usual Crew" of paradigmatic philosophers: Parmenides, Heracleitus, Socrates, Plato, Aristotle, and so on down to Husserl, Heidegger, Quine, Derrida, Kripke, et al.

But, as Euthyphro discovered in the case of "holiness," we need more than a list. We want a unified definition—a rule for deciding what is covered, and what not, by the term defined.[8] What single enterprise were these people engaged in that makes all of them philosophers? Clearly, writing—or, in Socrates' case, being written about. Anything else?

It is commonly said that they were all engaged in a search for truth. Quine put the matter thus, with his customary substitution of "logic" for "philosophy":

> Logic, like any science, has as its business the pursuit of truth. What is true are certain statements; and the pursuit of truth is the endeavor to sort out the true statements from the others, which are false.[9]

The idea that the history of philosophy is the written record of a search, or searches, for truth surely gives us an important component, if not the entirety, of the traditional conception of philosophy. To be sure, like all definitions of philosophy, this one can be used, justly or not, to exclude people—people such as Nietzsche and Foucault, for example.[10] But its problems do not end there. Characterizing the common enterprise of the Great Philosophers as a search for truth in fact has four further objections against it, of which the first three are as follows:

1. Philosophers have never found very many truths. If you want truths, go to science.
2. Who wants truth, anyway? I can give you a million truths about my living room:
   a. George W. Bush is not in it.
   b. Lady Gaga is not in it.
   c. G. W. F. Hegel is not in it.
   d. Elwood P. Dowd is not in it.
   e. Neither is his rabbit friend . . .
3. What is "truth"?

The first two considerations make us wonder why philosophers want to pursue truth at all. They rest on the now-standard view that truth is that property of a sentence, proposition, statement, or belief which enables that sentence, etc., to inform rather than mislead us. (I take this characterization of truth to be vague enough to include the three main theories current today—correspondence, coherence, and pragmatic.) The Usual Crew I began to list above would generally have agreed with it, before going their separate ways. According to both Martin Heidegger and Alfred Tarski, it even constitutes the traditional consensus on truth in Western philosophy.[11]

But when Heidegger and Tarski agree on something, we need to be careful. In fact, the traditional consensus on truth lasts only so long as truth is not pursued (see *TD*, 43–44). When we ask the Usual Crew what sort of "truth" each of them is after in his writings, the answers diverge spectacularly, and the divergence dates from ancient days. For Plato, the goal of philosophy—as of life—is, throughout the dialogues, not a set of sentences, etc., but nearness to *t'alēthē*, "the true things" or the Forms. Augustine, in his *Soliloquies*, suggests that truth is preeminently the divine being to whom philosophy is supposed to bring us; Anselm's *De veritate* follows him.[12] Commenting on Plato's *Parmenides*, Proclus distinguishes "falsity" from "error": if S is P, and I say "S is not P," I have asserted a falsehood. But *both* "S is P" and "S is not P" are in "error," because in them the mind moves from the subject to the predicate of the sentence.[13] Neither true nor false statements are adequate to the unity of the One, and that unity is the truth toward which Proclean inquiry moves.[14] *The whole Platonic tradition*, in other words, is outside the philosophical consensus on truth; and if all philosophy is really a set of footnotes to Plato, then philosophical truth in the "traditional" sense is found—if at all—only in the notes.

But it is not only Platonists who stand outside the consensus. In the Middle Ages, Thomas Aquinas claimed, in his *De veritate*, that a thing is "true" insofar as it "fulfills the end to which it is ordained by God." With respect to the human intellect, this means truth is found in the conformity of intellect to thing:

> Since everything is true according as it has the form proper to its nature, the intellect, insofar as it is knowing, must be true according as it has the likeness of the thing known, which is its form as a knowing power. For this reason truth is defined as the conformity of intellect and thing; and to know this conformity is to know truth.[15]

Aquinas thus arrives at the consensus view of truth as inhering in sentences, beliefs, and the like. But this is a view he *arrives* at, from his more basic view that to be true is to have one's proper form, and he arrives at it only in the case of the human intellect; angels, having different forms of intellect, would have different forms of truth. For Aquinas, in any case, the job of philosophy, as a pursuit of truth, is to give the intellect its proper form, the one God ordains for it: philosophy brings us not close to God but to the proper human distance from him.

Spinoza's *Ethics* first defines truth as "adequate to its object," which would sound traditional enough to people such as Heidegger and Tarski if they ever read Spinoza. But "adequacy" for Spinoza turns out to mean not "correspondence to an object" but "existence as in the mind of God" (him again!).[16] God knows an object in relation to its entire causal context, which is ultimately the entire universe: to know anything adequately is to know everything adequately. Though we cannot attain such adequacy in our knowing, the job of philosophy is to get us as close as we can to it; and we are back again to the notion of philosophical truth as nearness to God.

In short: the "traditional consensus" on the nature of truth is a myth. The kind of truth which these Great Philosophers actually pursue is not a matter of beliefs or sentences but of human proximity to the divine. This means that objection (2) above is put out of play, for no truth, on this view of truth, can be trivial.

One lesson of this is that while God has by now disappeared from overt definitions of truth, the word retains a semireligious power. It operates like an ancient icon which still moves us to reverence even though we no longer believe in what it represents. That, perhaps, is why Nietzsche identified truth as the last god:

> These "no"-sayers and outsiders of today, those who are absolute in one thing, their demand for intellectual rigour . . . these are very far from being *free* spirits: *because they still believe in truth.* . . . Precisely in their faith in truth they are more rigid and more absolute than anyone else. (*GM*, 118)

Nietzsche to the contrary, however, the problem with philosophical views of truth is that they are not nearly "rigid" enough. Overall, when it comes to telling us what the divine is, and what human proximity to it amounts to, you can hear almost anything you want to hear from the Usual Crew; the preceding discussion, brief though it is, shows that they are all over the map. And when we ask them what correspondence or coherence actually amounts to, we hear very little. This all makes it rather difficult to mean anything at all by defining philosophy as a search for truth.

So it looks as if Quine is overly generous: the history of philosophy is not only irrelevant to philosophers. It is worse than that. It is an embarrassment to all humanity, a confused groping for something which no one needs (2 above) and which philosophy never finds (1) because it doesn't know what it is (3).

But there is one more objection, the fourth, to characterizing philosophy as a search for truth: that it may really in fact be something else. What if the Usual Crew were in fact engaged in a common project, but a *different* one? And what if that other common project, unlike philosophy's "search for truth," was something definite and important, and that it largely achieved its goals?

Schmilosophy as an Obsession with Ousia

Actually, I am going to advance two other suggestions as to the common project of the Usual Crew. First, far more uniform across them than their views on truth is their obsession (I think the word is not too strong) with something else entirely—with a kind of ontological structure. My claim is that the common enterprise of the members of the Usual Crew is better captured by viewing them as clarifying, validating, and criticizing that structure than by viewing them as pursuing truth. I will be exploring this in subsequent chapters and so here will provide only a general sketch.

Because this way of conceptualizing the common enterprise of the Great Philosophers is my own,[17] intellectual honesty compels me not to advance it as an account of "philosophy." Instead, I will resort to Kripke's dodge and call what I am talking about "schmilosophy." The Great Schmilosophers are the same crew as the Great Philosophers, but they are seen as engaged in a very different project. It is like discovering that all those people running around on the open field are not playing rugby very badly but soccer quite well.

We cannot, I suggest, understand the game that philosophers are playing without understanding what it is that I am calling "ousiodic structure." I call it "ousiodic" because Aristotle first advances it as nothing less than the structure of Being itself—or as he calls it, *ousia*. Something has "ousiodic structure" to the extent that it exhibits three traits:

1. It has continuous boundaries, beyond which no part of it can be found ("boundary").
2. The order and functioning of what is inside those boundaries is generated and/or maintained by a single unitary component of the thing, called its "form" ("disposition").
3. That single component governs all interaction with the world beyond the boundaries of the thing ("initiative").

A few brief and sketchy considerations taken from the Great Schmilosophers can show that, beginning with Aristotle (for whom see Chapter 3), they got a lot of mileage out of this structure. When Aristotle himself applies it to the body, it gives him the concept of an organism under the control of the soul, its form. Applied to rational beings, it yields the concept of the moral agent, ordering moral matter—desires and actions—into a coherent *bios*. Applied to the family, it is the all-too-reassuring structure of patriarchy. Applied to the state, it yields a variety of structures, from unified parliamentary government all the way to totalitarianism. Applied to the cosmos, it is the unmoved, governing center of Aristotelian "monotheism"—as he quotes Homer at the very end of *Metaphysics* 11, "the rule of many is not good, one ruler let there be."[18]

The metaphysics of ousia, conceiving Being as the domination of form over matter, is not a "theory" of oppression in the sense that it consists of a number of sentences held to be true of all and only cases of oppression. Because its origins are independent of the phenomena to which it applies, we might, in a quasi-Kantian way, call it a "schema" for viewing, as well as instigating, real-world oppression. It serves as an abstract description of a kind of state to which actual givens may approximate in all sorts of ways. As such, for example, it loosely captures Marilyn Frye's less abstract characterization of the overall experience of oppressed people:

> The living of one's life is confined and shaped by forces and barriers which are not accidental or occasional, and hence avoidable, but are systematically related to each other in such a way as to *catch one between and among them* and *restrict or penalize motion* in any direction. (Frye 2005, 85; emphasis added)

This formulation is *loosely* captured by the ousiodic model in two senses. First, the model tells us what to look for on more specific levels: on Frye's level, we look for boundaries ("barriers") which restrict motion and so impede one's ordering of one's own life. In actual cases of oppression, the nature and effectiveness of these boundaries will be different, perhaps greatly so. Second, the capture is "loose" in that Frye's account does not trace the restrictions to the operation of a unified ousiodic form. This divergence from the schema can be explained by suggesting that Frye is describing a specifically modern form of ousiodic oppression, in which (as we will see in Chapter 4) a plurality of ousiodic forms combine to attack the individual from a variety of angles. There is a unity to these forms—otherwise their operation would not be, in Frye's word, "systematic"—but the unifying feature is not apparent.

This looseness on the part of the ousiodic schema frees it from the rigors of exact truth but does not put to rest all doubts about general accounts of oppression. In a now-classic article, Iris Young has argued that a single definition of oppression is impossible to give. Oppression can for her be characterized as "structural phenomena that immobilize or diminish a group," but that relatively empty characterization is the best we can do (*FFO*, 42). Instead, Young offers a Wittgensteinian "family" of characteristics, or "faces," of oppression.

My claim that we can flesh out Young's abstract characterization in terms of the three axes of boundary, disposition, and initiative is supported by the fact that the first three of these five "faces" of oppression correspond to those axes. "Exploitation," the "transfer of the results of the labor of one social group to benefit another" (*FFO*, 49), takes from the first group their effects on the world beyond their own boundaries—it appropriates their initiative. "Marginalization," the fate of people whom "the system of labor cannot or will not use" (*FFO*, 53), refers to people living within the geographic boundaries of a political system but excluded from the boundaries of its economy—from its factories and workplaces. Instead, they have traditionally been located in prisonlike institutions: "poorhouses, insane asylums, schools" (*FFO*, 54); today we find them in shelters or SROs or fending for themselves in parks and under bridges. And "powerlessness," the inability of people to "regularly participate in making decisions that affect the conditions of their lives and actions" (*FFO*, 56), is the appropriation of their power to order their own lives—their individual disposition is replaced by that of the state or economic system.

In addition to these three faces of oppression, Young lists two more: "cultural imperialism" and "violence." The distinction between these two and the first three is not made wholly clear; the former set is said both to concern the "social distribution of labor" and to be a "a matter of concrete power in relation to others" (*FFO*, 58). These are not the same thing, and I suggest that the second of them is nearer to the mark: exploitation, marginalization, and powerlessness are oppressive practices directed specifically against groups, in that they treat every member of a group within society in the same way and differently from members of other groups. The other two do not.

Cultural imperialism, in which "the dominant meanings of a society render the particular perspectives of one's own group invisible at the same time as they stereotype one's group and mark it out as the Other" (*FFO*, 58–59), operates *to the detriment of* a specific group (or groups), but it operates *on* all members of the society. Stereotyping people of color and women as intellectually inferior, for example, has to succeed both with them and with white males. As such, it is the imposition of a specific conceptual order on the minds of everyone within the society and so is a generalized exercise of dispositional power. Because it is thus generalized to the whole society, this face of oppression is the most closely connected with what I call the "speaking of matter," which is likewise generalized; this can be seen by replacing "invisible" in the quotation from Young with "inaudible."

Violence, for its part, is a "random, unprovoked attack" on a person and/or his property (*FFO*, 61). As such, it is the physical replacement of an individual's disposition over his own body or property with that of another. Often this happens because the person is a member of one group or another—be it a minority or majority group within society, as when someone sets out to kill someone else because he is black or white; be it the society itself, as when someone starts shooting people in the street; or be it humanity itself, as when someone goes to a foreign country and starts shooting people. Violence in Young's sense is thus directed against individuals because they are members of a group, but it does not treat all members of that group in the same way; it selects one or a few for violation. Since the members of the hated group have no individual characteristics which the perpetrator feels bound to respect, it is random: any member of the hated group will suffice.[19]

Young's five faces of oppression thus turn out to be cases of the three axes of boundary, disposition, and initiative. Those axes themselves, as I will argue in Chapter 3, are grounded in metaphysics. Their looseness as a schema means that a rigorous theory, or a univocal definition, of oppression is indeed impossible; but the operations of that schema in much that is oppressive in lives and societies cannot be overlooked. Neither can the role of philosophers in formulating and validating it.

Ousiodic structure is endemic to life today, certainly in what is called the Western world. A moment's thought about architecture, for example, will reveal bounded and centrally controlled spaces serving as homes, classrooms, courtrooms, churches, and factories, each disposed by the power of a parent, teacher, judge, cleric, or manager. A particularly telling example of such structure is the men's consciousness-raising group portrayed in *Infinite Jest*, which I discussed in Chapter 1. It is located in a windowless, and so strictly bounded, room whose center is occupied by Discussion Leader Harv, armed with his CD player and blackboard; the entire scene is a display of Harv's control over the room and its occupants, especially Kevin Bain. Meetings of Boston AA, by contrast, are held in the relatively open spaces of cafeterias and diners; no one person occupies the center permanently or even gets to choose who does. People are free to wander in and out and (within broad limits) to behave as they wish while inside.

The speaking of matter in general, moreover, contravenes the three traits of ousia; that is why the two are correlative concepts. Just as anyone is allowed to attend a meeting of Boston AA, so anything whatever is allowed into the speeches given there; though a speech is supposed to contain a recapitulation of the speaker's experiences, it can (as Gately's diatribes show) include anything whatsoever and so has no discursive boundaries. Since the speech is nonconceptual, in that its unifying factor, we saw, is not understood by the speaker, it has no thesis to argue and no arguments with which to do so; it therefore has no determinate principle of unification and so no dispositive form. Since its speaker has no expectations, she has no control over or interest in how others understand her words: the speech lacks initiative in that no message goes from speaker to hearer.

Schmilosophy and Ousia

Schmilosophy, as I define it, has been preoccupied with ousiodic structure ever since Aristotle. Much of the preoccupation has taken the form of efforts to validate it in various ways. For Aristotle, the domination of form is *metaphysically* necessary because matter has a tendency to fly apart, or to resolve itself back into its elements (earth, air, fire, and water):

> We must ask what is the force that holds together the earth and fire [in the bodies of living things], which tend to travel in contrary directions; if there is no counteracting force, they will be torn asunder; if there is, this must be the soul. (*De anima* 2.4.216a6–8)[20]

For Aristotle, the chaos of matter—what Nietzsche, in *The Birth of Tragedy*, would call "Dionysian"—cannot be disciplined into the ordered cosmos we see around us except by the activity of form. Ousia is thus metaphysically validated as basic to nature itself (its epistemological validation, as basic to knowledge, will be discussed later in this chapter).

Later on, the metaphysical validation of ousia leads beyond nature into theology—and runs into trouble when it arrives. For Thomas Aquinas (as we will see in somewhat more detail in Chapter 4), matter is not obstreperous but wholly docile. It cannot resist form, because the dispositive, ordering power of form is ultimately exercised by God, and resistance to God is sin—which is restricted to creatures with free will. Yet though God, for Aquinas, is responsible for ousiodic structure (which of course makes that structure something good), he does not exhibit it himself, or any other kind of structure: as Étienne Gilson emphasized, God for Aquinas is *ipsum esse*, sheer being itself (see Gilson 1956, 32–44).

Still later, ousia becomes a matter of philosophical psychology. In Descartes (who will also be discussed in Chapter 4), the mind is conceived as *res cogitans*.

Like any *res*, it has rather strict boundaries. They are given, in fact, in the *cogito* itself—everything that counts as "thinking" belongs to the intellect. Within those boundaries, moreover, order is maintained by a single component: the will (see *MO*, 109–127).

What is new for Descartes is that nature has lost its own ousiodic forms (what the medievals called "substantial forms") and has become mere matter in motion. Ousia is thus no longer validated by nature and requires justification from beyond it. This was most zealously sought by the schmilosophical figures generally known as the Rationalists—preeminently Descartes, Spinoza, and Leibniz. Rationalism of their general sort has traditionally been defined by its claim that unaided reason can give us knowledge of nonsensible reality. Equally important, from a schmilosophical point of view, is the *kind* of nonsensible reality of which the Rationalists claimed knowledge: it is divine. Not only Descartes's *intellectus* but his *deus*, along with Spinoza's *deus* (*sive natura*) and Leibniz's Kingdom of Grace, all exhibit various forms of the three traits of ousiodic structure I have adduced (see *MO*, 194–202). The "supersensible realm" of the Rationalists is thus ousiodic reality, rendered supernatural and thereby given divine sanction—though one very different from the kind of theological sanction it had in Aquinas.

When the Empiricists rejected those supersensible knowledge claims, they did not reject ousia—just the Rationalist vindication of it. Hobbes is an example (see *MO*, 128–144). We have seen the relish he takes in ridiculing Aristotle; but in spite of his contempt, Hobbes's quasi-totalitarian state is thoroughly ousiodic in structure. That he already suggests this with his subtitle means that we, the readers, have acquiesced in ousiodic structure before we have even opened Hobbes's book. An ousiodic conception of the state, in other words, is not argued for in the book but is presupposed by it, as a preliminary decision which makes reading the book possible. Thus, for Hobbes—as for other Empiricists such as Locke and Hume—the status of ousiodic structure as the basic ordering principle of the human realm is established neither from nature, as the Aristotelians did it, nor from supernature, as the Rationalists did it. It is simply presupposed (see *MO*, 128–179).

The Empiricists destroyed the Rationalists' attempt to validate ousiodic structure on metaphysical grounds; but the unargued brutality of their own presupposition of it left it open to increasingly sharp challenges, which have mounted and multiplied as humanity has learned more and more about itself. One of the first of these challenges was social contract theory, which I will discuss briefly in Chapter 4. When the American Founding Fathers claimed that sovereignty comes only from below (from what Hobbes might have called the "matter" of the commonwealth [Hobbes 1991, 128–132]), they were challenging the ancient ousiodic schema in the case of the state. Such challenges have come to define modernity. From Marx's early analyses of the ousiodic structure of the factory, Nietzsche's valorization (in his concept of power) of initiative above boundary and disposition, and Heidegger's non-ousiodic account of human life in *Being and Time* (see *MO*, 205–229), down to contemporary queer theorists, race theorists, and feminists who diagnose and protest the many ways in which people are relegated to the status of mere matter, challenges to ousiodic structure have come to coincide not only with philosophy itself but with virtually all of world history.

So: the history of *philosophy* as a search for truth, which is how Quine sees it, may well deserve dismissal as a confused and irrelevant waste of time. The history of *schmilosophy* as an obsession with ousia, though it covers basically the same figures, cannot be so easily dismissed—for ousia is the central structure of Western selves and institutions, and its fate affects us all.

When we look at the common enterprise of the Usual Crew in a schmilosophical way, it becomes very important indeed. But it does not exactly become appealing. It seems to amount to obsessive tinkering with an archaic and outmoded structure of domination—a structure which would best be tossed into history's wastebasket, were it not still so powerful today. Schmilosophers thus appear, like the philosophers in my Introduction, to be caught on the wrong side of history—defending not merely the exclusions necessary to the Enlightenment but an even more ancient picture of social relations as ineluctably oppressive.

But of course there is more.

The Wrong Side of History

There are a number of ways in which philosophers might come to be on the wrong side of history. In the Introduction I traced the problem back to the paradoxes of Enlightenment, but the notion of ousia as schmilosophy's most basic structuring principle enables us to trace it back even further. And not in a good way.

When feminists started writing about the history of philosophy in the 1980s, it was very quickly realized that philosophy was highly misogynistic and that the misogyny went well beyond the personal antipathies of philosophers. Over and over again, even philosophers who explicitly proclaimed the spiritual and intellectual equality of women espoused doctrines and used metaphors in other contexts which expressed and promoted patriarchy.[21] Race theorists such as Eze and Outlaw, to whom I have previously referred, made similar discoveries—except for the absence of explicit proclamations of equality.

Something was clearly wrong, then, not merely with the philosophers but with philosophy itself. But what? As Genevieve Lloyd put it in 1984, the history of philosophy was clearly not a mere "conspiracy by male philosophers" (MR, 109); philosophers themselves, at least a number of the "great" ones, seemed as likely to be trying to combat patriarchy as to uphold it. But if individual philosophers had goodwill toward women, their complicity with patriarchy must be something they had fallen, rather than jumped, into. The problem was thus considered, including by Lloyd herself, to be a passive complicity rather than an active one—to lie in a conceptual inertia which kept philosophers from rooting out sexist conceptual structures and patterns of thought. However deeply embedded within philosophy these were, at least they had not been put there by philosophers themselves. Lloyd suggests that they had instead been inherited from philosophy's ancestral roots in Greek nature worship (MR, 2–3) or from the sexist social structures in which philosophers, like other people, had been acculturated (see MR, 103). Susan Moller Okin, in a similarly path-breaking work, suggests that they are derived from the experience of growing up and living in a patriarchal family structure (see Okin 1979, 289).

More recently, Ann Cudd has suggested several more reasons: that philosophers generally come from privileged groups; that oppression is too emotional a topic to be comfortable for them; that it is not abstract enough to interest them; or that, as a case of injustice, it can be treated in the framework of a more general "theory of justice" (Cudd 2006, vii–ix). This externalism makes perfect sense: with respect to the universalism claimed by the philosophical tradition, any treatment of women is already a diversion (we saw Outlaw make a similar point with regard to race in the Introduction). If women, people of color, and nonheterosexuals are alien topics for philosophy, how can their oppression be anything else?

These considerations are, as far as I can see, entirely correct; but I do not believe they are complete, for they locate philosophy's complicities with oppression outside philosophy itself: in ancient religion, family structure, various psychological traits shared by philosophers, and a failure to appreciate its specific nature as injustice. When we turn from these specific forms of oppression to the general schema for oppression that I have advanced here, we uncover something rather more disturbing: a level which provides philosophical justi-

fication for sexual, racial, class, and gender oppressions by positing a single generic structure according to which any being whatsoever is securely bounded;
within its boundaries, one of its components (its "form") is privileged to generate and/or order the rest; and only that form controls entrance into and egress
from the bounded structure.

Various practices and traditions of oppression, including the gender oppression in the ancient household and ancient religions, certainly preexisted
the philosophical codification of ousiodic structure; such formulation does
not appear in philosophy before Aristotle.[22] But it did not originate *solely* in
traditions and practices of the nonphilosophical world. In Aristotle's ousiodic
ontology, as we will see in the next chapter, oppression has changed its nature:
instead of a number of disparate practices and traditions, it has become a single
project, validated by the comprehensive philosophical systems erected on its
base. Aristotle's metaphysics thus did for oppression what Kant says the Greeks
in general did for mathematics (*CPR* B, x–xi): Aristotle, the Euclid of oppression, took a disorganized set of inherited rules of thumb and converted them
into a systematic enterprise which could be methodically pursued. Preexisting
traditions and practices were actively reshaped by philosophy itself in such a
radical way that they can be said to have received a new birth, a more generic
and abstract one—and one all the more effective for that.

Philosophy did not merely inherit this general structure of oppression from
outside, and it is not merely tolerated by philosophers through lack of energy,
intellectual inertia, psychological predispositions, or the like. However critical
philosophers may have been of one or another of its specific manifestations, on
the more general ontological level philosophers have enthusiastically installed
and consolidated it almost without exception. From its never-questioned redoubt on the ontological level, it keeps returning, even where philosophers
themselves think it has been extirpated.

This means that one of the standard ways in which today's "theorists" deal
with philosophy, together with its history, is incomplete. What I have in mind
is taking over the results of earlier philosophers and using them as tools for
the critical exploration of various phenomena in art, politics, history, and the
like—"culture" in the widest sense. If my preceding considerations are right,
the history of philosophy is no benign storeroom of ideas. It is a booby-trapped
labyrinth, where the best-lit hallways are often dead ends and the real pas-
sageways are often hidden. The only way to see what tools are really available
within it is to explore it—very carefully. Which doctrines were really arrived

at, and which were simply shoved in for psychological or cultural reasons or merely for want of something to say? What hidden complicities and underlying quarrels have philosophers taken over unknowingly from their forebears? What, really, have they not gotten right?

Such investigation is most sorely needed, I will argue in Chapters 5 and 6, in the cases of Hegel and Heidegger. Simply casting Hegel as a metaphysical throwback, for example, obscures the real impact of what I will call his concept of "dialectical reflection," which is in truth free not only from Hegel's reported eschatology of Spirit or Consciousness but from *all* overarching themes, including that of class struggle. It can thus be employed in a very broad variety of contexts. Simply dismissing Heidegger as a Nazi hides the fact that his thought does not pulverize reason in toto, as Nazism does, but fractures it in careful ways.

For the moment, another problem is at hand. Aristotle's philosophical account of form and matter is as abstract as anyone could wish for in an ontology; and as such, it does not suffice for accounts of actual oppression. For these, we need to see the fundamental ousiodic schema put into operation; and this requires in turn the delimitation of a specific space in which to deploy that binary. The strictly *binary* terms which Lloyd (like so many others) invokes— "'superiority' and 'inferiority,' 'norms' and 'difference,' 'positive' and 'negative,' the 'essential' and the 'complementary'" (*MR*, 103)—thus do not suffice to clarify the nature of oppression. It also needs what Marilyn Frye calls an "enclosing structure of forces and barriers" (Frye 2005, 88), and so deploys a *triadic* structure which includes the boundaries within which those binaries operate. That is why Charles Mills gives such importance to the way the racial contract normatively structures space (*RC*, 42–53) and why (as we saw in the Introduction) Lucius Outlaw brings up the construction of a "subworld" to which people of color are consigned. Otherwise, people assigned to the "lower" ("material") elements of the binaries cannot be oppressed, for they always have available to them the freedom of the Maroon—the ability to relocate somewhere else.[23] The ensuing condition of a Maroon individual or group—self-excluded and alone, deprived of the benefits of the surrounding society as well as of its evils—has not received careful definition and study from philosophers; but that it is in some sense a life of freedom is not in dispute—otherwise there would be no Maroons. Conceptual binaries such as the ones Lloyd mentions (and Derrida deconstructs) are important components of oppression; but until they are deployed and take effect within determinate boundaries, they are merely conceptual tools in the drawer. The notions of *pater*, wife, and slave exhibit an unsavory strategy of intellectual subordination in Aristotle; but they become actually oppressive only when deployed within the walls of an *oikos*.

It is when we specify the bounded space of oppression, then, that our opposition to it changes from a merely intellectual critique of abstract conceptions—the kind of thing with which theory is so often taxed—to the kind of concrete analysis which can become a guide to action. The reason the emancipatory possibilities of postmodernity have so often been missed, including by postmodernists themselves, is that they do not always take this step. Not that they never do—in fact they do it more than one would perhaps think, because the "boundaries" in question need not be physically realized, in walls and fences; they can be the intellectual boundaries of a text or the customary boundaries of a practice. Nor should theorists be required to take that step, for abstract critiques are indispensable in their way and on their level.

Once we have identified the bounded space necessary for the deployment of a particular binary, we have what I call an "engine of oppression" (*MO*, 88–96). What then remains is, first, to identify who is oppressed within that engine, a category which may include several types of person (as in the ancient household); and, second, to identify the specific ordering principles which relegate those people to the status of matter. These, again, may vary with the type of person being oppressed: in the ancient patriarchal household as described by Aristotle, the slaves are oppressed by being ordered about; but the wife is oppressed, as we will see in the next chapter, by the husband's *karteria*—his "tolerance" of her.

Oppression and Intelligibility

The patterns and gestures by which philosophers have instated oppression as an inescapable, general human condition are too many and various to be summed up in a single argument. I have mentioned the metaphysical validation that oppression receives from Aristotle and will discuss it and its vicissitudes more extensively in later chapters; but another argument, one less wedded to metaphysical peculiarities, is at the core of much of it. If we are to deprive ousia of its ontological redoubt, that argument must be tackled head on. It runs, roughly, like this:

1. The world is partially *intelligible*: some things can be understood and others cannot.

2. To be intelligible is to be something and not something else: it is to be *determinate*.

3. The relation between the determinate and the indeterminate is one of the *domination* of the latter by the former.

Let us grant that intelligibility and determinacy go together and focus on the move from (2) to (3). Why must the relation between the determinate and the indeterminate be one of domination?

We can see what is at stake here by looking at an alternative account. Let us imagine a sorting mechanism which takes, at random, a ball from a jar and drops it into one of two side-by-side drawers. Half the balls are colored black and half are white.

Occasionally the balls will be equally distributed as to color, so that the two drawers have equal numbers of black and white balls. The drawers are thus the same overall color and, we may say, color entropy is maximized, so there is lack of determinacy and so of intelligibility; the drawers cannot be distinguished from each other. Also, occasionally, all the white balls will be in one drawer and all the black ones in the other; entropy is minimized. We can call this situation "partially intelligible": the color of each drawer is determinate because all the balls in it are of the same color, but why each ball has been assigned to the drawer it is in cannot be explained—it is random. Most of the time, however, there will be a preponderance of white balls in one drawer and of black balls in the other. Let us call this situation, which has many gradations, "quasi-intelligible."

Quasi-intelligibility is thus the usual situation, but partial intelligibility, the situation in which one drawer is unambiguously white and the other unambiguously black, comes about randomly from time to time. The point of invoking domination is to put an end to this randomness: to provide for *constant* partial intelligibility. The aim is to elevate partial intelligibility from something that is randomly thrown up by the machine from time to time to something that is always there.

For this, the machine can no longer operate at random; it needs consistently to put the black balls into one drawer and the white ones into another. In so doing, it determines what is allowed to be within the boundaries of each drawer, and so orders—though to a minimal extent—the balls in that drawer. This is the kind of principle which philosophers came to call "form"; the balls themselves, which get ordered by this, correspond to what philosophers came to call "matter." The activity of sorting thus exercises a form of what I call "disposition."

What this argument is actually saying, with its move from (2) to (3), is that partial intelligibility must be constant or nearly so (as Aristotle phrased it, it must happen "either always or for the most part," i.e., it must be "natural").[24] To take issue with this move is to deny that anything in the world can be assumed, in advance, to be even partially intelligible. Partial intelligibility, in that case, arises where and as it will, and we can be glad when it occurs. Situations of quasi-intelligibility—various unequal distributions of the colored balls—can then be viewed as degrees of it. Pure quasi-intelligibility would be the situation for the Plato of the *Phaedo* if he did not believe in the Forms: everything is a mixture of opposites but rarely an equal mixture (*Phaedo* 102b–103e). Plato, of course, had the perfectly determinate and eternally static Forms to guarantee the permanent intelligibility of their own world, but making the intelligibility of the physical world into something dependable requires forms in this world: it requires some version of ousia.

Schmilosophy and the Order of the Mind

While philosophers have been very open about their search for truth, they have not—as far as I can tell—explicitly avowed their schmilosophical side: they have not seen themselves as justifiers (and, occasionally, attackers) of ousiodic structure. That their own obsession has remained hidden from them is de rigueur for obsessions but rather scandalous for a profession that traces itself back to the Delphic injunction to "know thyself." There may be good reasons for it, but I think it ought to end—not only in the service of the lucidity advocated by the *Philebus* but because it is nothing to be ashamed of. Attention to the history of schmilosophy's concern with ousia shows that something positive and valuable has indeed come out of that history—and is still coming. We can get at this by asking, What does it take to validate ousia as the single basic principle for the human realm?

It clearly means much more than simply to *argue* for it. As I suggested earlier, schmilosophers have long been doing what they could to *establish* ousia as the basic ordering principle of the human world. They have been doing so in the most direct way imaginable: ordering things by it. What they have primarily ordered has been their own philosophical domain par excellence, human thought. So schmilosophy, especially in the modern era, has been deeply concerned with the quasi-ethical project of instilling the right order within the mind. This is not the same thing as installing the "right" (patriarchal, racist, heteronormative) order in the person, the family, or the polity. It is, for one thing, not nearly as evil.

When Kant wrote in the *Prolegomena to Any Future Metaphysics* (*AA*, 4:304) that "the business of the understanding is to think, and that of the senses to intuit," he knew that he was not accurately describing the human mind as he saw it operating around him in Königsberg. All around him, people were trying to use their senses to establish truths about the mind (the way Kant thinks Locke did) and to reason intuitively (the way he thinks Swedenborg did). This is why Gilles Deleuze refers to Kant's doctrine of the faculties as an "état civil" of the mind (Deleuze 1984, 27). The *état civil* in France was no mere census or genealogical archive; it regularized property titles and established identities as much as it recorded them. Similarly, Kant is trying to *regularize* the mind's faculties and *instill* the proper order into them. The *Critiques of Pure and Practical Reason* are thus performed, as Deleuze notes, by reason in its "subaltern," housekeeping function, which establishes the limits of each of its activities and orders them all to one another.[25]

That *into which* Kant seeks to instill such ousiodic order is, then, the "human mind," a set of "faculties" which probably never existed as Kant codifies it (except, perhaps, in Kant's own case). Descartes, more promisingly I think, seeks to put the correct order not into our faculties but into our ideas.[26] To put ideas into order is to relate them to one another, and the most intimate relation two different ideas can have to one another is when one is "part" of another, as Descartes would say—or as we would say, helps define it.

Thus we get the idea that philosophy is to produce not a well-functioning set of faculties (and certainly not a set of true beliefs or propositions) but a network of interdefined ideas—a network which is rational and so systematic. This does not entirely abandon the older aim of bringing us into proximity to the divine, for it was such a system of definitions that Spinoza referred to, in *On the Emendation of the Intellect*, as "the thoughts of God before He created the world" (Spinoza 1985, 31–32). To be sure, Spinoza's God never created the world and so had no thoughts before doing so. But even as a counterfactual or a metaphor, the idea that a system of definitions can approach divine self-cognition directs us to the ethical relevance of the mind's right order—as did Kant's version of it, which was designed to give reason the power to determine our actions by abolishing its claims to know a supernatural reality with which it needed to agree.

Modern schmilosophers, in their obsession with ousia, thus did not get as far away from the ancients as many people think they did. In particular, we now see that they adopted, without saying so, the ancient view that the business of schmilosophy is to instill the right order within the mind. In pursuing this goal, schmilosophers had to relate our ideas to one another—and that meant giving them definitions which would connect them up with one another in ways which would be consistent and nuanced. Schmilosophers have thus been engaged, from time immemorial, in the largely unspoken project of providing us with a critically vetted vocabulary.

This third view of the common enterprise of the Usual Crew emerges historically from the second, obsession-with-ousia one but is independent of it. We can see this by looking at Hegel, who reconceived ideas, which by that time had become Kantian *Vorstellungen*, as words—as the "element of thought" (cf. *CW*, 229–238). As we will see in Chapter 5, this transformed them from the given inhabitants of a supersensible kingdom called "the human mind" into materially embodied public objects, invested with conventional, and so humanly malleable, significance.

With this, the full scope and massive importance of schmilosophy's project becomes visible. For unlike ideas, words, as Wittgenstein showed again and again, are bound up with forms of life. They articulate the goals for which we strive and set us to doing things; they coordinate our common activities. It is in words that we understand ourselves, each other, and our communities. And the philosophically vetted vocabulary bequeathed us by the history of schmilosophy has been of incalculable benefit to all of us. It is an incredibly precious heritage—thirty generations of critically working over, or reshaping, our most basic words.

This vetting process explains why the analysis of philosophical words must become historical: there is nowhere other than history for philosophical concepts to come from. We do not read philosophical concepts such as "truth" and "justice" off the face of sensory experience the way we (perhaps) do "red" and "triangle"; Quine's many arguments about the underdetermination of theory by experience show this, but Plato already knew it.[27] Nor do we read philosophical concepts out of the nature of our minds, as Kant thought. You never saw a belief; you never heard a true utterance (as you hear a loud or a soft one).

In such cases, what we learn first is not the concept but the word, which we hear from people who already speak our language. Only when we have heard a word used on several different occasions can we begin to figure out what it means. And the way we do that is to guess from what we see of how those people use those words. The meanings of philosophical words come to us from previous users of the language, who learned them from previous users, and so on back through history. If philosophy has anything to do with self-aware discourse—with knowing what you are really doing when you think and speak—it cannot ignore, even for a second, the history of its basic concepts, for the history of those concepts is their source.

What I earlier called the "contamination" of later philosophers by earlier ones is thus not the whole story when we come to schmilosophy. Such contamination, we now see, is present every time a philosopher uses a word in a sense which is not wholly new. When this fact becomes the object of philosophical reflection, it becomes an opportunity for the critical and creative reshaping of that word.

The Importance of the History of Schmilosophy

Philosophers may be lousy provers, but schmilosophers are indispensable definers and even more indispensable redefiners. They became that way, I am suggesting, because of their obsession with ousia. In order to establish ousia as an ordering principle in human affairs, they had to establish it in language—which required establishing a set of critically worked-over, or reshaped, definitions for terms. The present aim, of course, is to continue the vetting while jettisoning those parts of it dedicated to validating oppression.

If I am right about what schmilosophers have succeeded in doing for the rest of humanity, then there are two lessons to be drawn about the history of schmilosophy: it is not irrelevant, and it is not over. The history of schmilosophy is not irrelevant because it provides rational structure for our vocabularies, which in turn constitute the intersubjective medium of our lives and communities. Indeed, it may not be too much to say that as the ongoing rational core of human interaction, the history of schmilosophy is what other things must be relevant *to*.

As Kant argues throughout the *Critique of Pure Reason*, if I ignore the sources of my knowledge I can get along for a while—but eventually I will transgress the proper boundaries of the employment of those concepts, boundaries which they have because of where they come from. In the case of philosophical concepts, ignoring their historical source means exempting them from history and, inevitably, taking them to be immutable. This can mean finding yourself on the wrong side when history takes another turn and the meaning of a concept changes—finding yourself high and dry because the basic terms of discourse have passed you by. An example of this is the previous century's discourse on "sense data." It is hard to say that there is a single aspect of philosophy today that would look different if that discourse had never existed. The sad thing is that there are still a few people around (when I first came into philosophy, there were lots) who wrote their dissertations on sense data theory, and who—wrongly assuming that what they were writing on was a matter of permanent philosophical concern—never bothered to learn anything else.

There is in fact no point at which the historical development stops and we can start doing "philosophy," for the history of philosophy extends to the most recent philosophical sentence uttered. To be sure, many efforts are made to draw such a line; all are specious. Some continental philosophers draw it, for example, with Derrida—they learn lots about Derrida but little about any philosopher prior to him. This requires them, however, to ignore the bulk of Derrida's own work, which is on the history of philosophy. Indeed, as Luc Ferry and Alain Renaut point out in their *La pensée 68* (published in English translation as *French Philosophy of the Sixties*), many of Derrida's insights derive from Heidegger, who articulates some of Derrida's basic themes better than he does; if more French and American followers of Derrida had known this, they would have understood him far better than they did (Ferry and Renaut 1990, 19–22). Similarly for the other Great Beginner of twentieth-century continental philosophy, Edmund Husserl. In what does his radical newness consist? In the use of the "epochē" to uncover "eidē" by distinguishing "noēses" from "noēmata," all in the service of "phenomenology"? If the whole thing is so new, why are so many Greek words used to convey it?

Similarly again, on the analytical side, for Russell and Frege. Logic had indeed made great advances during the nineteenth century, and their way of applying it to philosophical problems is indeed quite new. But the problems to which they applied it were basically the philosophical problematic of the seventeenth century, with its issues concerning absolute certainty, knowledge and mathematics, mind-body problems, realism versus idealism, the existence of God, freedom of the will, social contract theory, and so on. It is no accident that the great founding sentence of analytical philosophy—"That all philosophy must begin with an analysis of propositions is a truth too evident, perhaps to demand a proof"—was written by Russell in a book on Leibniz (Russell 1992, 9).

The history of schmilosophy is also not over, first because it has not been completed. As I noted above, its most recent American forms have focused on individual thinkers, or indeed on individual texts. We all know the merits of that focus, which is indispensable. But we must also recognize the dangers of trying to do Plato with no knowledge of Aristotle or Spinoza with none of Descartes. It is now time, I suggest, to go further and build on that individual-centered work in new ways. The overall sweep of the history of schmilosophy (and philosophy) needs to be investigated. How, exactly, do Hegel's views relate to those not merely of Kant or Schelling but of Plotinus? Was Derrida or Aristotle right about Plato's thesis of the *chōrismos*, the "separation" of Forms from sensibles (they cannot both be)?²⁸ Was it really faithfulness to Aristotle that got Thomas Aquinas condemned by the Church?

It is not yet time to go into detail about overall methods for doing history of schmilosophy. As I suggested in the Introduction, many of philosophy's contemporary problems derive from its allegiance to the Enlightenment. We have not yet considered that in sufficient detail to see beyond it, and we have not considered the two most important responses to the crisis it provoked, Hegel and Heidegger, at all. But I do have just one final point to make about philosophy and schmilosophy.

The Final Point

The history of schmilosophy is not over, not just because it is still incomplete but because it has been done wrongly; and it has been done wrongly, in part, because schmilosophy itself has been done wrongly. Schmilosophers have labored hard to create a vocabulary that would be clearly and distinctly defined, that would be consistent with itself and yet concrete enough to deal with the problems we actually encounter in philosophy and in life; that is schmilosophy's good side. But if I am right about its bad side, they have generally done all this with a view to installing one particular kind of structure into thought, language, and ultimately into life itself—a structure of ousiodic domination. This has affected at least some of the definitions they have produced.

Here is an example of what I mean. For Aristotle, everything that exists by nature must either be an ousia or part of an ousia—the form, matter, property, or accident of an ousia. So human beings must exhibit form and matter. In the human moral agent, the form of the human being is reason, "considered as being the man himself" (*NE* 9.8.1168b31–1169a1). Something also has to play the role of matter, and Aristotle defines desire (*orexis*) as doing so. Being matter, it is obstreperous and so is "by nature opposed to reason, resists it and fights against it." It is also able, however, to receive reason and obey it "as one does one's father" (*NE* 1.13.1102b16–1103a3).

Desire is thus defined by Aristotle, in entire accord with his metaphysics, as something which by nature opposes that to which it should be subordinate, namely reason. Women, children, and slaves are in turn defined as beings whose behavior is excessively conditioned by desire—or, as Simone de Beauvoir will put it thousands of years later, woman "thinks with her glands."²⁹ According to this conceptual framework, first put in place in Aristotle's metaphysics, women, as well as slaves and children, should be subordinate to the

Man of Reason, even though their nature "opposes . . . resists . . . and fights against" him.

Aristotle's definitions of woman as a creature of desire and of desire as properly dominated by reason rationalized and so facilitated thousands of years of oppression; they gave it metaphysical sanction and made its pursuit methodical. This was not merely a matter of Aristotle's own psychology, or of male psychology in general, or of Greek culture. Long before Kant and the Enlightenment, oppression took active philosophical root in the clotted depths of the ancient metaphysics of matter and form.

What this means is that we cannot do history of schmilosophy uncritically. When we look at how a later thinker reshapes the vocabulary of an earlier one, we must always bear in mind that the exigencies of thought in accordance with which he does so are not always purely conceptual and are not always openly avowed. The concepts we uncover in the history of schmilosophy are so important that we *as* schmilosophers have a moral duty to correct them where they are wrongly set up. In particular, I think, we are currently obliged to reshape the schmilosophical vocabulary we have inherited to eliminate traces of ousiodic domination such as the one I have mentioned above.

Quine was, as so often, right. The history of philosophy as he understood it, as a search for truth, is irrelevant today.[30] But the history of schmilosophy as the production of critically vetted definitions remains as pressing today as ever, and that is pressing indeed. Who knows—if enough people come to see things this way, my need for Kripke's dodge may disappear. The name "schmilosophy" will then be waved off with thanks, and a new kind of "philosophy" will have begun.

CHAPTER 3

MATTER, FORM, AND OPPRESSION IN ARISTOTLE

Engaging the Greeks:
Foucault and Arendt against Hegel and Reichenbach

If ousia is philosophically justified because it allows us to pursue what I have called permanent partial intelligibility, part of getting beyond it is to see that intelligibility—reason itself—has to be continually tinkered with. New words and tools are continually needed, which means that philosophy has to regard reason as "malleable," that is (in a first approximation, derived from the Introduction), as subject to change on all levels. In order to be changeable in this way, reason has to be in time; and once it is in time it inevitably becomes historical. For the move from time to history is just the move from abstract to concrete—from seeing reason as, in general, changeable to looking at the specific changes in it which have made us what we are. Before making that move, two methodological considerations impose themselves: one on why we need to make it, which is indicated by Michel Foucault; and the other on how to do so, which is exemplified by Hannah Arendt.

Let us characterize any origin which is not itself in time as "metaphysical." In this we (broadly) follow Kant, for whom time was the condition of all appearances (with space the condition of outer ones: *CPR* B, 50–51). Since we only know appearances, anything outside of time is for Kant "metaphysical," and we can have no knowledge of it. This rules out supernatural, and so atemporal, causes such as the will of God, laws of nature, the transcendental structure of the human mind, and even logical forms. Indeed, there is on this basis no such thing as a cause which begins a series of events but does not itself have a specific place within that series.[1]

Foucault's rejection of such extratemporal causes in his "Nietzsche, Genealogy, History" is hardly original; indeed, he himself locates it in "modern historicism" in general, which "places within a process of development everything considered immortal in man" (*FR*, 87). This characterization does not apply to Kant, for although Kant placed all objects of cognition in time—in a before-and-after ordering—he did not locate the faculties of the mind itself within any developmental process; that is why he became the kind of radical foundationalist I mentioned in the Introduction. Hegel, however, did; and Foucault's criticisms of metaphysical origins become sharper when we introduce Hegel as their target.

When Hegel places everything proper to the human world into historical development, nothing in or about us can remain immortal.[2] In contrast to the "Platonic" tradition discussed in Chapter 1, Hegel has no eternal divine being in terms of which to define truth. He allows only empirical origins to the phenomena of history—which means origins in time. Or, rather, origin: for philosophy in Hegel's view began only once, with Thales. It does not restart de novo every time a philosopher sits down at her word processor or even when she gets her PhD. When she does either of those, she comes into contact, not directly with some eternal inbreath of Philosophy Itself, but with a long and complex chain of intermediations.

Having assigned such a temporal, and so empirical, origin to philosophy, Hegel denies that it is unified from outside, by atemporal causes. But he is still "metaphysical" for Foucault insofar as he argues that unity is produced at all: to say that philosophy is historical is to say that there is only one philosophy which develops down through history (SL, 580). Indeed, for Hegel all of history, not merely its philosophical aspect, is the development of one idea—that of freedom. For Hegel freedom takes on different forms in different historical periods and has no existence outside the human history it unifies, so it is not above time itself but is present from beginning to end of the process it unifies. If something about freedom did not at bottom remain unchanged, we may say, there would be no unifying factor in the overall development, which means that it would not be a single overall development at all; history would be fundamentally disunified.[3] Similarly for philosophy.

Thus, though Hegel and other modern historicists make temporal developments basic to reality, they still see those developments as governed, if not by wholly extratemporal beings such as God and the Platonic Forms, then by what we may call relatively supratemporal "ideas" such as freedom and philosophy. Such history, like metaphysics in general, "assumes the existence of immobile forms which preceded the external world of accident and succession" (*FR*, 78).

The word "accident" here is as important as the word "assumes." That historical origins involve succession is obvious; they are events in time. But not all successions, we like to think, are accidental. Some things follow each other according to patterns or causal laws. Foucault rejects this predilection because it makes those patterns and laws themselves into atemporal and therefore metaphysical beings. Accidentality is then basic to history; Foucault's claim against Hegel is that to see successions of events as radically historical, ungoverned by extra- or supratemporal entities, we must see them as accidental. This in turn means decisively challenging all forms of legitimacy, for what is merely accidental cannot be legitimated.

We do not need a dogmatic acceptance of Foucault's views to see that they form the only possible starting point for a globally critical approach to history.[4] This is shown by the breadth of his target. Foucault's critique of metaphysics in history hits Hegel's most implacable twentieth-century enemy, Hans Reichenbach, at least as squarely as it hits Hegel. As Richard Rorty remarked in 1982, Reichenbach's 1951 *The Rise of Scientific Philosophy* (Reichenbach 1951) still provides today's philosophers with their unconscious background narrative of how philosophy became scientific (Rorty 1982, 211). But it is no Hegelian story of steady ascent from lisping Greek beginnings to contemporary Germanic flowerings. It presents, rather, the direct opposite: an embarrassing and painful groping among wrong paths before the right path—the path of logical analysis—was found. Hegel's and Reichenbach's stories thus have similar beginnings and endings, but what comes in between is as different as can be. For Foucault, Reichenbach was correct in viewing history as mere stumbling around and correct to see the arrival of scientific philosophy as a decisive rupture with that; but the rupture, while decisive, does not bring for Foucault an escape from more stumbling around—or, in Fine's term from Chapter 1, it brings no escape from shakiness.

If Foucault's criticism hits both the history-as-gradual-ascent view of Hegel and the history-as-stumbling-around-until-the-right-path-is-found view of Reichenbach, we are rather at a loss as to what it does not hit. The conclusion is that Foucault's emphasis on accidentality, taken nondogmatically as a working hypothesis rather than a dogmatic statement, eliminates the alternatives to it and must, today, be our starting point.

Reason is now beyond malleable; it is fragmented. The basic premises from which it begins cannot be viewed as somehow inherent in the nature of things, for that would take them outside of time. For the same reason, they cannot be viewed as logical, intuitive, or self-evident truths, or even merely as obviously true to intelligent people. We have to search for and find them in history, where they have the same epistemic and ontological status as other historical facts: they are accidents. And if reason is merely an accident, it loses normative claims and is no longer reason.

Hegel (whom Foucault has not read correctly) will show us the way out of this impasse in Chapter 5. For the moment, philosophy's engagement with history now takes a new direction. If there is no such thing as a cause which begins a series of events but does not itself have a specific place within that series, then we must look, for our origins, to a specific time. Since you can't "originate" anything without already existing yourself, the specific time in question must come at the temporal beginning; except in the view of metaphysics, there is no priority without temporal priority. In philosophy, this means turning to the Greeks. Hannah Arendt exemplifies this approach as lucidly as anyone ever has, at the beginning of *The Human Condition*:

> Our tradition of political thought . . . far from comprehending and conceptualizing all the political experiences of Western mankind, grew out of a specific historical constellation: the trial of Socrates and the conflict between the philosopher and the polis. (Arendt 1958, 12)

What is left to be the "origin" of philosophy, for Foucault, Arendt, and indeed continental philosophy in general, is a "specific historical constellation"—the earliest one, comprising the texts, concerns, strategies, and arguments of what we call Greek philosophy, or more broadly, Greek culture. We may say that Greek philosophy in toto supplies the basic premises for historical reason—premises which such reason, if it is to remain reason, must not only use in its own further arguments but must critically justify in contemporary terms. Hence, spelling out in more detail the overall view of the history of philosophy which I presented in Chapter 2 requires us to attend to the Greeks, and in particular to Aristotle.

Ousia, Presence, and Metaphysics

If Foucault is right about the nature of history, then philosophy can have arrived at the crisis I discussed in the Introduction only if it has lost touch not only with the specifics of its history but with its general nature *as* history. For it is only by overlooking the accidental nature of everything historical that we can take the present state of philosophy, with its current repertoire of themes, procedures, obsessions, and exclusions, to be the "right path" for all time. Both Kant and Reichenbach look at it that way, and the result in both cases is an inability to tolerate the unregulated discourses of the unenlightened or the unscientific. The separation of philosophy from the larger culture sketched in the Introduction can thus be viewed in terms of tolerance.

"Tolerance" is the appropriate word here because it represents a minimum level of acceptance: to tolerate something is passively to endure its presence, as a bearing wall "tolerates" weight and a body "tolerates" certain doses of a medicine. To tolerate is not to invade, annihilate, assimilate, or expel; but it is also not to welcome, embrace, or encourage. I "tolerate" that which is near me but to which I do not want to relate actively.

Tolerance and intolerance can be viewed from a variety of angles and can be seen, for example, not only as psychological traits but as political, social, and ethical phenomena. Everywhere we find one disenchanting fact: intolerance, the attempt to remove or destroy an offending phenomenon, seems to be the norm, while the tolerant enduring of it is merely a hoped-for, even utopian, ideal for which we must strive. This unfortunate priority holds across cultures and suggests that intolerance is more than a merely psychological trait. What if intolerance of others is as rooted in physiology as intolerance of pharmaceutical overdoses? What if, in other words, intolerance were a fact not of individual psychology but of human nature? What if it were even, say, a phenomenon of physics: would it be illuminating to say that positive and negative electrical charges cannot "tolerate" each other? Or that the north pole of a magnet cannot "tolerate" the south? What if the factual priority of intolerance went even beyond physics to infect all that is: what if intolerance were an *ontological* phenomenon, one inscribed in the nature of being itself—"to be is to be intolerant"? Such a thought is not only disenchanting, it is depressing indeed. For absolutely everything, of course, *is*.

If we locate intolerance in ontology, we must do as much for its opposite, tolerance. This seems strange, because the most basic term in ontology is, by definition, neither "tolerance" nor "intolerance" but "being": *to on,* or as Aristotle had it, *hē ousia.* Together with this, we may say, goes "presence" (*parousia,* literally "being against"). The former term designates whatever it is that distinguishes beings that exist from those that don't; the latter designates the relation of coexistence that things can have with one another solely in virtue of their being.[5] My argument here will be that tolerance is the ethical form of parousia, and that intolerance derives from that. In order to see this, however, we must go deeper than we have into Aristotle's ousia ontology; for we cannot understand par-ousia without understanding ousia. Nor, moreover, can we understand the metaphysics of ousia without understanding its relation to its older, but still vigorous, sibling, the metaphysics of substance, which is a metaphysics dominated by the notion of parousia.

Being as Substance:
From Aristotle through Nietzsche to Butler

Parousia does not in fact belong only in Aristotle's ousia ontology, which historically speaking is his second. It also plays a role in the earlier ontology from which he arrived at the ousia ontology and which, following long tradition, I will call the "metaphysics of substance." I begin by translating the opening words of the great treatise on ousia that stretches through books 7–9 of Aristotle's *Metaphysics*:

> Being is said in many ways. . . . For in one sense it means what a thing is, a "this";
> and in other senses it means quality or quantity or any of the other categories thus
> predicated. But, even though "being" has all these senses, it is obvious that the
> first of them is "being" in the sense of the "what-it-is," i.e., the sense which signi-
> fies ousia. . . . For none [of the others] is according to itself (*kath hauta*) or sepa-
> rable from ousia, but rather, if anything, it is that which walks that is among the
> class of beings, and that which sits and is healthy. (Metaphysics 7.1.1028a10–25)

Being is thus predicated in all the categories, but the primary sort of predication tells us *what* a thing is, as opposed to specifying its size, color, activity, the disposition of its parts, and so on. The priority comes from one of the two senses in which, Aristotle tells us here, ousia is "separable."[6]

First, the fact that things in the other categories cannot exist "according to themselves" is said to mean that they cannot be "separated" (*chōrizesthai*) from ousia. It, however, can be separated from them. Everything nonsubstantial, such as properties and relations, inheres in an ousia: an ousia can walk or not walk; it can "separate" itself from the activity of walking. But walking has to be the movement *of* something, from which it is therefore inseparable: the movement of an ousia. Ousiai can thus "separate" themselves from their properties and relations, but properties and relations cannot exist "separately" from the ousiai in which they inhere. It follows, though it is not stated explicitly, that ousiai are separable from each other as well. For if to inhere inseparably in an ousia is the prerogative of what is in the other categories, of non-ousiai, then no ousia can inhere inseparably in another ousia. An ousia is thus separable not only from other kinds of things but also from other ousiai.

A final implication is that if an ousia is separable from other ousiai but the properties it exhibits are inseparable from it, then no such property can inhere in more than one ousia. For if some property inhered in two things which could be separated from each other, then it could be separated from itself.[7] So ousiai individuate properties: the color of this particular object, as a quality of it, can never be identically the same as the color of another object. It can only resemble it.

At this point, Aristotle's ontology is entirely defined in terms of separability and inseparability; but we can go deeper. To be "separable" is not to be separated (in the sense of the philosophical separations discussed in the Introduction, for example); it means to be distinct-from-yet-together-with, and thus to be present-to. The metaphysics of substance thus implicitly defines beings in terms of parousia, of their capacity to be present to other things, rather than (for example) in terms of their inner structure. It holds that things in general are most basically mere inert beings, "substrates." In a substance, the substrate passively underlies the actions it performs, the properties it has, and the relations in which it stands; it is "present to" them all.

The metaphysics of substance is associated with parousia because a substance lacks the internal structure of an ousia as sketched in the previous chapter. Defined entirely by its separability and inseparability from other things and bereft of internal structure, a substance exists not only within its boundaries but, so to speak, on them; they are its only essential feature. This makes it, unlike an ousia, capable of being entirely "present" not only to other things but to us, the knowers. This kind of parousia became basic to modernity (as we will see in Chapter 4). In the modern perspective, to be present is to exist independently of everything except us. When Derrida says in "Force and Signification" that to be "present" means, most basically, to be "summed up [*résumée*] in some absolute simultaneity or instantaneity," in modernity it is we who do the summing up (Derrida 1978a, 14). This comes to mean that a present being is epistemologically ultimate and so an epistemic foundation.

There is more. When the parousia of substances is redefined from a relation substances have to one another into a relation they have in the first instance to us, the knowing subjects, the world itself becomes entirely knowable. We then pass from what, in Chapter 2, I called "partial intelligibility," in which some aspects of any thing are intelligible, to a situation in which everything is, in principle at least, wholly intelligible. Things conceived as substances do not have the partial intelligibility of form wresting truth from matter but are simply there to be known from the start.

The metaphysics of substance, though supplanted in Aristotle's own thought by the metaphysics of ousia, comes in its modern revival to ground a particular kind of freedom. As Nietzsche argued, if the substrate of a being is unchanged by its actions, then they are not essential to it, and it need not have committed them: people are thus free to act otherwise than they do. The strong, in particular, are "free" to be weak—so we should blame them for being strong (*GM*, 28–29).

One important thing about this kind of freedom, for Nietzsche, is that it is illusory. In reality, there are no such "substantial" individuals; all that exists for Nietzsche, both inside the human mind and outside it, is forces:

> It is just as absurd to ask strength *not* to express itself as strength . . . as it is to ask weakness to express itself as strength. A quantum of force is just such a quantum of drive, will, action, in fact it is nothing but this driving, willing and acting, and only the seduction of language (and the fundamental errors of reason petrified within it), which construes and misconstrues all actions as conditional upon an agency, a "subject," can make it appear otherwise. (*GM*, 28)

Finally, the metaphysics of substance plays a critical role in Judith Butler's theory of gender, for it represents the fundamental mistake she locates in previous gender theorists: they all appeal to a pregendered identity of some sort and posit those identities as enduring agents whose basic nature is unchanged by their actions (*GT*, 20–21). Genderfication, if we may call it that, is not, to be sure, an action; it is something we undergo. But we could have existed, on some level, as the people we are without it. The usual term for this pregendered form of identity is "sex," which is then viewed as natural, while gender is culturally enforced.[8]

When Butler abandons appeals to something fixed underlying gender, gender becomes a series of actions without an actor—or of performances without a performer. It then consists merely in the repetition of gendered behavior. To have a gender is to behave in ways in which others have behaved in the past; such behavior is "not expressive [of an underlying identity] but performative" (*GT*, 141). At its base we find not the actions of any substantive self or body but the sheer fact of repetition itself. But as thinkers from Kierkegaard through De-leuze have shown, repetition is never exact replication. As Derrida puts it in his discussion of "citationality," the repetition of anything occurs in circumstances different from those in which what is being repeated originally occurred and so *must* be, to some extent, different.[9] This means that repetition is always cre-ative. Butler puts it this way:

> The injunction to be a given gender produces necessary failures, a variety of in-coherent configurations that in their multiplicity exceed and defy the injunction by which they are generated. (*GT*, 145)

> This perpetual displacement constitutes a fluidity of identities that suggests an openness to resignification and recontextualization. (*GT*, 138)

The creative repetition of gender behavior, which Butler famously calls "parody" (*GT*, 138), is not necessarily the outcome of reflection; its inevitabil-ity means that it intrudes, even where the intention is faithfully to duplicate the perceived behavior of others (in which cases it is viewed as a "failure"). Such unconscious repetition is thus a version of the sympathetic vibration, the movements in one's own body occasioned by the movements in other bodies which I discussed in Chapter 1. Here the crucial factor is the necessary differ-ence between the sympathetic vibrations and the original ones.

We can now make some general points. For the metaphysics of substance, the substrate has no properties of its own but is capable of receiving them (see *Categories* 5.4a10–13). That is the aspect of the metaphysics of substance on which Butler and Nietzsche both concentrate their fire: the idea that there is some neutral identity underlying one's actions or gender. Their fire is, as we will see in a moment, well aimed. But Butler's critique of it is incomplete, because it leaves one very important question unresolved: How does it come about that certain forms of gender, such as homosexuality and transgender, are so widely and obviously not tolerated in Western societies while others are? On the cur-rent version of the metaphysics of substance, the substrate, being wholly inde-terminate, is equally capable of receiving any property whatsoever. If gender is merely a property residing in such an indeterminate substrate, then all genders should be equal. Why, then, is heterosexual behavior so widely tolerated when other forms of sexual behavior are not?

A condemnation of nonheterosexual behavior can be derived from the metaphysics of substance only when we modify it to say that the substrate is not wholly indeterminate but has, in the case of humans, a determinately heterosexual nature. Then we can say the following: What is distinct from me, but from which I cannot actually separate myself, is what I have to tolerate. Actions, from this point of view, must "tolerate" their substrates. I cannot, therefore, act in a manner which denies the kind of substrate that I most basically am. A human being, for example, cannot fly; if I leap off a cliff, we can say, I "deny my substrate" against the rocks below. Intolerance of homosexuality would then be argued for on the grounds that, as a denial of the individual's human substrate, homosexual conduct destroys that individual as surely as does falling from a cliff.

The power of such argument can be seen from the love antihomosexuals have for it: they assert continually that homosexual lifestyles are self-destructive. Like most metaphysical arguments, this one is empirically absurd. People contravene the "laws of gender" all the time without destroying themselves. And how can I identify the underlying human substrate, that is, human nature itself, as heterosexual? Even the Bible, in the passage most commonly cited against homosexuality (the story of Sodom at Genesis 19), does not call it unnatural (if the passage is about homosexuality at all, rather than, say, about rape). It is also not obvious why what is unnatural should be condemned; are we to condemn airplanes and televisions?

These are not Butler's problems; her analysis begins from the evident fact of such repression and leads to a critique of the notion of gender identity itself rather than a critique of gender intolerance. Constructing the latter sort of critique leads us also to metaphysics—but to a metaphysics of determinate substrates rather than to the metaphysics of substance. We must follow Aristotle further.

The Metaphysics of Ousia

The reasons why Aristotle does not remain with the metaphysics of substance are complex,[10] but two of them, both directed against the indeterminate substrate, are important here. One is that if the substrate is truly indeterminate, it cannot be separated from itself; it must be, so to speak, one continuous fog, for if of itself it had boundaries, it would not be wholly indeterminate. As *Metaphysics* 7.3 tells us (1029a7–26), if all properties are stripped away in thought from a particular quantity of matter (including, of course, its very "quantity"), then there is no way whatsoever to identify the subject of the predication. There is nothing left which is definite enough to be separate from anything else.[11] Separability thus fails as the basic category of ontology.

Second, if the substrate is indeterminate, it is equally capable of receiving any property whatsoever, and all changes will occur at random. They do not, however. In particular—a point which Aristotle makes no fewer than twelve times in the *Physics* and *Metaphysics* alone—"humans beget humans."[12] The quality of being human must pass from the parent to child, then; and since this passage is the creation of the child, human nature itself is defined in terms of reproduction and hence heterosexually.

On the most general level, the fundamental component of a thing (which Aristotle will call its "form" or "essence") must now perform three jobs. First, it must establish boundaries for the thing, lest it sink back into the continuous fog. Second, its determinacy excludes certain properties from the thing; when the properties are active, that is, tendencies to behave, it therefore orders the behavior of the thing. And third, it must be capable of passing beyond the boundaries of the thing to its offspring. Thus, it must establish the three axes of domination I discussed in Chapter 2; it must be an ousiodic form for the thing.

That humans beget only humans, and never horses or trees, means that "humanity" cannot be an indeterminate substrate—indeed, that it must be reproductive and so heterosexual. The way is now open to an argument against homosexuality which does not rest on the absurd claim that it necessarily destroys the homosexual but merely on the view that it is unnatural: sex is the fulfillment of human nature via reproduction; sexual activity outside the context of reproduction is therefore unnatural and so wrong; and this includes all homosexual activity, which is not to be tolerated. Where Butler's argument against gender identity could be formulated in terms of the metaphysics of substance, a critique of the specific intolerance of homosexuality must target the ousia ontology as well. And for that, we must understand it better.

For Aristotle, what is knowable is *to ti ēn einai*, to which the medievals gave the handier name of "essence." The first thing we are told when Aristotle begins discussing essence in *Metaphysics* 7.4 is that the essence of a thing is "what it is *said* to be according to itself" (*kath hauto*; 7.4.1029b14). To exist according to yourself no longer means merely to be separate from other things, then; now such separability is the effect of something else, something which can be captured in a spoken formula and so is intelligible. *Metaphysics* 7.10–12 goes on to tell us that the essence of a thing, the intelligible component according to which it exists, is its "form"; that in the thing which is other than its form is its "matter."

Form is portrayed by Aristotle as actively unifying matter, both with the form itself and with whatever other matter belongs to the thing thus constituted. Form is thus "the responsible factor (*aition*) by which matter comes to be a this" (7.17.1041b7–8). As Ellen Stone Haring puts it:

> Form, the primary intelligible reality, determines the whole individual. Thereby, it governs also the material parts of the whole. Severed from the whole, the parts lose their roles, that is, their power qua parts, and often even their structure. A finger severed from the body is removed from the aegis of soul, and is a finger in name only. (Haring 1956–57, 495)

If matter comes to be a "this" only by being brought together with form, then matter in itself has no form. Hence the negativity of Aristotle's definition, at *Metaphysics* 7.3.1029a19–21, of matter: "By matter I mean that which in itself is neither a particular thing nor of a certain quantity nor assigned to any other of the categories by which Being is determined." He goes on to say (7.3.1029a23–26) that matter is neither positive nor negative with respect to the categories; it escapes the basic properties of quantity, quality, and the rest altogether. Escaping them, it escapes more concrete properties as well and is in itself entirely unknowable (*agnōston kath hautēn*); only form or essence has a cognitively determinate nature (7.11.1037a27–28).[13] Hence, Aristotle moves to a version of what in Chapter 2 I called partial intelligibility: the form in a thing is knowable, but the matter is not.

To sum up: ousia is the most basic kind of thing in Aristotle's cosmos, but any ousia exhibits a further hierarchy of basicality within itself. Most basic is the essence or form: a complex but determinate set of predicates denoting a complex but unified activity which unifies the thing from within, establishing its boundaries and ordering its material parts. Matter, for its part, is unknown, unknowable, and passive. When Derrida speaks of the "theme which is debased, marginalized, repressed, displaced, but [which nonetheless] exercises a permanent and obsessive pressure from the place where it is contained,"[14] he calls it "writing"; but in Aristotelian terms, it can be nothing else than matter.

Because the form, or essence, of a thing is to have disposition over whatever happens within the boundaries of that thing, we may call it "intolerant" in a double sense. First, it will not tolerate the disposing activity of other forms within its own boundaries: no alien essences allowed. Second, it will not tolerate even its own matter except as something passive and indeterminate (which means, for Aristotle, wholly bereft in itself of form, the principle of activity and determination).

With this we have fleshed out the nature of ousiodic structure enough to see how it grounds both tolerance and intolerance. The former grounding is more evident in Aristotle's ethics; the latter can be seen from his theory of the household.

Metaphysics and Ethics

This view of Being, abstract and theoretical, does not remain so for Aristotle. In general, the middle term between his theoretical account of Being and the various concrete ethical and social phenomena it will structure is intelligibility. What we can deal with intelligently is what is intelligible, and what is intelligible, if only partially, is what has an essence, that is, is structured like an ousia. Since Aristotle's own discourse is an exercise in right knowing, ousia gains the power to structure and orient further Aristotelian discourses. And since human life itself is also, for Aristotle, largely a matter of right knowing, ousia comes to play this structuring role not only in his own discourse, or even in philosophy in general, but in nondiscursive practices that traverse the entire spectrum of human activity. Hence, if we want our marriages, alliances, families, societies, states, religions, and works of art—among other things—to be intelligible, we must see to it that they embody ousiodic structure.

Such structure is clearly visible in a key feature of Aristotle's ethical thought: the moral hierarchy that, in his view, covers the entire human realm. It is, to be sure, a male hierarchy rather than a human one. Women are out of the picture, if only because female bodies contravene ousiodic norms in a variety of ways. As Carole Pateman has written, "Women's bodies are permeable, their contours change shape, and they are subject to cyclical processes" (*SC*, 96). The main such "cyclical process," of course, is menstruation—a subject of much mystery to Aristotle, who was perhaps the last philosopher to take it seriously. That menstruation was believed to be caused from outside a woman's body is evident, if not from Aristotle's own texts, then certainly from the word he uses for it: *ta katamēnia*, "the things according to the moon."[15] Women's bodies thus have undependable boundaries and are, at least at some times of the month, disposed from outside.

There are four levels in Aristotle's moral hierarchy; but the names of the two middle ones suffice to show its overall nature. As the beginning of *Nicomachean Ethics* 7.1 has it, the lowest form of good man is the "continent" man (the *enkratēs*), while the highest form of bad man is the "incontinent" man (*akratēs*): literally, the man "in" dominance or mastery (*kratēsis*) and the man "without" it. It is not strictly the "man" who has mastery here. As Aristotle tells us, "the continent and the incontinent man are so called because in them reason dominates or does not, *reason considered as being the man himself*" (9.8.1168b34–1169a1; emphasis added).

The train of thought is clear: reason itself is the essence of man;[16] it is what a man most basically is. Indeed, as the form of the individual human being, reason is the only intelligible thing in him; beyond it is merely the unknowability of his matter. So if reason is not in control of our lives, then "we" are not in control of our lives; but if reason dominates, then "we" dominate. Ethical life for Aristotle is thus a confrontation between reason and matter.

The general model for such confrontation is sketched at *Nicomachean Ethics* 1.13. The soul, contains, in addition to reason itself, desire (*orexis*), which (as noted in Chapter 2) "is by nature opposed to reason, fights against it, and resists it" (1.13.1102b16–17). Desire, then, is the ethical matter that must be "mastered" by reason if we are to live a good life. Such mastery is possible because in spite of its irrational antagonism to reason, desire is, in a passive sense, rational. For it is able to go along with reason, to be persuaded by it: to come to agree with it over time. When desire agrees with reason from the outset, we have the virtuous man, in whom desire "speaks with the same voice" as reason (*homophōnei*, which can also be glossed as what in Chapter 1 I called sympathetic vibration). When desire opposes reason but the man is able to persuade it and to act as reason advises, he is "continent." The sympathetic vibrations of "homophony" now pass over into silence: in the continent man, desire "listens" to reason as one listens to one's father (*tou patros akoustikon*, 1.13.1102b33), is "persuaded" by it (*peithetai*, 1.13.1102b33), and "obeys" it as a higher authority (*peitharchikon*, 1.13.1102b31). In the incontinent man, by contrast, there is apparently a certain moral clamor: his desires resist and oppose reason. And when, on the lowest level of the moral hierarchy, a man's reason agrees with his desire, telling him that whatever he happens to want to do is in fact what he should do, he is "unhindered" (*akolastos*, literally "unchastised") in his evil; his reason, we may say, vibrates to his desires, serving to rationalize them—thus inverting the "natural" order of things, according to which desire should be subservient to reason.[17] Such a person is worse than an animal, because his better part—reason, which animals do not have—has been corrupted (7.6.1150a1–8).

The whole of *Nicomachean Ethics* 1.13 thus trades on various equivalences between reason's rule over desire and form's rule over matter. The good life resides in the ordering of desires, so that at any moment what you want to do is what you should be doing; in such a life, reason exercises what I call "disposition" over desire. And because these desires, though "within" the moral agent, are for Aristotle provoked by external objects (food, drink, money, sex), to act on them is to transgress the boundary of the person. To be unethical is thus to violate both boundary and disposition.

To be good, by contrast, is to exemplify boundary and disposition. The good man's ultimate desire is not for external objects but for the well-being of his own rational principle—of what he himself most is—and so he is not determined from outside.[18] The boundary of his body is in good order, as witness his relative imperviousness to eros (which besets the young, not the mature)[19] and his attention to diet—it is no accident that the *Nicomachean Ethics*' main example of moral deliberation concerns whether or not to eat "dry food" (bread) rather than "wet" (porridge; 7.3.1147a5–8).

Aristotle's account of the relation between the desires and reason, one of the keys to his entire ethics, is, moreover, couched in a metaphor of speaking and hearing. The good man's desires, unlike the incontinent man's, are, as I have noted, at the disposition of his reason to the point of "homophony." In the continent man, desires do not speak but "listen" to reason and "are persuaded" by it. There is, however, no explicit mention of an "allophony" of reason and desire. The closest Aristotle comes to a speaking of desire not in accord with reason—a "speaking of matter"—is also the closest he comes to a notion of tolerance. This is in his concept of *karteria*, which is the ability to hold out against desires or misfortunes and in that sense to "tolerate" them.[20] In the passages cited, *karteria* is connected closely to continence, for in both the desires are opposed to reason. In the continent man, the desires allow themselves to be persuaded by reason and so submit to it; in the *karteros* they do not, and he has to act with indifference to them. The difference, Aristotle tells us, is that between winning and remaining unbeaten (7.7.1150a36).

Karteria, which is occasionally translated as "tolerance" but is etymologically related to *karteros*, hard, thus amounts to not listening to desire—or would if Aristotle extended his metaphor of speaking and hearing to the lower levels of his moral hierarchy. The closest he comes to an interpersonal conception of this is perhaps his cryptic remark at *Politics* 1.13.1260a13–15 that while slaves lack reasoning power, women have it, but it is "without authority"; the picture seems to be of the Little Woman yapping away while Hubby buries himself in his newspaper.[21]

Karteria is not fully translatable as "tolerance" (and I have not translated it at all here) because there is in it a complete absence of goodwill; "tolerance" suggests at least a minimal level of that. Though Aristotle does not openly extend his metaphor of speaking and hearing to *karteria*, if he did so he would presumably have to say that desire speaks—for since it remains unpersuaded it does not listen, and if it must be ignored it must be making itself heard in some fashion. Since the desires are, as we saw, the "matter" of the moral life, it is here that Aristotle comes closest to what I discussed in Chapter 1 as the "speaking of matter."

What we must tolerate is what we do not like but cannot change or escape. In the first instance this is our own unruly desires, but Aristotle's more general term for such things is "the necessary" (*ta anankaia*). *Metaphysics* 5.5 grounds this type of necessity in compulsion, that is, in what acts on us contrary to our own natural inclinations.[22] Everything that inescapably engages us but does not fulfill our nature and so is not for us an end in itself must be tolerated as necessary; and what is an end in itself, for Aristotle, is what fulfills our own rational nature (see *NE* 1.7.1097a28–1098a18).

Most things outside us do not fulfill our rational nature. We should not try to change them, however, for they have forms of their own and so "manifest goodness and beauty both in their being and their coming to be" (*Metaphysics* 1.3.984b12–13). We also cannot flee from something unless we already know it, and knowledge of things outside us is by sensation and implies proximity (*De anima* 2.5). Thus, our dealings with things outside us which do not help us fulfill our rational nature are occasions, at bottom, for toleration.[23] It is telling, in this regard, that the two paragraphs of *De anima* 3.12 which discuss why animals have sensation, the distinctive trait of which is to relate us cognitively to things outside us (*De anima* 2.5.417b19–23), use one or another form of *ananke* no fewer than nine times. When an entity is construed as an ousia, then, the most basic way it can relate to other entities is to tolerate them: to endure their parousia while still trying to fulfill its own nature.

Tolerance, then, is a very broad concept for Aristotle. It stands to parousia as domination stands to ousia: it translates the term into the life contexts from which it arose and to which it is to apply. But this seems at variance with my beginning insight: that intolerance, rather than tolerance, is the norm in human affairs. How do we explain this?

Metaphysics and Social Structure

The organizing power of the concept of ousia within Aristotle's thought is extraordinarily wide. It claims not merely to render things dependably comprehensible but to provide "scientific" knowledge of what they *truly* are—or, in the case of ethics, of what they truly should be. The scope of this concept is apparent not only on the level of the individual organism in fields like cognition, biology and ethics but in both Aristotle's politics and his theology. The *Politics*, for example, like politics since, is structured on the following principle:

> In all things which are composed out of several other things, and which come to be some single common thing, whether continuous or discrete, in all of them there turns out to be a distinction between that which rules, and that which is ruled; and this holds for all ensouled things by virtue of the whole of nature; and even in nonliving things there is a sort of ruling element, such as harmony. (*Politics* 1.5.1254a28–32)

Or, in the famous closing words of book 12 of the *Metaphysics*—themselves quoted from an even more ancient authority, Homer—"the rule of many is not good; one ruler let there be."[24]

It is unsurprising, then, that the way Aristotle analogizes the relationship between reason and desire to that between father and child should suggest that the same basic structure—ousiodic structure—is to be found in both cases. Incontinent and bad men, however, are not the only humans whose human form cannot play an effective, disposing role in their lives: "For the slave has no deliberative faculty at all; the woman has, but it is without authority; and the child has, but it is immature."[25]

Young males, to be sure—unlike the others—will one day be moral agents; but that comes about only after decades of maturation and instruction, not by mere decision or action. The defective reasons of women and slaves, by contrast, are irremediable. What members of these latter groups must do, for their own good, is participate in reason in the only way open to them: by adhering to a structure in which a single active reason informs not merely its own body but several others as well. This is the household, with a mature male at its head. The structure of the household is thus, like that of the relation of reason and desire in the moral agent, very similar to the relation of form and matter articulated in the *Metaphysics*:

> And it is clear that the rule of the soul over the body, and reason [*nous*] over the passionate part, is natural and advantageous. . . . Again, the male is by nature superior stronger [*kreitton*], and the female inferior; and the one rules, and the other is ruled; the same manner is necessary for all humankind. Where then there is such a difference as that between soul and body, or between men and animals, . . . the inferiors are by nature slaves. (*Politics* 1.5.1254b5–18)

The ancient family, of course, exhibited the traits of an Aristotelian ousia long before Aristotle codified them. The *pater familias* (a term for which there is, thankfully, no English equivalent) not only bought the slaves but approved the marriages of his children and (technically) had the right to have them exposed at birth; in all three activities he established and secured the family's boundaries. His wife and children, to say nothing of slaves, had to obey his orders and heed his advice as a matter of course; they were at his disposition. In Aristotle's codification of it, the family has, strictly speaking, only one moral agent: the *pater*.

This overall binary of oppressor (master, husband)[26] and oppressed (slave, wife) should not obscure the fact that the dispositive power of the *pater* is implemented differently in each case. The dominance of the master over the slave, *kratēsis*, is of the kind that the master's reason has over his own desires, for the slave lacks active reason and has only the ability to apprehend it in another. The master's reason is thus what governs the actions of the slave, who is merely a "separated" (*kechōrismenon*) part of the master's body (*Politics* 1.6.1255b11–12). Since the well-being of the master's reason is the goal or *telos* of his acts (see *Politics* 7.14.1333a17–24; *NE* 6.2.1139b3–4), it is the slave's *telos* as well. The free man is the one who "exists for his own sake and not for that of another" (*Metaphysics* 1.2.982b25–26), and the slave by contrast would be the man who lives for the sake of another, and who, we now see, desires to do so; for the master's good is his *telos*.

With regard to the wife, the situation is different. She has an active reason, and in accordance with what we have just seen its well-being is her own good; her actions ought to be directed to that. Because she has active reason, moreover, she can speak. But she should not; Gorgias, says Aristotle, was right to say that "silence is a woman's glory" (*Politics* 1.13.1260a30). In a woman, the human form (reason) has failed to gain complete domination over its matter,[27] which means that she, though rational, is ultimately a creature of desire. She, like the slave, is fit only to obey (*Politics* 1.13.1260a23–24). A woman's reason is therefore "without authority," and though she can speak, she is not to be listened to. The *pater*'s dispositive power over her is thus not a matter of *kratēsis* but of *karteria*. She is not "dominated" in the way that a slave is but is merely "tolerated."

Tolerance and intolerance, then, are domestic: what I must or cannot tolerate falls within relevant boundaries, those of my family or polity. Being domestic, it cannot be escaped. But what is the distinction? What makes something intolerable?

According to the metaphysics of ousia, the space within the boundaries of an ousia is to be structured in certain sorts of ways—if it is a social space, by a certain set of ideas, practices, customs, and traditions which are at bottom unified and function as its ousiodic form. Those formative structures must be evidenced in (have disposition over) every point in that space. Thus, any speech or action which runs counter to those ideas, customs, practices, and traditions can be regarded in one of three ways: as a spontaneous upsurge of matter (as when a slave does something "at random," without being ordered to (see *Metaphysics* 12.10.1075a20–23); as the presence within that space of an alien form which has and seeks no authority (the speech of the good Aristotelian wife); or as the intrusion into that space of an alien form which does claim authority and so contests the dispositive power of the *pater*. In any case, it will be regarded as irrational and unethical, but in the first two cases, I suggest, it can be tolerated. What cannot be tolerated in the household or in any ousiodically structured being is a second ousiodic form claiming authority, that is, dispositional power. Indeed, when a creature of desire claims the authority which can rightly come only from reason, it is a case of *hybris*; the correct response is not toleration but anger (see *Rhetoric* 2.2.1378b23–1379a4).

Consider again the common argument against homosexuality I ran through earlier: Human nature is reason; the reason for sex is reproduction; sexual activity outside the context of reproduction is therefore wrong; and this includes all homosexual activity, which is not to be tolerated. This, though familiar enough from, for example, the teachings of the Roman Catholic Church,[28] is not Aristotle's view. He has no particular problem with homosexuality per se, as is evident in the way he tells the following anecdote in the *Politics*:

> The Syracusan constitution was once changed by a love-quarrel of two young men who were in the government. The story is that while one of them was away from home his [male] beloved was gained over by his companion, and he to revenge himself seduced the other's wife. They then drew the ruling class into their quarrel and so split all the people into portions. (*Politics* 5.4.1303b20–26)

There is no moral distinction drawn here between heterosexual and homosexual affairs; the damage, in fact, is done by a heterosexual seduction which intrudes an extra man into the wife's bed. It is all very well for a young husband to have his male lover; but when this leads, however indirectly, to adultery, it interferes with the ousiodic structure of the household. The real damage here, however, is not to the household; it is to the state itself, for the young man, being of the ruling class, seduces his lover's wife in the context of a quarrel with another man of that same class. The evil to which Aristotle calls attention is thus brought about not by the two homosexual affairs referred to but by the *plan* of the lover to gain revenge by seducing his lover's wife, thereby splitting the state. Aristotle's own moral to this story is not that homosexuality is wrong or unnatural but merely that we must pay attention even to seemingly trivial quarrels among the rulers, lest they grow and damage the city.

Erotic attraction for Aristotle is an excess of friendly affection (*NE* 8.6.1158a11–12, 9.10.1171a11). As an excess, it is not good; but no desire is for Aristotle "intrinsically disordered," as the Catholic Church calls homosexuality. Rather, it is when such an excessive desire is chosen and acted upon—when it receives the sanction of reason and gives rise to a plan—that it becomes evil. For then it is a case of what we saw Aristotle call unhinderedness: of reason following desire, rather than the reverse.

Similarly for women. The woman, be she wife, daughter, or slave, is free to speak because the *pater* will not listen. As long as she does not claim dispositive power, her speech can be tolerated. If others do listen, however, trouble arises—sometimes tragically. Antigone's sister Ismene is free to "rave" about Creon's edict regarding the burial of Polyneices and her sister's plan to disobey it; Creon "sees" her but does not stop to listen. It is when Antigone acts, and still more when Creon's son Haemon sides with her, that she must be done away with, "lest it be said that we were bested by a woman."[29] When someone in a domestic or political space presumes to speak from an irrational desire *and demands to be heard*, then that desire claims the status of form. Thus, it is desire acting as form that is *hybris* and so intolerable; as long as it is merely desire and does not claim the authority proper to form, it can be tolerated by the *karteros*. The speaking of matter in general, then, can be tolerated so long as it is ignored; for it is in ignoring it that the "toleration" consists.

Intolerance, then, is the angry response to the presence within my boundaries of an alien form—whether from outside or as an upsurge from matter. This holds not merely for homosexuality but for all otherness: for slaves and for women who speak.

Conclusions

The historicality of reason requires that we return to the Greeks; but when we look at their most influential philosopher, we find anything but historical awareness. Instead we find reason itself instated as the unalterable core of the human being. True, the ordinances of reason for Aristotle, what it actually tells us to do on specific occasions, change with one's circumstances; but the fundamental rational structure of ousia, which reason helps to validate and which in turn gives it its high status, is universal. Deviations from it, where possible at all, are immoral.

This rigidity of reason, in turn, traps it in a metaphysics which gives surprising weight to tolerance and intolerance. Parousia, which in the context of the metaphysics of substance signifies the presence of one thing to another, becomes *karteria*, the hardness with which reason "tolerates" matter when it cannot silence it or reduce it to the homophony of sympathetic vibration. This *karteria*, when conjoined with the lack of interior structure implied by the metaphysics of substance, assumes (as we will see in the next chapter) the epistemic rigidity of modern mathematics, which tolerates the multifarious mutations of the real world without changing its own nature.

Within the ousiodic framework, what has to be tolerated is matter, the factor of change and variety—and in particular, we saw, domestic matter, matter that cannot be moved away from because it is within relevant boundaries. Such matter, morally speaking, is desire, which for Aristotle should speak only to agree with reason and should listen only to be persuaded by it. Matter which manages to state its own case, speaking with its own voice as does a woman, goes almost unmentioned by Aristotle. Since speaking as rational is the prerogative of form, matter which speaks is trying to usurp the function and status of form. It is not to be tolerated but destroyed or expelled. Thus, as we saw, desire itself—heterosexual or not—is perfectly acceptable to Aristotle as long as it remains *merely* desire. Desire which gives rise to a plan, to *logos*, is what leads to problems.

If reason is to be able to listen to matter, it must become malleable. Then it can abandon the *hybris* of *karteria* and will be able to hear and identify with the speaking of matter. Butler's philosophy shows us one way this works. Though her sophisticated thought is hardly mere matter speaking, it shares certain features with it. Among these, we now see, is a kind of "Bottom," which in Butler's case follows from the inevitability of parody: we cannot repeat exactly and we cannot start from nothing, so we are condemned to parody as long as we are alive. It is, then, not AA or death, as in Wallace's account; it is parody or death.

CHAPTER 4

MODERNISM IN PHILOSOPHY

FULFILLMENT AND SUBVERSION IN KANT

The Late, Great Modernism Debate

Chapters 2 and 3 argued that modern philosophy, far from being a radical departure from ancient practices, was in important ways a continuation of them. If this is the case, then recent attacks on and defenses of philosophical modernity, the larger context of Kantian Enlightenment, have misconceived it; for common to both is an emphasis on the autonomy of reason. The idea that reason alone is capable of evaluating our social and individual lives is held by both sides to be a radical departure in philosophy and definitive for modernism.

The successes and failures of what I will call the "Great Modernism Debate" in philosophy were clear by the time of Robert Pippin's *Idealism as Modernism* (1997). Though the debate ostensibly focused on whether the various postmodern critiques of modernism had any merit, its more basic point, as with many debates, may have been to identify the participants. What was being defended, and what attacked? If, as we saw Cohen and Dascal suggest in the Introduction, basic structures of the philosophical world were under assault and needed to be either defended or jettisoned, what were those structures in the first place? And who were the attackers?

Pippin's account, which is paradigmatic for the whole issue, answers the first question in an admirably brief and lucid way. Philosophical modernism is the attempt to ground individual and social life in "a wholly self-authorizing or self-governing reason" (*IM*, 8). Modernism so conceived is clearly inspired by Kant's concept of Enlightenment but in Pippin's view progressively expands

Kant's relatively abstract recipe into broadly Hegelian accounts of "the allegiance demanded by modern institutions and practices, legal, scientific, aesthetic, as well as political and social practices" (*IM*, 6). The sum of this process of concretion is the defining imperative of modernism: Kant's abstract *sapere audere*, "dare to know," becomes Pippin's concrete "live freely" (*IM*, 24).

Problems arise for Pippin, as for so many others, when he gets to the other side of the debate. What or who is opposed to modernism? Pippin has two ways of characterizing modernism's philosophical enemy. One, the more casual, is to give a list of what "counter-Enlightenment" thinkers "celebrate":

> the priority of imagination in sense-making, of an organic tradition and of some sort of creative "expressivity" in accounts of meaning; a considerably more relativist and heterogeneous spirit than any single notion of modernity could encompass; a fascination with novelty; an appreciation, even celebration, of instability and change. (*IM*, 2)

This list is a strange one. Some of its components are in contradiction, or at least tension, with each other: people who value imagination tend not to value organic tradition, and people who celebrate tradition tend not to appreciate instability and change. Other parts of the list seem to include people far beyond postmodernists: fascination with novelty is a notable characteristic of primates in general, in philosophy and outside.

Such a broad and contradictory list is justified, of course, if the postmodernists are a broad and contradictory group of people—a motley crew coming at modernism from several directions at once. Even if we accept this as an account of postmodernism, however, any list which could not fit in such exemplary figures as Deleuze, Derrida, and Foucault certainly has problems. But the "critique of the subject" driven by them and other postmodernists does not leave room for assigning priority to imagination, launching expressivist accounts of meaning, or praising organic traditions.[1] So it is not surprising to find Pippin also referring to this list as "hypermodern," or that a few pages later, having clarified modernism a bit more, he abandons the whole idea of a list and simply says that "the enemy of such a modernism (whether in the name of premodernism or postmodernism) is dogmatism" (*IM*, 7).

In advancing this characterization of modernism's enemy, Pippin has reversed his earlier definition of modernism in philosophy: to adhere to a dogma is precisely what it is, in philosophy, *not* to live freely or by self-authorizing reason. But who are the philosophical dogmatists? Dogmatism, after all, was banished from philosophy by Kant; "dogmatic philosophy" is today, as it should be, an oxymoron. The question arises of whether it is even possible to be a philosophical opponent of philosophical modernism. Indeed, Pippin's suggestion that his list of counter-Enlightenment traits is really hypermodern implies that opposition to modernism is not philosophically possible, a point he had made in his earlier *Modernism as a Philosophical Problem*:

> While it certainly may be the case that some particular modern version of human autonomy secretly or unconsciously reflects . . . mythic fears or subterranean passions, "exposing" such dependence and its unintended consequences itself already reflects the insistence on critical self-consciousness and so the ideal of genuine independence characteristic of philosophical modernism. (Pippin 1991, 165)

This is a *tu quoque* ("you do it too") applied to postmodernists, who are said to rely on the distinctively modern notions of critical self-consciousness and (or as) autonomy. It has long been accepted by postmodernists themselves ("indeed we do"). Michel Foucault, for example, had done so in 1976:

> The simple fact of speaking about [sex], and of speaking about its repression, has something of the allure of a deliberate transgression. Whoever possesses this language places himself, up to a certain point, outside of power; he anticipates, however little, future liberty. (Foucault 1976, 13)

So it appears that philosophical opposition to modernism, as Pippin defines it, is indeed impossible: those who claim to express it are either modernists themselves, as Foucault admits to being, or, as Habermas has it, they are premodern and unphilosophical throwbacks (Habermas 1990).

If attacks on philosophical modernism always either presuppose it or subserve it, we can understand why, as James L. Marsh points out, the postmodernists never produced an effective response to the many critiques of their positions by Habermas, Pippin, and others (Marsh 2000, esp. 556). What it does not explain is why the postmodernists, without defending themselves, have kept right on doing what they were doing. Could it be that the modernist critiques all missed the target, shooting off into the intellectual waters like poorly aimed torpedoes?

It is perhaps not surprising that the Great Modernism Debate in philosophy, like so many philosophical debates in recent times, did not achieve any sort of resolution but simply faded away into exhaustion and became institutional:

the modernists, as I noted in the Introduction, are in the philosophy department and the postmodernists in comparative literature. In order to bring the debate to a more productive conclusion, we would need to understand the nature of the parties; and, as we have seen, no intelligible definition of postmodernism is possible, because there is no way to define an intellectual approach that would oppose modernism's emphases on critical self-consciousness and autonomy. This only raises another problem, for then modernism in philosophy is simply—philosophy. Does the term "modernism" then mean anything at all when applied to philosophy?

But perhaps that is still not the real issue. In Chapter 2, I contrasted two views of the history of philosophy: that it was a search for truth and that it was an obsession with ousia. Modernism in philosophy, it seems, has understood the nature of the search for truth well enough that philosophical opposition to that understanding is impossible. On that level, modernism wins; but if that were the only level, the losers would have faded away. Can we understand the persistence of postmodernism by looking at its history in terms of ousia? Does the debate somehow become more real, and perhaps even more adjudicable?

I will argue that it does, which means that the fundamental issue between modernists and postmodernists in philosophy does not in fact concern the critical capacities of reason. The real issue concerns ontology, the study of what Being is. When we see the debate in these terms, we come to a new understanding of modernism in philosophy—one which allows us to see not only why the Great Modernism Debate was an important one but where it should lead us.

Where Did Modernism Come From?
A Primer on Premodern Ontology

Modernism's view of reason as the ultimate judge of our lives and allegiances was, I suggest, predicated on a more basic shift, one concerning what Aristotle (at *Metaphysics* 7.1.1028b2–4) characterized as "that which was from ancient days, and is now, and always will be sought after and despaired of: what is Being?"

I discussed Aristotle's two answers to this, the metaphysics of substance and that of ousia, in Chapter 3 and suggested a couple of reasons why Aristotle moved from one to the other. A third consideration, which looks like a reason for the move but is not, leads us beyond the Greeks to a broader view of "premodern" philosophy.

Aristotle thinks, we saw, that boundary and disposition (initiative is not relevant here) are necessary features of a natural being because its matter tends to fly off in different directions (up and down) and so must be held together by something—the bounding and ordering power of form:

> We must ask what is the force that holds together the earth and the fire [in a living thing] which are carried in opposed directions; if there is no hindering force, they will be pulled apart; if there is, this must be the soul and the cause of nutrition and growth. (*De anima* 2.4.416a6–8)

This means that in any being, its form and its matter are working against one another. As Mary Louise Gill puts it:

> When the elements have been worked up into a higher object . . . the potentiality *not to be* that higher construct but to be some simpler stuff instead is a potentiality that determines the very nature of the material genus, because the properties that constitute the genus can specify the nature of a simpler body. The elements thus achieve their fullest being when they are separate in a state of uncombined simplicity. To put the point metaphorically, the elements do not "strive" upward toward complexity but downward toward simplicity.[2]

The matter of an oak tree or a human being tends to resolve itself into its primordial constituents—earth, water, air, and fire; the former two tend to move downward and the latter two upward, unless there is some further principle holding the being together. That, in turn, is the form, which is why the relation between form and matter is to be most basically understood as a relation of domination, in which matter is held away from its own nature by form. But that things fly apart without form is not a reason for adopting a hylomorphic ontology, because the idea that matter seeks to return to its basic nature only makes sense *once we have accepted* that ontology. In the substance ontology, there are no such forces to begin with—only properties dropping into and out of passive substrates. There is no reason to attribute to things a tendency to fly apart in the first place and no reason to invoke form to stop them.

What Gill calls the "tension and commotion" of Aristotle's cosmos[3] was eventually subdued, philosophically speaking, by the Christian creator-God. The attribution of the three ousiodic traits to that God is beautifully carried off by St. Augustine at the beginning of his *Confessions*, where God is addressed as *ex quo omnia, per quem omnia, in quo omnia*: all things are "out of" God (via the divine initiative, that is, the creation of the world by the Father); "through" him (via his ongoing disposition, or providence through Christ's sacrifice); and "in" him (particularly within the boundaries of the religious community, or the Holy Spirit).[4]

That the Christian path is advancing to modernity becomes clearer with Thomas Aquinas.[5] For Aquinas, what exists in a thing prior to the arrival of its form is not matter in simple, elemental states but sheer potentiality. Such potentiality, even in its purest form—that of prime matter—exists only because it has been created by God. This is what Étienne Gilson views as Aquinas's key insight:

> Now, the Pre-socratics had justified the existence of individuals as such. Plato and Aristotle had justified the existence of substances as such. But not one of these seemed ever to have dreamed that there was any occasion to explain the existence of matter. (Gilson 1956, 131)

Since it is sheer potentiality, matter does not have an elemental nature of its own as it did in Aristotle. Created by God to receive form, it cannot by its nature reject or resist form; if it does, then such resistance must be either accidental or (in the case of human beings) sinful. Hence, where for Aristotle the elements resisted form on behalf of their own natures, for Aquinas they do not. Instead, as he phrases it in *On Being and Essence*, they "operate only according to the exigencies . . . which prepare matter to receive form" (Aquinas 1949, 49).

Matter no longer resists its domination by form. In Gilson's words:

> Matter is only a potency determinable by the form. But the form itself is the act by which the matter is made to be such or such a determined substance. The proper role of the form is, therefore, to constitute substance *as substance*. (Gilson 1956, 32)

For Aristotle, we saw, form made matter a "this" (see also *Metaphysics* 7.17.1041b7–8). For Aquinas too, matter is necessary to composite substance (see Gilson 1956, 88). But its only role is to efface itself in its reception of form— just as Gilson's locution here effaces it. Matter is so docile in this destiny of effacement that its disruptiveness in Aristotle can go entirely unnoticed, even by so astute a scholar as Gilson, for whom only form has a "proper role" in constituting substance as substance.

Aquinas's philosophy, of course, springs from and articulates—in my word, codifies—a world which is radically different from Aristotle's. Such notions as createdness in metaphysics and Christian love in ethics are not merely un-Aristotelian but unthinkable for Aristotle. But the matter-form binary is still in place on the level of natural beings, and Aquinas's main innovation upon Aristotle with respect to this is what I call the "docilization" of matter. Matter no longer exists as elements whose nature is to *resist* form; it is now mere potentiality, whose entire nature is to *receive* form. Resistance to the domination of form is now unnatural or sinful—and in either case rationally unthinkable. Ousiodic domination has been consolidated throughout the universe. Gilson again:

> Precisely because every operation is the realization of an essence, and because every essence is a certain quantity of being and perfection . . . the universe reveals itself to us as a society made up of superiors and inferiors. (Gilson 1956, 359)

This, then, is the metaphysical situation which gave birth to modernism in philosophy. It is itself highly unmodern. The oppressive side of Aristotle's ontology of ousiodic domination has been extended and consolidated to the point that there is nothing left to be oppressed. This means, however, that *form has no empirical work to do*. For Aristotle, it was easy to see what in our experience had an ousiodic structure and what did not: anything which visibly persisted in its own nature without flying apart was resisting the elemental pulls of its matter and therefore must contain an active form. When Aquinas makes matter entirely receptive of form, form's victory is complete; nothing is left for it to do. Form loses its empirical purchase and will in modern philosophy become a target not merely of critique but, as we saw with Hobbes in Chapter 2, of ridicule.

How Ontology Became a Contract

When there is nothing left for the ousiodic structure of active form dominating passive matter to do, it vanishes (or, as I put it elsewhere, it is "evicted") from nature (*MO*, 105–108). Objects, bounded but unformed clumps of matter, replace ousiai, Aristotle's bounded and formed entities, as the fundamental components of the natural world. It is at this point that the metaphysics of substance, which I discussed in the previous chapter, makes a fateful return into the history of philosophy. Parousia, the existence of things on their boundaries, now becomes central, and the "look" of things, rather than the feel of their internal structure, becomes equally central. What Charles Mills calls the racial contract (Mills 1997), allocating the roles of oppressor and oppressed on the basis of visual appearance, thus joins the sexual contract, which differentiates mainly by touch (women for Aristotle are cooler and moister than men; see McCumber 1988). Just as philosophers have enthusiastically participated in the oppression of women, so now they give themselves over to the slave trade.[6]

Ousiodic hylomorphism continues in modernity, however, to be the basic structuring principle of the human world, even though it no longer applies to nature. This means that the human world will continue to be viewed as a set of unitary forms (sovereigns, fathers) controlling bounded spaces (nations, families).

Two features of the way the schema of ousia is deployed in modernity enable us to call that deployment "contractual." First, the ousia ontology is adopted in modernity as the result of a free decision. The decision is "free" because there is no longer any compelling metaphysical reason in favor of it: if ousia has no work to do in nature, what work need it do in society? Perhaps there are other ways than the imposition of a single unifying form (or sovereign) to keep society from flying apart. The decision not to pursue such possibilities is "free," at least in the sense of being metaphysically unconstrained.

Second, as with a contract, that decision is reached by a group of equals, a feature which requires some explanation. Its motivation can be seen in Cartesian physics. For Aristotle, what distinguished natural beings from artifacts and divinities was that every natural being "contains within itself a principle of motion and rest" (*Physics* 2.1.192b14–15). This principle, of course, was its ousiodic form. When such form is evicted from nature by way of the Christian creator-God, natural motions in nature can no longer be traced to something immanent to natural beings and must be sought for elsewhere. Fortunately, the cause of this problem is also its solution—God:

> I consider matter, left to itself, and not receiving any impulse from elsewhere, to be perfectly at rest. And it is pushed by God who conserves in it as much movement or transport as he put in it at the beginning.[7]

As Daniel Garber puts it:

> Descartes rejects the tiny souls of the schools only to replace them with one great soul, God, an incorporeal substance who, to our limited understanding, manipulates the bodies of the inanimate world as we manipulate ours.[8]

Nature, then, is not a set of ousiai, as it was for Aristotle. It is more like a single giant ousia, with God as its dispositive form. Instead of natural forms disposing of bounded packets of matter, we now have a single supernatural form whose operation covers the whole material universe. With the differentiated hierarchy of ousiodic forms evicted from it, all of nature becomes mere matter—a set of objects, each as "objective" as the others. Nature under God thus becomes a single egalitarian unit—what Joseph Needham has called a "great empire, ruled by a divine logos."[9] The aspirations of sovereigns are free to spread across the entire globe, and modern imperialism is at hand.

The very divinity of the universal logos means in a Christian context that its unifying source cannot be found anywhere in the empirical world, for God is other than his creation. Cartesian modernity thus presents us with a giant case of *ousia abscondita*: ousia has vanished from nature, only to reappear as divinity (see *MO*, 194–202). But even for Descartes, God is not knowable enough to enable us to found political and social arrangements on his will (earthly rulers are for Descartes inscrutable, and God must be more so).[10] When the Empiricists push this view to its end and deny that we can have any knowledge at all of supersensible beings, ousia's reassignment to divinity fails. God has not only absconded from the universe, validating ousiodic form from outside it; he has effectively died. The sons are all that is left.

Ousiodic structure in the human world has now lost both the ancient validation in terms of nature that Aristotle had given it and the modern validation in terms of the creator-God that Descartes (and the other Rationalists) had tried to give it. Political legitimacy must now come from below—from "atomized" human individuals who are as equal to each other as material objects are on the level of nature. Hence, the metaphysically unconstrained decision on the ousiodic ontology is reached not by intellectual authorities but by the educated public in general. Descartes himself, for example, writes his *Discourse on the Method* in French, because "I expect that those who use only their natural reason in all its purity will be better judges of my opinions than those who give credence only to the writings of the ancients" (*DOe*, 6:77). As Carole Pateman has pointed out, however, such contracts—ontological, social, sexual, racial—retain, like Cartesian physics, a reference to the departed Father, in that the parties to them are bound by ties of "fraternity" (*SC*, 78). Not everyone, it appears, is a "son" of God; in spite of its aspirations to universality, the free agreement to retain ousia is restricted to a particular group and directed against other groups—the women and people of color who live in the "state of nature."[11]

The racial and sexual contracts cannot operate in modernity without a free acceptance of the ousiodic schema; for without that schema, there is no category of nature as "mere" matter into which to place women and people of color, and so no way to erect what we saw Lucius Outlaw call the "subworld" of racial (and sexual) oppression. The acceptance of that schema in the modern world is through a "contract" among the fraternity of people (European males) who, as rational, can comprehend its logic. But however convenient this was to the gentlemen concerned, the ontological contract was also necessitated on philosophical grounds. It was developments within philosophy, exemplified by Aquinas, that forced ousia from nature and led, across the failure of rationalism, to the contractual empiricism of the surviving sons.

Descartes and the Self-Authorization of Reason

Modernism in philosophy achieves its fullest expression in Kant, and after some further stage setting in the form of a brief look at Descartes, I will turn to him.

Descartes's introduction of self-authorizing reason as the means of settling all disputes is traditionally regarded as the birth of philosophical modernity, but it was no innocent creation of an isolated genius; as Pippin puts it, "Descartes should not be understood as a brilliant philosophical puzzler, an individual genius manufacturing 'how do I know I am not dreaming' brainteasers" (Pippin 1991, 23). Descartes's enthronement of reason was in fact prepared by a variety of historical developments in addition to those I have noted. For one, the religious wars of the Reformation had made pressing the need for something beyond religion to adjudicate human disputes. For another, the rise of modern science had shown that myriad traditional opinions, long thought to be settled, were in fact false. But it is one thing to see that many things one has believed are false, and another to arrive at the first major step in Descartes's philosophy, the project of doubting everything. Aristotle, for example, never conceived of such universal doubt, though he was presumably bright enough to do so and had certainly encountered false opinions.[12]

Why, then, was it Descartes who first came up with the project of doubting everything? Pippin sees, at the core of Cartesian doubt, the possibility that everything we experience may be a dream (Pippin 1991, 23–24). If we want to know how Descartes ever came up with the project of universal doubt, we thus need to answer the question, How did Descartes ever come to imagine that our entire waking life might be merely a dream?

For Aristotle, we saw, matter was known through its (disruptive) effects on natural beings. When it is rendered docile, in the context of the Christian creator-God, those effects cease, and there is nothing to prevent the next step—dispensing with matter altogether. When the matter of external things is gone (it will of course return later for Descartes, in the form of the passive objects of his physics), we are left with merely their forms (including, to be sure, the "sensible forms" which constitute the entirety of their perceived properties). A set of sensible forms with no matter underlying them would be a sort of dream image, entirely folded into its parousia to the mind—and since matter now does no empirical work, there is now no way to distinguish the experience of an external thing from that of such an image.

Aquinas never takes this step, but it might have made sense to him. It would likely have made none to Aristotle, for whom ousiodic form has to inhere in matter because its active nature is to dominate matter; when Aristotle discusses dreams in the *De somniis*, one of his main problems is to ascertain just what matter it is in which dream images inhere—given that, being forms, they must inhere in some matter or other.[13]

It is because matter is eliminable in this way for Descartes, I suggest, that it makes sense to say that the whole world might be a dream. This represents the next crucial step beyond Aquinas: the possibility that matter, instead of effacing itself in form, never existed in the first place. This in turn both makes room for and necessitates the introduction of self-authorizing reason as the adjudicator of all beliefs. It *necessitates* it because if it is even possible that the world may be a dream, we cannot get dependable knowledge from our senses; only reason is left. It *makes room for* it because once the mind is freed from dependence on the senses, it can develop its own methods of adjudicating things. Modernism in philosophy thus begins with the realization that, as Marx will put it, "all that is solid melts into air," or as Heidegger will put it, when the world becomes a picture (Marx 1988, 212; Heidegger 2002a).

The loss of an epistemic role for matter is not merely a philosophical development. For one thing, it is related to mathematics by way of the fact that the science of the time, as Heidegger points out, was invested in calculability (Heidegger 1977). In order to make exact prediction possible, mathematics needed to deny matter's disruptive forces. But they were only there in the first place, as I noted above, within the framework of hylomorphic ontology; as subsequent science has amply shown, there is no *empirical* reason to maintain them. Once they are gone, we are no longer saddled with what, in Chapter 2, I called partial intelligibility. Objects now exist entirely on their boundaries, as inert units to which mathematics can be applied, and are thus—in principle, anyway—entirely knowable. The epistemological argument for ousia—that it could account for dependable intelligibility in a world continually disrupted by matter—is thus circumvented.

A second historical complicity, which I have already mentioned, is more sinister. When matter is lost, the "look" of things gains importance; indeed, in the case of dream images, all they are is how they look. The stage is thus being set for the application of ousia to people based on the color of their skin: racism will join sexism in the pantheon of oppression, and people can be reduced to matter because of the color of their skin.

There is one further preparation for Cartesian doubt, more philosophical and clearer in the early *Principles of Philosophy* than in the *Meditations*. That is the doctrine of free will. Proposition I.6 of the *Principles* explicitly grounds Cartesian doubt in this:

> By whomever it is that we are made, and however powerful and deceptive he may be, we nonetheless experience in ourselves this freedom, that we can always refrain from beliefs which are not plainly certain and examined, and we can thus guard against ever being deceived. (*DOe*, 8A:6)

According to Descartes, the human mind has two fundamental faculties, understanding and willing. Understanding gives us content in the form of what Descartes calls clear and distinct ideas. But for a judgment, the mind must also *affirm* or *not affirm* its ideas, and these are actions of the will (8A:17–18). When we withhold assent from all our ideas at once, we are engaged in Cartesian doubt; and that is an act of our freedom. Such doubt is justified for Descartes only on special occasions; we should not go through our entire lives doubting everything. The ideal is to give assent only to ideas that are clear and distinct, thus avoiding the difficulties that arise when we affirm or deny ideas whose relation to reality is not entirely certain.

This requires, however, the proper balance between the understanding and the will. If the will outstrips the understanding, we will assent to uncertain ideas and make erroneous judgments. If it lags behind, our knowledge will be incomplete. In order to form true judgments, then, for Descartes the will needs to gain what Aristotle would call "dominance" (*kratēsis*) over its own capacities and those of the understanding. It needs to make the ideas of the understanding clear and distinct, and it must limit assent to only those ideas. As we began to see in Chapter 2, knowledge for Descartes is thus not simply a matter of happening upon true judgments but of the will establishing the right order among one's faculties.

The will's ordering power, or what I call "disposition," is thus a normative goal for the mind, and its achievement is the aim of philosophy.[14] Philosophy therefore has an ethical function for Descartes, as it did in the Platonic tradition mentioned in Chapter 2. There it was the attainment of truth as nearness to the divine. Here, it is the process of achieving the proper ordering by the mind of its own faculties. One who achieves the proper philosophical balance of the faculties will in fact obtain all other virtues:

> For whoever possesses a firm and constant resolve always to make use of reason
> to the best of his power, and in all his actions to do what he believes to be best,
> is truly wise . . . and by this alone he is just, courageous, moderate, and possesses
> all the other virtues. (*DOe*, 8A:3)

In philosophy the will orders and arranges ideas, and in this exercises what I call dispositive power over the Cartesian mind. The mind also has secure boundaries, for it is independent of other things. This is shown, Descartes says, by the "this mere fact alone, that each of us . . . is capable, in thought, of excluding from himself every other substance. . . . It is certain that each of us . . . is really distinct from every other thinking substance" (*DOe*, 8A:28).[15]

In good Aristotelian fashion, the mind's boundaries, like its right order, are secured by the mind itself, which is able to think itself as distinct from all other beings. These boundaries are so secure, in fact, that only the truthfulness of God (established in *Meditations* 4) enables us to see beyond them, either into the nature of external things or into other minds.[16]

With Descartes, the basic outlines of modernism in philosophy become clear. On the one hand, ousiodic structure is gone from nature, because with matter rendered docile by the Christian God there is nothing for it to do. Natural beings have no immanent forms to draw their boundaries, order their internal components, or govern their interactions with other beings. They are merely material objects, and nature is a realm of matter in motion. Natural beings are thus absorbed into their parousia: their presence to us is all that they are, and everything is, so to speak, on the surface of our minds. This means that everything we experience may be a dream. We are cast back into our own minds—minds which turn out to exhibit their own versions of the ousiodic traits of boundary and disposition. We thus arrive at a general formula for the dual ontologies of modernity: ousia in the human world; substance in the natural world. This is the *content* of the ontological contract.

Its contractual *form* is arrived at through Descartes's instatement of free will as the mind's ousiodic form, exercising the bounding and disposing powers of Aristotelian form. This exercise culminates in philosophy and so is rational: the well-ordered mind is ordered according to reason. From the ousiodic perspective, then, the first role of reason is not to attain truth but to play the ancient role of the ordering and bounding form within the human mind; truth will arrive once this has been done.

But what authorizes reason to play this role? Why should the will be the mind's ousiodic form?

In general, God is defined as the most perfect being (a definition from which his necessary existence follows (*DOe*, 8A:10). All perfections, including those of our souls, exist for Descartes preeminently in God:

> Nor can we have within us the idea or image of anything without there being somewhere, either within us or outside us, some archetype which contains in reality all the perfections belonging to the idea. And since the supreme perfections of which we have an idea are in no way to be found in us, from this we rightly conclude that they reside in something distinct from ourselves, namely God. (*DOe*, 8A:12; see also 8A:11)

The virtues which the good man achieves by rightly ordering his mind are thus finite versions of properties of God. And Descartes goes so far as to hold that anything finite can be conceived only on the basis of our knowledge of infinitude. Our minds can be understood, then, only in terms of their difference from God's mind.[17] From this point of view, once the existence of God itself is established by reason, reason loses its prerogatives and from then on, that is, in all concrete cases, is guided by the idea of God. For it is from that idea that we learn the proper balance of our faculties, which in turn guides us in their proper use, which leads us finally to truth. Descartes's view of the self-authorizing of reason turns out to be a kind of counterpoint to the deistic philosophies of the Enlightenment: just as the God of the deists creates the world and then steps aside to let it govern itself, so reason for Descartes authorizes itself in Cartesian doubt and then steps aside.

But Cartesian doubt itself may already be conditioned by the idea of God. Consider the ousiodic trait of disposition. According to *Principles of Philosophy* 1.24 (*DOe*, 8A:14), we can understand our own dispositive form, our rational will, only by comparison with God's infinite version of such disposition.

We are to be rational, in the sense of willing ourselves to order our minds philosophically, because that is what makes us most like God. Reason's original project of doubting everything is thus the beginning of this ordering activity; and that beginning takes the form of an act of free will, that is, in the withholding of assent from our ideas. Cartesian doubt, the opening act of Cartesian reason, is thus already an effort to find the right balance of the faculties, and as such presupposes, if only indistinctly, our knowledge of those faculties in their perfect forms—which, I suggest, is part of our innately clear and distinct idea of God (*DOe*, 8A:11, 13). When (in Timothy Reiss's words) Descartes "virtually equated will, God, and the ground of truth" (see *Meditations* 4 [*DOe*, 7:57]), he "virtually" implied that the project of Cartesian doubt is grounded, however indistinctly, on the idea of God (Reiss 2005, 31). Here, truth is not equated with nearness to God, as with the Platonists, but is grounded on such nearness—on the right order of the mind. Reason would thus not be, in the end, entirely self-authorizing for Descartes; even in its beginnings, it would be authorized by the idea of God. Whether reason for Descartes is divinely authorized from the start or becomes so later on, divine authorization is crucial to it.

In general terms, we may say that viewing philosophy as a search for truth goes hand in hand with viewing reason itself as the way we conduct that search and so as self-authorizing. When we view philosophy in what I called in Chapter 2 schmilosophical terms, as the establishment of ousia, we see a second and more basic role for it: that of establishing ousiodic structure within the human mind as such. And in that role, reason is not self-authorizing; it is guided by the idea of God. There is now, for present purposes, only one further question: How does Descartes know what God is like?

Kant and the Completion of Modernity

This question was, of course, posed most pressingly by David Hume, one of the Empiricists. For Immanuel Kant, once awakened by Hume from his "dogmatic slumbers,"[18] any such question is ill formed. His critical philosophy is the study not only of the limits of the mind but of its powers or faculties, for the only way to determine what a faculty cannot do is to see what it can. Knowledge of God is beyond our powers because knowledge itself for Kant consists in the application of the categories of the understanding to sensory intuitions. This leads Kant to his views on Enlightenment, which constitute the most complete expression of philosophical modernism we have. In the critical philosophy nothing is grounded on the existence of God, and only so can human reason authorize itself.

Kant's overall critique of metaphysics also leads him to a critical treatment of the application of the metaphysics of substance to the mind itself (his application of the metaphysics of ousia will be far less critical). Like all our categories, that of substance cannot be applied beyond the field of sensory experiences. But because the categories apply universally within the field of appearances, we are tempted to think that they can apply beyond them. This happens to substance in the First Paralogism of Pure Reason. A paralogism is a fallacious argument which is nonetheless grounded in the nature of pure reason itself; the first one begins (in the first edition, *CPR* A, 348–351) from the point that substance is what is permanent in our experience. One permanent feature of my experience is that it is "mine": any awareness that I have must be capable of having "I think that" added to it. Hence, it is only natural to conclude that this "I" is a substance—that it forms the substrate of all my awarenesses, with specific awarenesses or thoughts as its accidents: "I, as a thinking being, am the *absolute subject* of all my possible judgments, and this representation of myself cannot be employed as predicate of any other thing" (*CPR* A, 348). The echoes of Aristotle's *Categories* are clear: the "I" is the subject of all judgments; all things can be viewed as predicated of it. It, however, cannot be predicated of anything else.

Though natural, and in a sense even logical, this inference is for Kant illegitimate: the substance to which it reasons would be one which can never be encountered in any individual intuition and hence is one we cannot know. Thus, he argues here, the "I think" is not an intuition and has no content of its own over and above the thought itself. All it expresses is the logical possibility that I *can* give unity to all my experiences—for example, by a thorough application of the categories of cause and effect. The thought of this empty unity is what Kant calls the "transcendental unity of apperception," and it serves as a condition of more specific thoughts: I cannot think anything determinate without also being able to think that the empty "I think" could accompany that thought. The idea of the substantiality of the soul is thus a *mere* idea—not one to which any underlying or objective reality can be known to correspond.

But if the "I think" provides no basis for attribution of Kant's version of substantiality, it is different for the "I will." For when we examine the nature and function of the Kantian will, we discover once again the ousiodic traits of boundary and disposition. They are evident, in fact, in some of the commonplaces of Kant's moral philosophy.

> For the single principle of ethicality (*Sittlichkeit*) consists precisely in independence from all matter of the law (namely, from a desired object), and at the same time in the determination of arbitrary choice (*Willkür*) simply through the purely universal legislative form to which a given maxim must conform. (*CPrR*, 133)

The will must, in virtue of its moral nature, determine itself independently of any other grounds, such as desire or prudence. As thus purely formal, it determines arbitrary choice. Moreover, the action of the will *remains* within the mind:

> Practical laws relate only to the will, without regard to what might be accomplished through the will's causality, and one can abstract from the latter (as belonging to the sensory world of sense). (*CPrR*, 21; see also 144–146)

The moral self thus defined is ordered by the will and has very definite boundaries. Unlike Aristotle and Aquinas, Kant does not locate ousiodic structures within the natural or empirical world: we do not experience hylomorphic beings around us. Unlike Descartes, he does not relocate it to the divine or supersensible realm. The ousiodic structure of the moral self is established not with the aid of claims about nature or God but through the critical investigation of the mind itself. Such investigation shows that we ourselves, as moral beings, are or must become ousiodic: we must recognize the boundaries of the moral will and allow it to order our other faculties. Where for Aristotle reason was our active disposing form, then, for Kant as for Descartes it is the will. Kant has thus completed the "modern" project of presenting the human self as an ousia existing in a non-ousiodic nature. For if the will is to be truly the source of the self's internal order, it cannot itself be ordered by anything beyond it—whether by nature, as with Aristotle, or through comparisons with God, as with Descartes.

Kant and the Subversion of Modernity

There is, however, a problem with Kant's account. The activity by which the mind actualizes itself Kant calls "legislation." Legislation in general is for Kant the determination of an action or event as necessary.[19] One kind of legislation we may call natural. Our mind legislates patterns to nature through the categories, and in Kant's famous phrase, it serves as the "lawgiver to nature." The other kind of legislation is moral. When an action is declared to be morally necessary, it is again prescribed by the mind in virtue of a universal pattern—a law, in this case the moral law. These two legislations are ultimate: there is, Kant says in the second "Introduction" to the *Critique of Judgment*, no higher legislation to unite them (*CJ*, 174–176).

Cognitive or theoretical legislation is carried out by the understanding; the laws that it prescribes are those inherent in the categories (e.g., the law that every event has a cause). In supplying these overall forms to sensory material, the understanding arranges or disposes the material of intuition in accordance with the categories—into causes and effects, substances and accidents, and so on. This in turn enables that material to be brought under less general patterns which, as empirical, are not necessary and therefore are not laws (or categories) but merely empirical generalizations or concepts. The legislative, or as I call it, dispositive, power of the understanding over sensory material is thus limited to what the twelve categories allow it to do. The object of such legislation, the domain constituted by its orders, is nature, which as the first *Critique* tells us, is "appearances as regards their existence according to necessary rules, that is, according to laws" (*CPR* B, 263, 446n).

The legislation of the understanding to nature is possible because the categories of the understanding and empirical appearances, though very different from one another, both stand in relation to time: the categories can be defined in terms of time, which is the form of all appearances. This is established in the "transcendental schematism," in which the categories are given definitions in terms of time: substance, for example, is defined in the First Analogy of Experience as what is relatively permanent in appearances (*CPR* B, 224–232). The constitution of appearances itself depends on the correct employment of the understanding; and so, it follows, does truth: "without reason [there is] no coherent employment of the understanding, and in the absence of this no sufficient criterion of empirical truth" (*CPR* B, 679). Such legislation then establishes the proper relation of the cognitive faculties and in this sense is for Kant the actualizing force of theoretical mind.

In the case of practical mind, the legislating faculty is reason itself. What reason prescribes is not, again, merely empirical maxims of conduct (which, like empirical concepts, are not necessary and hence are not laws) but the universal form of good acts, the categorical imperative (*CPrR*, 19–20). The pure will, as transcendental, can only be grasped by investigating it entirely within the boundaries of the human mind, "without regard to what might be accomplished through the will's causality, and one can abstract from the latter (as belonging to the sensory world of sense)."[20]

The object of this legislation, then, is not phenomena but the supersensible or noumenal realm: "thus supersensible nature, insofar as we can formulate a concept of it, is nothing other than nature under the autonomy of pure practical reason" (*CPrR*, 43). The supersensible domain has content of its own, for we can "fill it up" (*besetzen*) with moral ideas (*CJ*, 175). These ideas, as rational, are not merely adventitious but organically ordered. As Kant puts the matter with regard to theoretical reason:

> Pure speculative reason has a true structure (*Gliederbau*). In such a structure everything is an organ, i.e. everything is here for the sake of each member, and each individual member is there for the sake of all. Hence even the slightest defect, whether it be a mistake or an omission, must inevitably betray itself when we use that plan or system. (*CPR* B, xxxvii–xxxviii)

We cannot know if such a domain exists outside us, or if those ideas have objects in some really existing but non-empirical realm. But we do know that the supersensible realm is at least to be conceived of as ordered by reason and governed by the moral law. This governance, again, is purely formal; for it is the pure form of law, that is, necessary universality, which Kant asserts to be the "highest condition" of all purely moral maxims (*CPrR*, 109). Practical reason thus disposes the supersensible realm insofar as the principles of its disposition—those same moral maxims—are purely formal.

The relation of these two legislations to one another is now what causes problems—a multitude of them, as is attested by the length and complexity of the third *Critique*, which is intended to solve them all. From the present point of view, there are two major and distinct difficulties. One is the problem of the radical disparity of the two domains of legislation. If, on the one hand, we say that the understanding legislates to nature, while reason legislates to the noumenal realm, then the two realms fall apart: there is no way, let alone justification, to think that morality can make any difference at all in the "real" world. This, roughly, is the standpoint of the *Critique of Practical Reason*, which as we saw eschews talk of moral actions and carries the legislation of reason only as far as a (predictably tortured) account of respect for the moral law (*CPrR*, 72–89).

In undertaking the *Critique of Judgment*, Kant explicitly rejects this view: "the concept of freedom is to actualize *in the world of sense* the purpose enjoined by its laws" (*CJ*, 136). But if the two faculties both legislate to the sensory world, then we must confront the fact that their legislations are in conflict: the understanding claims that all actions are causally determined while reason claims that some of them (at least) must be free. This, then, is the state of the problem when Kant undertakes the *Critique of Judgment*; he writes the book, according to its introduction, to solve it.

The second problem, which is not explicitly posed but underlies many of the issues treated by the third *Critique*, concerns the relationship of the legislating faculties themselves:[21] How can one being, the human mind, have two distinct highest legislators, with no third legislation above them to unite them? It seems, to use my terminology, that two different ousiodic forms are trying to inhabit the same being. Must not one of them, in accordance with rules of tolerance that go with the metaphysics of ousia, be expelled? To put this somewhat differently: for Kant, the empirical world is to receive, not only the forms prescribed by the understanding but those legislated by reason as well. What can enable it to receive these two very distinct sorts of form?

The third *Critique*'s answer is: the imagination, which functions in both legislations and so unites them. In one of these functions, the imagination readies sensory material for the forms supplied by the understanding (the schematized categories). It does this by eliciting a "form" for that sensory material: its boundedness (*CJ*, 244), together with the interconnection of what lies within those bounds, or what Kant calls the "harmony of its manifold to a unity" (*CJ*, 227–228). An object which has been formed in this way, that is, imaginatively experienced as bounded and interconnected with itself, is ready to come under (receive) the categories of the understanding and then to become what it is not yet: an "object."

The form of a sensory object is thus the unity of the manifold of its various appearances in space and time. When this unity is a concept, its relation to the original manifold of which it is the unity is what Kant calls "judgment." Judgment thus has the form of, for example, "this is a horse," where "this" denotes a manifold of sensory data and "horse" is the overall unifying aspect to them.

The various concepts employed in judgments can, moreover, be united with one another in higher-order judgments ("this horse is a living thing"), until we have, ideally, a systematic unity of all empirical concepts—or, what is the same thing for Kant, of all the empirical laws of nature. When judgment compares and generalizes, drawing more and more general conclusions from its empirical data, it is acting on the presupposition of such a system.[22] But the presupposition is not derived from the sensory data themselves, which do not decide the issue of whether they can be harmonized into a single overarching system. The presupposition of a universal system of nature is thus an a priori or transcendental principle of judgment, one in virtue of which judgment legislates.

This legislation is *of* judgment and *to* judgment: it is not "autonomous" but "heautonomous." It is judgment which legislates here, and only to itself: the presupposition of system mentioned above is what it legislates, and that is not a principle that affects any of the other faculties. In particular, the understanding does not legislate to the properly aesthetic judgment, the judgment of taste, because there is (as we saw in Chapter 1) as yet nothing determinate to be legislated: sensory material has been recapitulated so as to be able to receive a concept but has not yet received it. Understanding and imagination thus stand not in the necessary sub- and superordination characteristic of legislation but in a "free play" which brings them into contingent (rather than necessary) accord (*CJ*, 191). As Rudolf Makkreel has put it: "The subjective agreement between the imagination and the understanding in an aesthetic judgment is not based on subordination of one to the other, but involves the free coordination and the mutual play of the two faculties" (Makkreel 1990, 47). It is only on the basis of this free play, once sensory material has achieved imaginative boundary and unification, that a concept can be applied to the now-formed sensory material and this, in turn, subsumed under a truth claim. Thus, the cognitive legislation of the understanding—and with it the ousiodic structure of the Kantian knowing subject—depends upon a previous relationship of the understanding to imagination which is one not of ousiodic domination but of "coordination and mutual play."

The other relevant functioning of the imagination is with respect to reason. In this, the imagination is unable to elicit a "harmony of the manifold" from sensory material, in part because the material is given as unbounded and in part because it is also not connected up with itself: the raging sea and the starry heavens are famous Kantian examples. Unbounded and internally disconnected, the sensory material is given as infinite, and the imagination's attempt to capture it in a form is an attempt to delimit something unlimited. Unable to do this, the imagination confronts its own *in*ability to fulfill a demand of reason, which can *think* the infinite and therefore demands that the imagination present the infinite on the imaginative level. The imagination's inability to achieve such a presentation awakens the sublime feeling of "respect" for reason, a faculty which is great enough to produce the idea of infinity in the first place (*CJ*, 250). And with this we get a first effect of reason in the sensible world: the experience of respect for reason which is ultimately produced, if not occasioned, by reason itself.

In this, reason does not "legislate" to the imagination. It merely demands that the imagination present an "image" of something infinite; since that demand cannot be met, it cannot be the determination of such an image as necessary and cannot count as legislation. Thus, the imagination and reason engage here again in a free play, in which the imagination operates by its own principles but unsuccessfully, as it tries to present something infinite and unbounded as something delimited and unified. This free play is the ground of moral legislation, in that only if reason is able to exceed the imagination while still being the substrate of appearances can such legislation be conceived to be possible and powerful in the empirical world. The ousiodic legislations of the Kantian acting subject are therefore grounded in a non-ousiodic free play of reason and imagination. According to the *Critique of Judgment* it is that free play, rather than the ousiodic ordering power of reason explored in the *Critiques of Pure and Practical Reason*, that we now find as the "unifying" core of the mind.

Kant's ousiodic account of the mind as functioning in virtue of fixed, synthetic a priori principles has run up against the fact that the two basic dimensions of that functioning—theoretical and practical—have principles which contradict one another. We cannot understand the world unless things in it are caused; we cannot act upon it unless some things, namely our actions themselves, are free. At this point, instead of trying to come up with some still-higher legislative principle, Kant looks downward: the unity of the two legislations is established not from above by reason, as with Descartes and the first two *Critiques*, but from below, by the imagination.

The imagination seems to function in this like a sort of switch. When it comes across a sensory manifold that it can recapitulate as bounded and unified, it refers that to the understanding and to truth; when it comes across one that cannot be thus recapitulated, it refers it to reason and to freedom. But the objects which occasion one or the other sort of free play are rather special—or, to put it more clearly, not special enough. Kant, in fact, is unable to arrive at a clear definition of aesthetic form: his descriptions of it are, as Rudolf Makkreel has written, "indistinct and varying" and do not "really move it beyond simple perceptual form" (Makkreel 1990, 59, 60). But anything we perceive has *that* kind of form, and hence commentators are tempted to say, with Ralf Meerbote, that "Kant may have to declare *all* sense-perceptible objects beautiful"—including the otherwise sublime raging sea and the starry sky.[23] If, for example, an object with aesthetic form is (in the terms I quoted earlier) one whose manifold is given as both connected with itself and disconnected from everything else, then it is hard to see how beauty's distinction from sublimity is anything other than a matter of degree.

Without a clear definition of aesthetic form, Kant cannot show how perceived objects differentiate themselves into beautiful and sublime ones. Nor should this surprise us. For the aesthetic unity of the manifold is not, we saw,

given directly by sensibility; it requires the recapitulative activity of the imagination. So beauty, for Kant, can be imagined where it is not present, as in experiences of a fire or a babbling brook, neither of which is necessarily bounded
or unified with itself (see *CJ*, 243). Similarly with the sublime: as ¶ 23 of the
Critique of Judgment argues, no object we experience is truly sublime—only
reason is. The boundlessness of natural objects, such as the raging sea or the
starry sky, serves only to lead us to an appreciation of what is truly sublime and
"powerful," which is nothing else but reason.

What is beautiful and what is sublime is therefore, at least in part, up to
us. Various things *can* be experienced in each way, but none *need* to be. Given
enough transcendental ingenuity, anything can instigate either kind of free
play; whether a manifold exceeds or does not exceed the mind's synthesizing
power—whether it is beautiful or sublime—is up to the mind. Not entirely, to
be sure: the raging sea is relatively difficult to fictionalize as beautiful, while a
thoroughbred horse standing in a field is hard to conceive of as sublime. Imagination thus serves as more than a shunting device: it serves its two masters
in part by "deciding" how to conduct its own recapitulative activity. It in fact
can prepare the same sensory matter for two different kinds of free play. The
imagination (or, as we will see, the thinking person) thus comes to exercise
considerable discretion as to whether to allocate a particular recapitulated form
to reason or to the understanding.

Since the categories which will be applied to the sensory material are temporally defined (in the schematism), the activity of reflective judgment of the
beautiful has what we may call a temporal bearing. In the free play of beauty,
the mind has run through and brought together the different components of a
manifold and has summed them up as a harmonious form; to judge something
"beautiful" is thus to view it against the background of our previous experience
of it and so to take a stance toward the past. When we judge something to be
"sublime," by contrast, we are saying that there is something the mind has yet to
run through, something not yet summed up; and this is to take a stance toward
the future (one which, to be sure, is unschematized because its object—what is
going to be run through—is still unknown).

These two forms of reflective judgment constitute what could be called
Kant's "transcendental grounds" of past and future; for though he does not
say so, they trace those aspects of time to a priori origins in the judgments
of the beautiful and the sublime. Where Kant's canonical discussions of time
refer to what John McTaggart calls the "B series," a set of events ordered by

the relations of "precedes" and "follows," here Kant has shown us how to move to a form of time structured by the three positions of past, present, and future—the time line we are actually on, or what McTaggart calls the "A-series" (McTaggart 1993, 23–34).

Kant has begun to show us, in other words, how we situate ourselves in time. Such situating, which I will discuss in more detail in the next two chapters, must be constantly redone. For, on the one hand, the unity achieved in the experience of the beautiful is always merely provisional. Any particular unity we may perceive will be undone when new sensory materials make us perceive something else, whether that is a whole new object or not; aesthetic form is a tenuous achievement. Achieved out of a particular set of sensory givens, it never fully transcends the space and time of its origin.

On the other hand, the experience of the beautiful renders the experience of the sublime merely preparatory. For the sublime object, however boundless it seems, will eventually encounter its boundary *in our experience*: when we pass on to something else. The sublime object always ends in something which, because it has limits, is less sublime—and so more beautiful. Chaos will pass, and unity will be temporarily restored. The imagination serves two masters, but it serves them in turn.

We now see that what I have been calling the "speaking of matter," the pre- or partially conceptualized discourse that enlightened philosophers must abjure, has temporal bearing. When we have no concepts, we are directed to where we are coming from and the possibility that we might go somewhere else; in terms of Boston AA, we recapitulate our experiences with the Disease and end up confronting two possible futures, AA or death. Only achieved concepts take us out of the temporal flow, into the long sojourn in the present tense that has traditionally constituted "philosophy."

If we tried, experimentally, to conceive of the imagination as conducting a sort of discourse, what would that discourse be like? First, it would be noncognitive, for since the imagination has no concepts, it cannot refer to things or claim to state truths about them. It would also, for the same reason, be nonpractical: it could not issue commands, moral judgments, or prudential admonitions. The imagination's discourse, as heautonomous, would thus be entirely self-referential, consisting in nonconceptual information it conveyed about itself (*CJ*, 185). Since the imagination is an activity, this would be information about what the imagination has been doing. The discourse of the imagination would express its own recapitulation of its experiences of an object.

The speaking of matter, particularly as it emerged in my discussion of David Foster Wallace in Chapter 1, is much like this. A speech at Boston AA is the recapitulation of the speaker's own experiences and has no claim on truth; it begins, indeed, with truisms that the speaker usually doesn't believe. The series of events it recapitulates—even if as accidental as Don Gately spewing forth his hatred of AA—is unified in that it consists of one's own recollections but has no more unity than that; even the speaker, we saw, does not understand how his speech works. Hence, the unity is no more than an empty "I recapitulate," a sort of aesthetic "unity of apperception" which can arrive, temporally speaking, only after the recapitulation has been performed—when the speech ends in the sublimity of the Bottom.

If the speaking of matter and its temporal bearing are to become philosophical, the two forms of aesthetic free play, that of the beautiful and that of the sublime, must be given principles and standards. For they are the ways we situate ourselves in time, and that seems to be something that can be performed well or badly; indeed, my criticisms of philosophy in the Introduction can be boiled down to the charge that philosophers today (and before) do it rather badly. When the two forms of aesthetic free play receive such standards, they become what I call "narrative" and "demarcation," respectively. But Kant does not deal with these issues; that is for Hegel and Heidegger.

Conclusion

We can now answer the question of modernism in philosophy and adjudicate the modernism debate. The fundamental innovation which Descartes and Kant make on the ancient and medieval philosophers is to deny ousiodic structure to the natural world while retaining it as the basic structuring principle of the human mind. Having discussed Berkeley, Hume, Leibniz, Locke, and Spinoza in these terms elsewhere (*MO*, 128–202), I am ready to elevate this way of handling ousia into an overall "definition" of philosophical modernity: *Modernism in philosophy is that epoch of Western history which casts ousiodic form out of nature while retaining it as the basic structuring principle of the human world.*

Since, as Charles Mills has shown, the "state of nature" in modern philosophy is the nonwhite world (*RC*, 42–47), it has no forms that "we" Europeans must respect—only substances we can exploit. Because those substances have been absorbed into their parousia, into the ways they are present to us, we (Europeans) can classify them by their color—in the case of humans, as black, yellow, and red. Whence we (Europeans), finally, class ourselves as white—which after Newton meant as all of the above (and before him meant none of the above). White is now the default color of humanity.

This basic framework will persist well beyond Kant, as will modernism in philosophy. Carnap and other logical positivists of the twentieth century, for example, will make physics the basic natural science, thereby accepting the view that nature exhibits no ousiodic structure. They will then devote endless pages to issues of how to reduce the other sciences to physics, a project which—if it had ever gotten very far—would have resulted in a perfectly ousiodic hierarchy of sciences, unified and ordered by mathematics and pursuing its single inherent goal, or *telos*, of scientific truth.

Modernity is not only, in Habermas's words, an "incomplete" project (Habermas 1983), but it is incompletable. It is a halfway house in which nature and the human realm—subject and object—have become radically different from one another. Objects are mere matter in motion, exploitable beings inexorably following immutable natural laws, while humans are free to violate moral rules and to pursue purposes. Nature being merely a realm of matter in motion, as Descartes maintained, it can provide no moral guidance. Kant shows that knowledge of God can provide no such guidance either, for God is beyond our understanding—a matter for religious faith, not philosophical knowledge. Kant thus provides an account of the human mind existing in a material world which makes no appeals beyond the mind itself and so radicalizes the project of modernity. But he does not, until the *Critique of Judgment*, fundamentally change the rules of its game. Reason, the faculty of principles, has the power to order the rest of the mind's faculties; within the transcendental boundaries of the mind, it plays the role of disposing form.

Pippin (and many others) notwithstanding, the most basic characteristic of modernism in philosophy is not the elevation of reason to the status of universal adjudicator. Rather, its basic concern is how to use ousia to structure the human realm once its Aristotelian warrant—that ousiodic structure is resident in the "whole of nature"—is no longer available. Descartes justifies his use of ousia by relocating it to the divine realm, which is something we need to imitate—but then he has problems showing how we can have knowledge of that realm. Kant operates without divine grounding—but his attempt to give a unified account of the mind's fixed principles runs up against the fact that the mind is in time, and its confrontations with past and future are too complex and disparate to be reduced to a single set of such principles without contradiction. His attempt to do so leads him to contest the basic presupposition of such principles and install free play rather than ousiodic form as the underlying source of the mind's unity.

Given these problems, it is not surprising that modernism in philosophy has been attacked in a variety of ways. Some of these, to be sure, have been aimed at reinstating ousiodic form in the human world after its ejection from nature or, with Kant (and the Empiricists: see *MO*, 128–179), from heaven. These attempts often rely on viewing that world in quasi-naturalistic terms derived from Aristotle and often appeal to the notion of "organic tradition" mentioned by Pippin. They therefore qualify as *pre*modern. But others are aimed in the other direction: at the continued use of ousia as the structuring principle of the human mind and communities. These, I take it, qualify as *post*modern.

Thus, when we look at the writings of such people as Derrida and Foucault, we discover that many of their ways of thinking are in fact directed against ousia.[24] When Derrida says that "there is nothing outside the text," for example—actually what he said is better rendered as "there is no outside-of-the-text" (*il n'y a pas de hors-texte*)—he is saying that texts do not have boundaries, as ousiai do:

> The text *affirms* the outside. . . . If there is nothing outside the text, that implies, with the transformation of the concept of text in general, that [the text] itself is no longer the snug airtight inside of an interiority or of an identity to self.[25]

When Derrida finds elements in a text which escape and subvert its dominant theme and concerns, he "ruins its hegemonic center, subverts its authority as unity"[26] and thereby—in my terms—shows that its internal disposition is impeached. When he insists that there is no right way to read a text, he is saying that its claim to what I call initiative, which would be its capacity to affect its readers by transferring its meanings and theses unchanged into their minds, is unjustified.[27] For Derrida, good reading is never the accurate reproduction of a text's finished and well-formed meaning but is inevitably creative or parodic—at once faithful and violent.[28] That Derrida does all these things to basic texts in the history of metaphysics means not that he is avoiding all concrete and worthwhile questions, as he is so often accused of doing, but that he is carrying the battle straight to the enemy.

Similarly for Foucault (and for other postmodernists, but I will stop here). His famous critical treatment of the Panopticon, the model for a prison conceived by Jeremy Bentham, explicitly attributes to it boundary and disposition (see *PF*, 111–115), and his warnings about the growth of the prisonlike or "carceral" (*SP*, 205–207, 298) suggest that the entire human world is becoming disposed not directly by power but by the various ousiodic formations that power, accidentally to be sure, throws up.

The lesson of the postmodernists is thus that we should take modern philosophy to task for the covert ways in which it continues to presuppose and reinforce ousiodic ontology in the human realm. When such philosophy says that *all* social decisions must be reached "contractually," through the free assent of a reason whose procedures are clearly defined and known in advance (as they are for Kant, for example), it is attempting to impose a single form on all debate; and that is wrong. When it says that all actions should conform to a rational imperative, it is trying to do the same thing; and so on.

I think that if philosophers had been more attentive to history, both that of their own discipline and that of the very different cultures in which it is embedded, they could have ended the Great Modernism Debate some time ago. To be sure, there would still be battles: some people are going to defend the ousiodic ontology as universally applicable to the human realm, or even to nature itself, and others are going to oppose that. But at least the issues could have been joined.

But if ousiodic ontology, which underwrites appeals to authority and top-down structures, is actually inimical to what I think is best about being human, some other ontology would be a good thing to have. And here we come not to an answer but to what I think is the great philosophical problem of our time: How do we eliminate ousia as the structuring principle of the human realm, or even limit it, without returning to a view of society as merely a realm of drifting heaps—of, for example, all-powerful power?

CHAPTER 5

THE MALLEABILITY OF REASON

HEGEL AND THE RETURN TO HERACLEITUS

Many years ago, the *New York Review of Books* had a policy of getting aging analytical philosophers to review works about dead continental ones. One of the analysts, P. F. Strawson, said of Martin Heidegger that while Heidegger was not much of a philosopher, he was very good at positioning himself with respect to the history of philosophy (Strawson 1979).

I don't think we should buy too deeply into this distinction, especially if it means that you can reverse it and be a good philosopher while not being much good at positioning yourself with respect to the history of philosophy. Even if we do accept it, I think Strawson gave away a bit more than he intended. For what you get out of "positioning yourself with respect to the history of philosophy" is a philosophical project—a task that needs to be done but has not yet been done. Finding a task like that often requires very sophisticated philosophical "positioning." Heidegger was indeed good at this—but I doubt that Strawson much liked its result, the project of Heideggerian *Seinsdenken*.

In any case, that kind of positioning-as-project-derivation, however separate it is from philosophy as such, is what this chapter will be about: trying to get clear on Hegel's position with respect to the history of philosophy, in order to shed some light on his philosophical project. That project—rightly understood—is crucial to solving the paradoxes of Enlightenment and getting philosophy onto the right side of history, for it presents as thorough a vision as we have of the malleability of reason.

Stories About Hegel

One hundred eighty years after his death, the nature of Hegel's philosophical project is still obscure. There are in fact two main stories about Hegel's position with respect to the history of philosophy and hence about his project. The more traditional of these, told by multitudes of thinkers from Marx through Derrida and after, is that Hegel's philosophy—certainly his mature philosophy, contained in the "systematic" works written after the 1807 *Phenomenology of Spirit*—represents a wholesale reinstatement of metaphysics after Kant's criticism of it. According to this story, Hegel rejects Kant's critique of metaphysics and undertakes his own highly metaphysical account of ultimate reality, or "the Absolute."

The other story dates only from the work of Klaus Hartmann in Germany and was brought to this country in the 1980s, primarily by Terry Pinkard and Robert Pippin. It sees Hegel not as *rejecting* the Kantian critique of metaphysics but as *continuing* it.[1] According to this story, indeed, Hegel seeks not merely to continue but to complete the critical philosophy by undertaking something Kant did not: validating Kant's "categories of the Understanding" by constructing them out of one another. (To read the *Critique of Pure Reason*, you would think that Kant had just come upon them while reading his logic book: *CPR* B, 95–109.) In the course of Hegel's construction, the categories apparently go from being a mere 12 to around 577, since there are 577 sections in Hegel's *Encyclopedia*, each one defined in terms of what went before and in that sense "constructed out of it."

The two stories are obviously incompatible, but they do have one point of agreement: both of them take Kant's critique of metaphysics for their *point de repère*. They both claim that Hegel's position in the history of philosophy, and so the nature of his philosophical project, is decisively determined by his stance toward that critique.

Since the two stories contradict each other, they cannot both be right. Both, however, could be wrong. This is no merely logical possibility, for each of these stories has what seem to be rather serious problems. On the first story, Hegel would reject the *central* claim of the *central* achievement of the *greatest philosopher* of his youth—the founding argument of the Critical Philosophy itself, its demonstration that metaphysics has no cognitive value. Hegel would reject that, moreover, without explanation or argument—for he never in fact provides any; he never tells us why or where Kant's critique of metaphysics ran aground. He just sets about doing philosophy in his own absurdly difficult way.

The other story also has problems, at least two of them. First, Kantian categories are a priori, and if Hegel is constructing them out of each other his construction, to be Kantian, must proceed entirely without empirical input. But expanding the categories from 12 to 577 greatly enriches the a priori realm. Are we to believe, for example, that the categories of "cephalopod" and "mollusk," both to be found in the *Philosophy of Nature*, can be constructed a priori? Robert Pippin, the most strenuous contemporary advocate of this approach to Hegel, gives up at this point:

> So many concepts [of Hegel's logic] are clearly as they are because the world is as it is, and cannot possibly be considered categorial results of thought's pure self-determination, that Hegel's project cries out for a more explicit, clear-cut account of when and why we should regard our fundamental ways of taking things to be "due" wholly to us, in the relevant Hegelian sense. (Pippin 1989, 258)

No one to date has taken up Pippin's challenge.

The second problem with this approach is not generally recognized but even more serious. It is that by seeing Hegel as a continuation of Kant, and in particular of Kant's critical rejection of his predecessors, it ends by postulating a self-contained national philosophical tradition—the "German tradition."

The first thing to note about national philosophical traditions, in Germany or elsewhere, is that there are no such things. Gilbert Ryle reviewed *Being and Time* (Ryle 1978), Aquinas freely cited Maimonides and Averroes, even Plato claimed to have learned from Egypt. This is all, definitely, as it should be: national traditions among philosophers can only be grounded, where they exist, in the kind of "palling around" I decried in the Introduction. As for Hegel's own "Germanism," G. R. G. Mure showed in the early years of the last century[2] that you cannot get from Kant to Hegel without a massive injection of Greek philosophy.[3]

So I am going to ask about Hegel's relation not to Kant but to a major member of the Greek philosophical tradition: Heraclitus—a man whose every proposition the later Hegel claimed to have accepted (Hegel 1892, 1:279). This choice of Greeks may seem surprising, but I hope to see it justified by the light it sheds on the nature of Hegel's philosophical project, on its position within the history of philosophy, and on how we should view that project today.

What does it mean to locate Hegel with respect to Heraclitus?

Philosophy's Return to Heracleitus

The first thing it means is figuring out some things about Heracleitus, who was already known in ancient times as "the obscure one" (*ho skoteinos*).[4] The saying most often associated with him—*panta rhei*, or "all things flow"—is often taken to deny all stability to the world and to instate flux as the only reality; but that is going too far. For one thing, there are other, clearer ways to express that thought in Greek (e.g., *hē rhoē panta*, or *monōs hē rhoē estin*). For another, the view that there is no stability at all in the world is closer to Heracleitus's pupil Cratylus than to Heracleitus himself, for it was legendarily Cratylus who, when his master said that no one steps into the same river twice, went him one better and said that no one steps into the same river even once, because it changes as your foot goes in. (Cratylus, again legendarily, gave up language altogether and simply pointed to what was speeding past before him.) If Heracleitus maintained that view as well, the two must have agreed—in which case there is no point to the legend. Finally and more philosophically, the denial of all stability would reduce everything to the temporal flow itself, submerging everything in the abstract movement of time. Hegel himself explicitly denies that Heracleitus meant to do this; rather, "enduring oppositions" must exist if there is to be a movement between them.[5]

Heracleitus is thus saying, for present purposes anyway, that there are things, on the one hand—but that they all (*panta*) "flow" (*rhei*), on the other: they come to be, change, and pass away. All of them do, even the relatively enduring oppositions among them. There is then nothing that is not in time. And since there are no timeless or eternal things, there are no timeless or eternal truths about them, either.

This is not as radical as the no-stability-at-all view, which I will call "vulgar Heracleiteanism," but it was radical enough that it did not gain lasting support in philosophy. Plato denied it, asserting (with Parmenides) that true Being never changes. Since everything we see and live with does change, true Being for Plato was to be found in another realm—the *hyperouranios topos*, the "place beyond the heavens" of the Platonic Forms. Decrying what he called the "separation" of Platonic Forms from sensible things,[6] Aristotle, in both the versions of his metaphysics discussed in Chapter 3, redirected the philosophical gaze from the unchanging world of Forms to unchanging components of this world, essences—but he did not deny that ultimate reality, the essences within things which made them what they were, was unchanging.

When the modern world evicted Aristotelian form from nature,[7] the philosophical gaze was redirected again—this time to the human mind, where

Descartes found his *fundamentum inconcussum* in the form of the *cogito*: "I think therefore I am" is always true, since where its protasis is false it cannot even be asserted. Even the skeptical David Hume believed in unchanging mental principles:

> I must distinguish in the imagination betwixt the principles [of the association of ideas] which are permanent, irresistible, and universal . . . and the principles, which are changeable, weak, and irregular. . . . The former are the foundation of all our thoughts and actions, so that upon their removal human nature must immediately perish and go to ruin. (Hume 1896, 225)

Unchanging principles of mental activity are also, of course, basic for Kant, who as we saw in the Introduction thought that not only the principles themselves but his own philosophical account of them would never change—at least not for the better. The view that philosophy is concerned with truths which hold independently of time continued after Kant, of course, and took new forms as old ones failed. In Quine, for example, the atemporal realm becomes something of our own doing, and his innovation here is important enough to be quoted at length:

> Our ordinary language shows a tiresome bias in its treatment of time. Relations of date are exalted grammatically as relations of position, weight, and color are not. This bias is of itself an inelegance, or breach of theoretical simplicity. Moreover, the form that it takes—that of requiring that every verb show a tense—is particularly productive of needless complications, since it demands lip service to time even when time is farthest from our thoughts. Hence in fashioning canonical notations it is usual to drop tense distinctions. We may conveniently hold to the grammatical present as a form, but treat it as temporally neutral. Where the artifice comes in is in taking the present tense as timeless always, and dropping other tenses. This artifice frees us to omit temporal information, or, when we please, handle it like spatial information. (Quine 1960, 170)

Atemporality, for Quine, is not a characteristic either of true being or of the human mind; it is something we philosophers constitute through the strategic "omission of temporal information." The argument now is about philosophy: whether there are atemporal realities or not, philosophy deals in atemporal truths just as it always has, because it *makes* truths atemporal by omitting certain types of information.

That philosophy, the age-old search for wisdom, should begin by omitting information is perhaps bizarre, and that it should do so in the name of "convenience" even more so. My point is not to criticize Quine, however, but to isolate an important thread in the glorious but confused tapestry of the history of philosophy: the "traditional" thread which holds that philosophy deals, one way or another, in timeless truths. It tries to find them in a space beyond the heavens, or in this world, or in the human mind. When all that fails, philosophy will even make them itself—but deal in them it will, or it is not "philosophy." "Malleable reason" is therefore an oxymoron.

Only in the nineteenth century does a different voice chime in. Consider the following statement:

> [Philosophy] includes, in its comprehension and affirmative recognition of the existing state of things . . . also the recognition of the negation of that state, of its inevitable breaking up; because [such thought] regards every historically developed social form as in fluid movement, and hence takes into account its transient nature not less than its momentary existence; because it lets nothing impose upon it, and is in its essence critical and revolutionary.

This is Karl Marx's characterization, in *Capital*, of "dialectics" (Marx 1906, 26). At around the same time, Søren Kierkegaard is saying that eternity cannot be understood by us and can intrude into our world only as absurdity:

> What now is the absurd? The absurd is—that the eternal truth has come into being in time, that God has come into being, has been born, has grown up, and so forth, precisely like any other human being, indistinguishable from other individuals. (Kierkegaard 1941, 188)

Cognitively speaking, we are for Kierkegaard wholly temporal beings, and the idea that eternal truth could reach us is absurd. Even if our spiritual destiny is eternity, we can understand nothing at all about it.

A couple of decades later, another German thinker—Nietzsche—is saying:

> Everything, however, has come to be (*alles aber ist geworden*); there are no eternal facts, just as there are no absolute truths. *That is why historical philosophizing is necessary from now on.* (Nietzsche 1986, 13; my translation, emphasis added)

It is, however, Heidegger who, in 1927, first explicitly formulated the rejection of eternal truths as a return behind an entire philosophical tradition beginning (in his view) with Plato.[8] I will discuss the book he published that year, *Being and Time*, a bit more in the next chapter; its overriding purpose (*BT*, § 5) was to reinstate the connection between Being and time, after millennia of denial. Following him in this are such people as Jacques Derrida, who writes concerning *différance*:

> Each so-called "present" element is related to something other than itself, thereby keeping within itself the mark of the past element, and already letting itself be vitiated by the mark of its relation to the future element. (Derrida 1973, 142)

Finally, Michel Foucault notes—with approval—that Nietzsche's project of "genealogy" aims at placing things into temporal sequences:

> The role of genealogy is to record [the development of humanity as a series of interpretations]: the history of morals, ideals, and metaphysical concepts, the history of the concept of liberty or of the ascetic life; as they stand for the emergence of different interpretations, *they must be made to appear as events on the stage of historical process*. (Foucault 1984, 86; emphasis added)

There are thus two remarks to be made about what I am calling the "return to Heracleitus":

1. From the names just given, the return appears to amount to what is normally called continental philosophy—minus, perhaps, the "transcendental phenomenology" practiced most notably by Husserl.
2. From the names just given—indeed from that of Karl Marx *alone*—it also appears that the return to Heracleitus is the single most important intellectual development of the last two hundred years, not only within philosophy but in all intellectual fields worldwide.

The return to Heracleitus is thus important enough that we need to understand how any major thinker stands with respect to it—especially Hegel, who lived and worked just prior to the first two of the people I have mentioned, that is, Marx and Kierkegaard. Is he a late resurgence of what I call "traditional" philosophy, as both the standard stories I told earlier would have him? Or is he a forerunner of the return to Heracleitus?

Is the End of the *Phenomenology* the End of Time?

If Hegel is a metaphysician in the precritical sense, he is obviously dealing in timeless truths. And if he is a Kantian category theorist, then by Kant's own testimony he is doing so as well: for critique, we have seen, is "established forever."

But Hegel also seems, sometimes, to think in the Heracleitean mode. The *Phenomenology of Spirit*, his first published book, begins with "Sense-Certainty," a chapter which concerns the inability of language to capture the passing play of sense—and which concludes with consciousness trying to point to things, which provides a cameo for Cratylus (*PhS*, ¶¶ 90–110; 58–66).

The reason that neither of the stories I gave above locates Hegel within the return to Heracleitus—and why not a single thinker of that return thinks Hegel belongs in it—is that they all believe that at the other end of the *Phenomenology*, Hegel somehow thinks he climbs up and out of time and history, achieving an atemporal or eternal standpoint. From there, he can explicate the "Absolute," which is either a single mighty Being—a sort of depersonalized godhead—or the totality of our a priori categories.

Hegel's account of philosophical reason is presented in his post-*Phenomenology* works— the *Science of Logic*, the *Encyclopedia of the Philosophical Sciences*, and the *Philosophy of Right*. If he truly climbs out of time at the end of the *Phenomenology*, looking in those works for an account of malleable reason seems hopeless. But *does* Hegel climb out of time at the end of the *Phenomenology*? Does he even think that he does? Unfortunately, "Absolute Knowing," the final chapter of the *Phenomenology*, is a terrible place to have to look for answers to anything. Like the rest of the book, it was written under extreme duress.[9] I admit to having dismissed it myself, elsewhere, as a mere "stew of words" (*CW*, 21).

Fortunately, we need not go far into it. The chapter's opening clearly identifies its task as the "overcoming of consciousness as such" (*PhS*, ¶ 788; 479).[10] What does this mean?

From "Sense-Certainty" on, consciousness has been defined by two oppositions: that between subject and object, on the one hand, and between the static and the dynamic—between that which is fixed and stable and that which is transforming or self-transforming—on the other. It seems only natural to suppose that "overcoming consciousness" means overcoming the first opposition. But almost every time Hegel contrasts consciousness and its object in the *Phenomenology*, he does so by identifying one of them as static and the other as dynamic.[11] Perhaps, then, we should look to this distinction as well; certainly doing so is in keeping with my "Heracleitean" project.

In "Sense-Certainty," the opposition between static and dynamic appears as that between the unchanging (because empty) universality of space, time, and the empty "I," on the one hand, and the passing individuality of what Hegel calls "dynamic examples" (*Beiherspielende*), on the other. As befits the empty nature of the "I" here, consciousness contains these as passing plays (*PhS*, ¶ 91; 58) but cannot refer to them because they go by too fast—hence the pointing.

When the book ends in "Absolute Knowledge," consciousness no longer sees itself as a static container; the developments of the intervening several hundred pages have led it to view itself as dynamic. There is now nothing fixed on the part of consciousness that can qualify as a property of "consciousness as such," and overcoming it now means, in another phrase of Hegel's here (*PhS*, ¶ 788; 479), "surmounting [*Überwindung*] the object of consciousness." This means showing that said object is, like consciousness, itself dynamic:

> [This surmounting] is to be taken more specifically to mean not only that the object presented itself to the self as *vanishing*, but rather that it is the *externalization* of consciousness. . . . The negative of the object, or its self-supersession, has a positive meaning for self-consciousness, i.e., consciousness knows the nothingness of the object, on the one hand because it externalizes its own self. . . . This is the movement of consciousness, and in that movement consciousness is the totality of its moments. (*PhS*, ¶ 788; 479; my translation, emphasis added)

Consciousness and the object have now changed places. Consciousness at the beginning of the *Phenomenology* was an empty, and so static, container; it is now dynamic and mutable. Its object, which began as an "example" flashing past, is now static. The final overcoming of their opposition is, we see, to be achieved by overcoming the opposition between what is dynamic and changing—here, consciousness itself—and what is stable and unchanging—here, the object. Once this is done, we will be able to see the object as itself dynamic—indeed, as having the same sort of dynamism as consciousness, thus being its "externalization." Or at least we hope so.

Showing that the object is dynamic is apparently to be done by the object itself, in that it "presented *itself* to the Self as vanishing"; the supersession *of* the object must be a "self-supersession" *by* the object. For the object to show itself to be dynamic means, further, for it to show itself as an interplay of three levels:

> (I). That on which it is simply an immediate being, a thing (*Ding*) as such;
>
> (II). That on which it is related to other beings and to itself, and so shows itself to be internally complex (since there is a difference between that aspect of it which enters into any such relation and the rest of it);
>
> (III). That on which it is the essence (*Wesen*) or universal. (*PhS*, ¶ 789; 480)

These correspond, Hegel then claims, to the three basic levels of consciousness as it has developed in the book: immediate (or sensuous) consciousness, perception, and understanding, respectively. But these three levels, so defined, also bring back the individual/universal opposition. For Hegel goes on to say:

> [The object] is, as a whole, the *syllogism* or the movement of the universal through the particular to individuality, as [well as] the reverse, the movement from individuality through itself as sublated, the particular, to the universal. (*PhS*, ¶ 789; 480)

Now we see what has been added to the static universal/fleeting individual distinction over the course of the book: the middle term (II), or the "particular" as the specific relationality of the object to other beings and to itself.[12] It is in virtue of its "mediation" by the particular that the object, itself an individual thing (I), can acquire a universal essence (III).

The complex mediations between individual, particular, and universal constitute the nature of what Hegel, in his *Logic*, calls the "concept" or the "notion" (*Begriff*; *SL*, 577–595). The relevant considerations may be summarized as follows: A "universal" must (to speak Kantian for a moment) comprise a number of things "under" itself. No universal has a single instance, then, and the individual things a universal instantiates are related to one another by the same thing that makes them instances of that universal itself: by the fact that they all exhibit some particular property. As particular, this is not a property of the universal itself but one which only some instances of that universal have. Thus, any property of a thing has what we may call a relational dimension: it relates that thing both to the property itself and to the other things that have it. Through that relation, they are related to the universal "essence" which they share. As an example: I, an individual human being, am related to the universal "humanity" not directly, in that I exhibit rationality and animality, but in virtue of various properties I share with some but not all other human beings, such as the properties of being male, an American, a philosopher, and so forth; these are all particular ways in which an individual animal can come under the universal predicate "human."

The "vanishing" of the object is the mediation or interplay of these three levels, which shows it to have the same structure as consciousness. In that interplay, each level transforms the others, and so all are constantly "vanishing." Since consciousness and its object are now structured by the same trilevel interplay, the way is open for their final identification. But here we encounter a problem. On the one hand, as we saw, the object is to present *itself* as vanishing and so as the externalization of consciousness. But because the object here is static, it is also passive; it cannot "do" anything and appears to be "a number of shapes which *we* bring together, and in which the totality of the moments of the object and of the activity of consciousness can only be shown as dispersed" (*PhS*, ¶ 789; 480).

Hence, Hegel also says that the "vanishing" of the object—the mediation of its three levels—is carried out in it not merely or even primarily by the object itself but "more specifically . . . rather" by self-consciousness (*PhS*, ¶ 788; 479). We thus have two views, and in the same paragraph, of the self-mediation of the object: that it is brought about by consciousness and that it is brought about by the object itself. How to reconcile them? Who or what carries out the mediation of the object?

The solution, clearly, would be to show that the vanishing or self-mediation of the object is carried out *both* by it and by "us," or consciousness, together. If either side does it alone, a disparity will remain between the two, because one side will have been active and the other passive. But how can Hegel show that the object and consciousness *together* effect the final mediation of the object?

Here, instead of an answer, we get a further puzzle. For Hegel's argument that the object carries out its own mediation of its individual, particular, and universal aspects turns out to be merely a short recapitulation of the *Phenomenology* itself up to that point (*PhS*, ¶¶ 790–797; 480–485). Instead of talking about "the object," he talks about the *Phenomenology*. Almost the whole of the chapter in fact concerns the nature not of the object but of the *Phenomenology* and its relation to science and to history—to time.

Why should Hegel apply this strategy at all? The *Phenomenology*, pretty clearly, is the story of the development, the mediation, of consciousness. Why would Hegel think that merely recapitulating that would show us that the development of consciousness is also the self-mediation of the object? The answer can only be that the *Phenomenology's* original story was also the story of the self-mediation of the object. But this possibility raises yet another issue, for if the *Phenomenology* was *about* that, then Hegel could have gotten it wrong. Even if his presentation of the development of consciousness was correct, in other words, it might not have applied to the development of the object.

Let me rehearse in slightly more detail what I take the situation to be; my construal will be supported by the solution it provides to the problems it presents. Hegel has written a book about the development of consciousness; its original subtitle, as Heidegger reminds us, was "Science of the Experience of Consciousness" (Heidegger 2002b, 86). In the introduction to that book (*PhS*, ¶¶ 73–89; 46–57), Hegel sets forth a number of procedures by which the book will be constructed. Among these are that consciousness is to assume various "certainties"; examine them; find them inadequate; and formulate a new certainty which resolves the inadequacy, at which point the process is repeated. As Hegel writes the book, he often stops to make sure that he has performed these procedures correctly.[13] The book's validity as presenting the development of consciousness is thus established as it goes along. But now, at the end, we suddenly discover that what has been narrated was also the mediation of the *object* of consciousness. Objects have been present, here and there, of course, but they were never explicitly the theme of the whole thing. So how are we to know that Hegel has presented a valid account of that as well?

He never even brings up the issue. This cannot be a mere oversight, for as I noted he has brought up issues of validity all along, starting in the introduction, and it is not too much to say that here at the end, everything is hanging on it. Nor can he be silently attributing perfection to his own work—an attribution which would be not only unphilosophical but absurd.[14] Rather, I suggest, the absence of any discussion of the validity of the *Phenomenology* as an account of the object is a consequence of the fact that there is no *room* for Hegel to have been mistaken in his presentation of the self-mediation of the object, because the presentation and the self-mediation are one and the same. The *Phenomenology* is not *about* the mediation of the object—it does not refer to or describe it. Rather, it *is* that mediation.

Which means that the "object" whose mediation the *Phenomenology* presents is just the *Phenomenology* itself. "The object" at the beginning of Absolute Knowing, the one whose surmounting was supposed to produce the "unity of subject and object," is not objects as such or in general. It is the *Phenomenology* itself. When consciousness comes to be identified with the trilevel interplay of the object, it is identified with the book's own tripartite structure of sensuous consciousness, perception, and understanding.

And what is "consciousness"? At minimum, just what the *Phenomenology* says it to be: the book's protagonist, the binding element in its overall story. But that story, as the introduction tells us, is the story of consciousness's whole project of attaining unchanging truth. That project itself, we now see, is not something which something preexisting called "consciousness" undertakes—it is definitive of consciousness itself. "Consciousness" and "the object" are identified at the end because both turn out to be the *Phenomenology* itself and nothing more. In the end, the *Phenomenology* proves to be entirely self-referential.

It therefore makes no truth claims, for any such would have to refer to outside realities of some sort.[15] As with the putative discourse of Kantian imagination presented in Chapter 4, the *Phenomenology*'s unity can be recapitulated—but not as the realization of a general concept: if its unity is as the story of "consciousness," then "consciousness" itself is merely that whose story has been told; we cannot know what it is until the story has reached its end, and the book thus recapitulates what Kant would call the search for a concept.

Since their concepts are not found until the end of the book, terms such as "consciousness" and related terms—"certainty," "truth," "spirit," "in-itself," "for-itself," and so on—can change their meanings as the book goes on. They do so both continually (i.e., they never leave off doing so) and continuously (the changes are only minimal at each stage).[16] The language of the *Phenomenology* is therefore malleable indeed; and the language of Hegel's system, we will see, must retain that malleability.

The *Phenomenology* thus ends by recapitulating its own development as a series of conceptually unguided experiences—as does a speech at Boston AA. Matter speaks, then, throughout the *Phenomenology*, by way of its confusions, divagations, and "blank cunctations," until it ends in the Hegelian Bottom: either move to the System or stay with Death (the death, indeed, of God; *PhS*, ¶¶ 752, 786; 455, 476). To understand how philosophy is to respond to this, we need a short discussion of the nature of Hegel's system. For it is possible to view Hegel's entire systematic philosophy as a series of lessons in how to read the *Phenomenology*.

The Malleable Hegel: System and Language

At the end of the *Phenomenology*, "subject" and the "object" both turn out to be the *Phenomenology* itself, which amounts to a spectacular collapse into self-referentiality. Where does this collapse leave Hegel?

I hope it is clear that it *cannot* land him where either of the standard stories I have mentioned places him: in traditional, atemporal philosophy. For that into which consciousness and its object have both collapsed is nothing metaphysical, or even categorical. It is simply a book, a set (or, as I put it elsewhere, a "company") of words. Language itself is thus the wider middle term between subject and object, of which the *Phenomenology* is what Hegel, in the later *Science of Logic*, calls an "example."[17]

Pace Hartmann, Pinkard, and Pippin, Hegel is not a Kantian category theorist; *pace* everyone else, he is not a metaphysician. As he puts it in *The Science of Logic*:

> What we are dealing with in logic is not a thinking *about* something, which would exist on its own outside thinking and as a base for it; [it is not a matter of] forms which are supposed to give only distinguishing marks of truth; rather, the necessary forms and proper determinations of thinking [*Bestimmung des Denkens*] are the truth itself. (*SL*, 50)

This quote alone suffices to put metaphysical interpretations to rest; Hegel cannot possibly be a reinstatement of traditional metaphysics after Kant. But it also shows that he cannot be a continuation of Kant, for the "thinking" outside of which the object of logic cannot exist is not thinking in general, or such principles of mental activity as the Kantian categories; if that were the case, the thought would have to be true to something beyond itself, namely, "thought" in general or the categories, of which it could at best claim to give "distinguishing marks." It is merely the thinking of the logician at the moment she thinks.

And this is linguistic, for the "determinations of thinking" to which Hegel refers are words:

> We know about our thoughts and have determinate [*bestimmte*], real thoughts only when we give them the form of *objectivity*, of being *distinguished* from our *interiority*—only, then, when we give them the form of *externality*—of *such* an externality, to be sure, as bears the imprint of the highest *interiority*. The only such interior externality is the *articulated tone*, the *word*. . . . The word therefore gives to thoughts their worthiest and truest existence. (Hegel 1971, 220)

Though he never quite calls himself that, Hegel is a philosopher of language.[18] His view of language is unusual, however, in that it focuses on vocabulary at the expense of syntax. Hegel is interested in words rather than sentences or propositions, and it is striking how often he refers to his system as a set not of propositions or arguments but of definitions. In addition to the famous comments about systematic philosophy being a series of "definitions of the Absolute" or of God,[19] he demands that in the development of the system, determinations must "arise, define and justify themselves" (*zu entstehen . . . sich dadurch zu definieren und zu rechtfertigen*; *SL*, 79).

Philosophy of Right § 2 Zus. virtually equates philosophical science with the production of definitions (*PhR*, 26–28). Hegel there contrasts his systematic procedure not with historical investigation or mathematical proof (as the discussion in the preface to the *Phenomenology* might lead us to expect; *PhS*, ¶¶ 42–46; 24–27) but with the usual procedure by which definitions are formed. This, according to Hegel, is to compare a formulated definition with ordinary thought and usage (*SL*, 50; Hegel 1975b, 40, 53). In philosophy, by contrast, ordinary thought and usage are not the most important thing; rather, "in philosophical cognition . . . the chief concern is the necessity of a concept, and the route by which it has become a result [is] its proof and deduction" (*PhR*, 27).

These comparisons culminate in the revealing "Supplement" to Section 99 of the *Encyclopedia Logic*:

> Throughout philosophy we do not seek merely for correct, still less for plausible definitions, whose correctness appeals directly to the popular imagination; we seek approved or verified definitions, the content of which is not merely assumed as given, but is seen and known to warrant itself, because warranted by the free self-evolution of thought. (Hegel 1975b, 146)

Ordinary or "nonphilosophical" definitions relate a word to other words in its language and to the meanings that people associate with those words. Hegel's "verified" definitions are to do something else. Such a scientific or logical definition "has its proof only in the necessity of its emergence" (*SL*, 49; my translation). Just what Hegel intends by equating the "free evolution of thought" with "necessity" will be discussed shortly; right now, what the emergence, or production, of a definition ties it to is not other words in its language but the sequence of definitions which constitutes the system itself. Hegel's system is thus universally valid because it has been produced in accordance with rules which can apply not merely to nineteenth-century German but to any language at any time.[20]

But Hegel is, once again, an odd sort of universalist. When subject and object both collapse into the *Phenomenology*, they do not collapse into "language" itself; they collapse into words of one particular language, early nineteenth-century German (see *SL*, 53–54). Hegel's philosophy becomes universal when it becomes systematic—*after* the *Phenomenology*. Produced by the "free self-evolution of thought," which as free is unaffected by such contingencies as culture, the meanings of the system's terms—unlike its sounds—are not those of early nineteenth-century German though they match them in various ways (for which, see *CW*, 319–324).

But if that is the case, then the famous Hegelian "Absolute" is merely a set (or a "company") of words. And if it is merely that, it is hardly atemporal or eternal. If Hegel's philosophy presents, as Derrida suggests, the fulfillment of the philosophical tradition (Derrida 1982b, 73), it is also a decisive break with it. The eternal truths of metaphysics and the unchangeable truths of critique have been replaced, as the core of being, by mere words whose sounds and meanings change over time. Hegel's return to Heracleitus comes not when he claims that "all things flow," or that they are a "unity of opposites,"[21] but when he makes reason linguistic and therefore malleable.

We can begin to understand that malleability when we note that one of the basic formation rules for Hegel's system of "verified definitions" is that no term can occur in a *definiens* which has not itself already been systematically defined (see *SL*, 40; *CW*, 130–143). When it is time to expand the system by introducing a new term, Hegel thus cannot go beyond the set of terms he has already defined. But he is free to combine any subset of those terms into the new definition; that, then, is what he means with his reference to the "free self-evolution" of thought. In the context of such freedom, the "necessity" of Hegel's system cannot mean that it is incapable of being other than it is. Hegel's claims of necessity usually attribute it to "content" (as at Hegel 1975b, 3, 13, 16–18, 41–45), and we can interpret this quite straightforwardly as the claim that any term in the system has the content systematically assigned to it: that is defined solely in terms of moments which have preceded it. So generated, the "content" of such a term is unaffected by contingencies of nature and life. They cannot make it other than it is.

But philosophical thought itself can. This all gives Hegel's system enormous resources not only for defining new terms but for redeploying previously defined terms in order to revise definitions already established. As a glance at the tables of contents of the various editions of Hegel's systematic works shows, his own practice of such revision was, though unacknowledged, ruthless.[22] Hegel's system is thus far more flexible than it is given credit for being, and Hegelian reason is malleable indeed. Its malleability, as we have seen it so far, comprises the following views:

1. Reason is linguistic, an activity of arranging words. As such it is public and its medium, being mere sounds of the voice, is itself entirely malleable.

2. Reason is not language bound but language transforming: the words of Hegel's German are malleable enough to receive new meanings bestowed entirely by thought.

3. Reason generates universality. Universal validity is not a given, as on views which see reason as proceeding from necessary premises, but comes to be as new definitions are formed. Since this process is entirely immanent, anyone with a basic understanding of how it works can follow it, no matter what their home language or culture may be.

4. The process of generating new definitions is a continuous redeployment of definitions previously arrived at.

The Hammer of Language

But "malleable," from the Latin *malleus*, or hammer, means to be capable of being *hammered* into new shapes. Where do the blows come from, and who or what wields them?

If my account of the end of the *Phenomenology* is correct, the blows are wielded by matter itself: by conceptually unguided recapitulations of experience, with which philosophy must somehow "resonate." We can gain an abstract understanding of such resonation by looking at what, following Michael Hardimon,[23] I take to be the basic concept of Hegel's entire social philosophy: reconciliation.

Reconciliation, as it is treated in the *Phenomenology*, begins from a situation in which consciousness, fleeing the world in order to maintain its moral purity, disowns both its acts and its words:

> The absolute certainty of itself thus finds itself, *quā* consciousness, changed immediately into a sound that dies away . . . but this created world is its speech, which it has likewise immediately heard and the echo of which returns only to it. This return, therefore, *does not mean that it is present in that speech* in and for itself; for the essence [of the matter] is for it nothing in-itself, but its [own] self. (*PhS*, ¶ 658; 399; my translation, emphasis added)

Cutting through the verbiage, we see the moral self presented here as the height of what David Foster Wallace would call "irony": it is not present in its own speech because its own purity requires its elevation above its very words in such a way that it disowns them. When such consciousness confronts another consciousness, it confronts a being whose pure self is similarly elevated above its words (and acts); but the *specific* words above which the second self is elevated differ from those of the first self, for otherwise the two selves would be identical. Reconciliation begins when one of the two consciousnesses confesses to the other—no longer disowning its concrete content but affirming such content as a past sin (*PhS*, ¶ 658; 405).[24] When such affirmation is mutual, the two consciousnesses recognize that their previous speech is not something they can disown but is also not something they are bound to: they can move beyond it, and in mutually recognizing this they forgive one another. This mutual forgiveness is "reconciliation." Reconciliation thus corresponds to what Wallace, as we saw in Chapter 1, calls the "Bottom," the realization that one's own situation—trapped between the deathly stasis of denial and the AA-like dynamics of confession—is "fucking similar" to the situation of the other consciousness.

As for the speech of the moral selves, so on the philosophical level for the words in which they express themselves. The words which consciousness has developed up to now are its words, which have penetrated into all its thought and so define it; but they need not define it for all time. Consciousness's "reconciliation" with its own language is thus not a commitment to carry it forward unchanged but includes the recognition that language—and so thought, and so reason itself—are malleable.

The scope of such reconciliation is wide indeed, for language shapes the entirety of our world:

> In our day it cannot often enough be recalled that what distinguishes humans from animals is thinking. Into everything which makes thinking something internal . . . there has penetrated language, and what we make into language and express in language contains, whether concealed, confused or elaborated, a category. (SL, 31–32)

Indeed, language for Hegel has penetrated the human world so deeply that, as with the later Wittgenstein (see Wittgenstein 1958, 11–12), no sharp line can be drawn between what is linguistic and what is not. Social practices in general attain full clarity when they are put into words; the achievement is a gradual matter.

Since all thought occurs in words, no thought that anyone has ever thought is exempt from Hegelian philosophical comprehension—from having the terms in which it is couched receive immanent, "verified" definitions. When this happens, moreover, there is a sense in which we understand our own words fully for the first time. To show this, I must quote Hegel at some length:

> The forms of thought, and further the viewpoints and principles which have validity in the sciences and constitute the ultimate touchstone [*Halt*] for the rest of their material, are for all that not peculiar to them, but are common to the culture of a time and people. . . . Our consciousness contains these representations, it allows them validity as final determinations, it moves forward on them

as its guiding connections. But it does not know them, does not make them themselves into the objects and interests of its examination.

To give an abstract example, every consciousness has and uses the wholly abstract determination, "Being." "The sun is in the sky," "the grapes are ripe," and so on forever. In higher culture there are questions of cause and effect, force and expression, etc. All [our] knowing and representing is interwoven with such metaphysics, and governed by it; it is the net in which is caught all the concrete material that occupies us in our ways and doings. But for our ordinary consciousness, this web and its knots are sunken in multilayered material. It is the latter which contains the interests and objects which we know, which we have before us. Those universal threads are not set off and made objects of our reflection. (Hegel 1892, 1:57; my translation)

Presented here are two acceptable but less than optimal ways of understanding the meaning of a word. One is the way of "every consciousness," which makes use of highly abstract terms but does not reflect on them. Such consciousness, we may say, is like Euthyphro at the beginning of Plato's dialogue of that name: he does not know the meaning of the word "holy" but thinks he recognizes holiness when he sees it. He is, of course, wrong; prosecuting your own father for murder is not a "holy" act. Unless we "set off" word meanings and make them "objects of our reflection," we cannot use our words properly.

The sciences of "higher culture," for their part, have done this, but only for words as they themselves use them. Physicists and lawyers may both talk about causality in highly sophisticated ways, but neither group knows anything about the other. They therefore do not take account of the fact that a term such as "cause" is not the property of any one science but is shared by all sciences and by speakers in general.

It is philosophy, with its system of verified definitions, that solves both problems. To the fluid terms of ordinary language it gives definitions which, being systematically developed, are well formed in that each term has in its definition all and only the terms which are needed to define it (see CW, 322). And it gives to the specialized terms of the various arts and sciences definitions which show how those meanings relate to those in the wider community. Philosophy thus enables the common folk to talk to the learned and the learned to talk to each other. In that sense, it serves as an underlaborer to the public use of reason that Kant called "Enlightenment." But philosophy is more than an underlaborer. When Hegel says that the forms of thought serve consciousness as "guiding connections" on which it moves forward, he is implicitly installing philosophy as the central switchyard in which human discourses come together. Without it a human community not only cannot be enlightened; it cannot even be coherent.

Hegel thus remains true to Aristotle's view that it is speech, which can set forth "the expedient and the inexpedient, and therefore also the just and unjust" (*Politics* 1.2.1253a14–15), that binds us into communities and so makes us truly human. But for Hegel, who already lived in a time when speech was becoming specialized, it is not language in general which automatically does this (as it might in less specialized civilizations such as Aristotle's), but philosophical language. Philosophy's position as the unifying center of all human discourse, and so of humanity as such, gives it a position akin to that of an ousiodic form; and in a perhaps unguarded fragment from an early notebook, Hegel attributes to it what sounds like dispositive power: "Philosophy rules representations, and these rule the world" (*HWe*, 2:560).

For the later, systematic Hegel, this is not the case. If philosophy's job is to comprehend terms from ordinary and expert languages, revising itself when necessary, then it operates under the impulsion of the nonphilosophical world. This impulsion is particularly evident in the case of empirical science:

> On the one hand the empirical sciences do not stop at the perception of *single instances* of appearance; but through thinking they have prepared the material [*Stoff*] for philosophy by finding universal determinations, genera, and laws. In this way they prepare the content [*Inhalt*] of what is particular so that it may be taken up into philosophy. On the other hand, they contain the requirement [*Nötigung*] for thinking to advance to these concrete determinations. . . . Thus, philosophy owes its development to the empirical sciences, but it gives to their content the most essential form of the *freedom* (the *a priori*) of thinking. (Hegel 1975b, 37; my translation)

The discourse of science so understood is thus for Hegel, as it was for Boyle, a highly reflective form of the speaking of matter. It begins, like Kantian reflective judgment, with individual sensory objects; and, like such judgment, it seeks, in one way or another, to find concepts for them.[25] When such concepts are arrived at by science, it is philosophy's job to integrate them with itself through new definitions. It is thus science, and more generally reflection on human life itself, which hammers philosophy into new shapes. The blows of that hammer are the new words which people come up with as they try to articulate their experiences of life and the world. A nonscientific example is the

Phenomenology itself, the story of a search for words which define the nature of consciousness as it emerges from the work. As is true of the speaking of matter in general, the *Phenomenology* has an ambiguous location, both "inside" and "outside" philosophical thought (see *CW*, 148–154).

Philosophy itself, as pure thought, is free to develop its content according to thought's "self-evolution"; but the philosopher should seek definitions which apply to words actually in use. Only when she responds, at every step, to such language—and, when necessary, adjusting thought itself to the impacts of new words and new meanings—can philosophy be "reconciled" to the languages of the world. Only then can the result of the philosopher's efforts be called not merely thought but "philosophy."

Philosophy and World: A Matter of Hierarchy

We can thus characterize philosophical reason for Hegel, as reconciliation with the speaking of matter. Sometimes, however, the words with which we must be reconciled are ugly ones. If nothing that anyone has ever thought is exempt from philosophical definition, philosophy for its part has no exemptions either. It is not free to pick and choose what will be its *Stoff*, any more than a seed can choose the soil where it will land. This means that philosophers must be willing to confront some very strange *Stoff*. As Hegel puts it with regard to the macabre aspects of some religions:

> [We must] recognize the meaning, the truth, and the connection with truth; in short get to know what is rational [i.e., linguistically communicable] in them. They are human beings who have hit upon such religions; therefore there must be *reason* in them, and amidst all that is accidental in them a higher necessity.... To get a grasp of the history of religions in this sense means to reconcile ourselves even with what is horrible, dreadful, or absurd in them, *and to justify it.* (Hegel 1970a, 200; emphasis added)

If this is a protest against philosophical removal from the world, it sounds as if it goes too far—and intersects with one of the standard pictures of Hegel as someone who thinks the whole world is in good order just as it stands. But for Hegel, as we saw above, to "justify" (*rechtfertigen*) something is to define it; and the definition in question may reveal the thing to be defective: "a bad state is an untrue state, and the bad and the untrue as such consists in the contradiction which obtains between the determination, or the concept, and the existence of an object" (Hegel 1975b, 41).

In order to locate such a contradiction, of course, we must know what the concept—the verified philosophical definition—of something is. Only when we know that the philosophical definition of the state includes equal rights for all its adult inhabitants, for example, do we know that the United States is still far from being de facto a "state," though because of its mid-twentieth-century civil rights legislation it has largely become one de jure.

An Hegelian social philosopher thus cannot do what Charles Mills chastises recent Anglo-American social philosophy for doing—ignore the racist basis of the modern state (*RC*, 121–123). The Hegelian social philosopher cannot simply abstract away from things like race and gender in her accounts of society and the state, for part of her job is to define "state," and when she does she must take account of the relation of the state to those who live within its boundaries. If she avoids bringing gender and race into this and simply assumes that all people in the state have equal personhood, she will get caught in the disparity between the definition of "state" and the way the word is actually used around her.[26]

Since reason for Hegel is malleable, such a philosopher might still be able to define the state as inherently sexist or racist—Hegel himself certainly did the former, at *Philosophy of Right* §§ 165–166, and his remarks about Africans are legendarily offensive. We cannot, of course, be Hegelians without reservations—indeed, without many of them. The need for a further one is indicated by the dots in the quote above on religion. The sentence I have omitted reads: "We must do them [strange and abhorrent religions] this justice, for what is human and rational in them is our own too, although it exists in our higher consciousness as a moment only."

This exposes a problem with Hegel's view of philosophy as the reconciliation of reason and language. On the one hand, we own, and cannot *dis*own, foreign and even repellent discourses; we cannot elevate ourselves above such words. But we have them today only as echoes of the originals. Hegel thus understands Greek religion, but only because it still vibrates within his modern German soul; its vibrations have been softened and rationalized by the hammer blows of intervening history (Christianity being in Hegel's view an especially powerful hammer). Philosophy for Hegel therefore stands not only at the end of a development but at the top of a hierarchy; it deals only with material (*Stoff*) that has been worked up by science and other reflective enterprises.

We can flesh out this hierarchical dimension of Hegel's thought by asking the following question: What for Hegel makes the end of a development the top of a hierarchy? What guarantees that reflection's movement onward is a movement upward as well? If Hegel ignores this question, then he is simply taking it for granted that whatever has been around for a long time is ipso facto justified. We are back at the long-discredited image of him as a Prussian arch-conservative whose dictum "The real is rational" simply means "Whatever is, is right." But if Hegel does not simply take it for granted that movement onward is movement upward, he has to *show* that it is—in every case. He does this by a process that I will call "dialectical reflection."

Malleable Reason as Dialectical Reflection in Hegel

The *Phenomenology*'s hierarchical dimension points us to a contrast between two ways in which, on an Hegelian approach, matter speaks: in the original experiences which constitute the bulk of the book and in their recapitulation at its end. In contrast to Wallace's presentation, discussed in Chapter 1, both are explicitly discursive. Tracing the development of words through history, dialectical reflection for Hegel is supposed to show how the hammer blows of language organize themselves over time, until they reach the point where they impact philosophy itself—the point where philosophical thought can and must provide them with "verified definitions." As such, dialectical reflection is a procedure for grasping the speaking of matter and organizing its resonances in us. It is also a method which can be used independently of Hegel's own employment of it, to trace the developments not merely of words but of all sorts of historical phenomena, including social practices and groups.

Hegelian dialectic is often viewed as a silly exercise in historical mythology, powered by self-contradiction. Actually, it is a way of reconstructing the unique histories of historical phenomena without imposing conceptual guidance on them and of doing so in a way which can be called "rational." According to the procedural points I noted in the *Phenomenology*'s introduction, the rationality of such a history consists in meeting three criteria, which can be roughly stated as follows:

1. The history contains a sequence of attempted definitions of a word.

2. Those definitions succeed one another because each one fails at a certain point: something is encountered which in one way comes under that definition but in another way doesn't—in other words, something which both does and does not come under that definition.

3. Each new definition solves only the problem encountered by the old definition and no others.

It is important to note, in regard to (2) above, that in the *Phenomenology*'s introduction Hegel specifies that the discovery of something that does not fit under the opening definition does not come about "by way of a second object which we come upon by chance" but "through a reversal of consciousness itself" (*PhS*, ¶ 87; 55–56). Self-reversing reason is malleable in the extreme, but the present passage (like others) is often taken to mean that the development of the *Phenomenology*, like that of the system itself, is an entirely immanent one, in which the successive contradictions consciousness encounters are all present, somehow, at the beginning, so that consciousness itself would be a self-enclosed realm which develops without impetuses from outside. The alternative reading would claim that chance objects may furnish occasions for a "reversal of consciousness," but no one of them is enough to compel it (see Quine 1960, ix). This would enable us to generalize the kind of narrative produced in the *Phenomenology* to a wide variety of historical phenomena.

The latter reading, I take it, is the correct one. The self-referentiality of the *Phenomenology* comes only at the end—that is why I called it a "collapse"—and consciousness is continually, in the course of the book, making empirical discoveries (recall its original subtitle: "Science of the *Experience* of Consciousness"). Desiring consciousness, for example, "learns through experience that the object is independent" (*PhS*, ¶ 168; 106; see also ¶ 175; 109), and the battler to the death learns "in this experience that life is as essential to it as self-consciousness" (*PhS*, ¶ 189; 115). When Hegel writes about "consciousness" and "self-consciousness" in the *Phenomenology*, then, he seems to have had various experiences of the "external world" in mind.[27] The complex relationships between dialectical reflection and the discourses and realities on which it reflects can never be taken for granted: at each stage, we must ask ourselves what (if anything) is really "out there" being reflected on and what in our reflection is really due to the way we are reflecting.

The development of the *Phenomenology* is thus not "objectively" unified in the sense of portraying the kind of unified historical development that we saw Foucault criticize in Chapter 3. Thematic unity is hammered into the *Phenomenology* by consciousness's experiences. The only points at which the sequence of definitions relates to reality are, in fact, the points at which it fails to capture it ([2] above). The overall position is akin to Karl Popper's view that scientific theories can be falsified but not verified: we can say that an attempted definition must have gotten something wrong, but we cannot say what, if anything, it has gotten right (see Popper 2002, esp. 57–73). Nor is it internally unified by a common thematic present from beginning to end. What most basically organizes the sequence of attempted definitions is (again contrary to Foucault, as discussed in Chapter 3) not some overarching theme or insight but merely the fact that each definition fixes one problem with the previous definition. Nothing else need hold the sequence together (see *CW*, 148). Such "thematic" unity as the *Phenomenology* has comes only at its end, when its final collapse into self-referentiality shows us what the book was about all along—itself. This final insight, once given explicit formulation, can count as a "concept" produced by the development it unifies—but it is a concept which is validated only because it retrospectively unifies that particular development and does not necessarily apply to any reality beyond that.

In that it pushes toward a unifying concept which it does not have at the beginning, as well as in the indeterminacy of its own location with respect to the "outside" realities with which it "resonates," dialectical reflection seeks to capture the recapitulation presented in such speech not by submitting it to a definite end but as a continuous self-redefinition. Dialectical reflection is thus attentiveness to the speaking of matter.

Because language is so intimately interwoven with the rest of life, the methods of dialectical reflection (even in Hegel) are not limited to words; to understand a word, we must understand the practices with which it is associated. Dialectical reflection thus applies across the board; in Chapter 7 we will see Abraham Lincoln apply it to a conspiracy he thinks he has uncovered.

For Hegel's own philosophy, however, it is words themselves which are the primary objects of dialectical reflection, and in his systematic philosophy Hegel deals only with words that have already been through this process—those whose definitions have been tested and reformulated many times. The end of that process is the "expert discourse'" of Hegel's Berlin. Its raw beginnings in humanity's earliest experiences of nature and life are largely unknown to us, but must have been wordless or almost so: something like the Cratylan pointing that occurs in the *Phenomenology*'s discussion of sense-certainty. At the beginning of dialectical reflection, then, we would find an inchoate groping for words which are not yet there—what I have called the speaking of matter. But Hegel himself comes in at the end, that is, at the top. This may go some way toward explaining Hegel's repugnant statements about Africans, Chinese women, and others: they are rehashings (and sometimes sharpenings) of views current in the educated circles of early nineteenth-century Berlin.

A more adequate and nonhierarchical account of the unreflective origins of matter's speech cannot be gleaned from Hegel; we will have to await the next chapter for that. But the underlying point has been made: once reason becomes linguistic and so malleable, it must attend to the speaking of matter rather than exclude or degrade it. Otherwise thought does not know how to progress; without the hammer blows of speaking matter, thought's "free self-evolution" turns into arbitrary emptiness.

Example: Hegel on Gay Marriage

As an example of how Hegel's thought underwrites malleability, I adduce an Hegelian thematic which I discuss in more detail elsewhere:[28] the philosophical definition of marriage advanced in the *Philosophy of Right*.

I noted above the importance of definitions for philosophical method as Hegel discusses it in the introduction to that book (notably at § 2). Marriage for Hegel is systematically defined as a way of coping with nature, and the part of nature with which marriage primarily copes is, of course, maintaining the "actuality of the species"—reproduction (*PhR*, 200). Though marriage does not begin without impulses of mutual attraction and, indeed, of passion (*PhR*, § 162), it goes beyond this in that a married person can no longer take account merely of his or her own selfish desires. Each partner has to care as much about the needs and desires of the other as about his or her own: "In this respect, their union is a self-limitation; but since [the parties] obtain their substantial self-consciousness within it, it is in fact their liberation" (*PhR*, 201–202).

What the partners gain by this "self-limitation" is what is defined as the immanent goal of all spirit: freedom. In marriage as an ethical bond, the individuals constitute a new person, leaving behind their old, natural individuality, which is defined (like everything natural) as "transient" and "capricious," as well as "contingent" (*PhR*, 202). In that process, Hegel tells us,

> consciousness emerges from its naturalness and subjectivity to concentrate on the thought of the substantial. Instead of reserving to itself the contingency and arbitrariness of sensuous inclination, it removes the marriage bond from this arbitrariness and . . . makes itself over to the substantial; it thereby reduces the sensuous moment to a merely conditional one—conditioned, that is, by the true and ethical character of the relationship, and by the recognition of the marriage bond as an ethical one. (*PhR*, 205)

Disciplined by the marriage bond, the drives and desires of the partners are thwarted and lose force; sexual desire, in particular, is fated "to be extinguished in its very satisfaction" (*PhR*, 202). The married person is then no longer at the disposal of powerful but whimsical natural desires and becomes a true moral agent, able to act independently of them. Marriage thus plays a powerful role in the self-constitution of the moral agent (see *PhR*, 201–202).

This account of marriage as liberation from the contingency of natural whims and desires can apply to gay couples as much as straight ones. Hegel, who some evidence suggests was what we today would call gay (see Pillow 2002), does not in fact specify that the mutual attraction which leads to marriage must, in order to be "natural," be heterosexual. What he does specify, oddly enough, is that it does not even have to be what we would call sexual. Though at *PhR* § 163 he characterizes such attraction as the "natural drive," he also calls it "sensibility" (*Empfindung*), the mind's awareness of bodily messages in general (*PhR*, 200–201; see also Hegel 1975b, 29–31). He also calls it "passion," in which one's entire being (*alle Saite seines Wesens*) is focused on another person (*HWe*, 7:313). It could, then, just be delight caused by the presence or thought of another person, whether sexual, heterosexual, or not "sexual" at all. Thus, marriage can perform the same function for gay men and lesbians that it performs for heterosexual couples. Indeed, if we assume that drives are originally polymorphous (as Hegel does: a drive "has all kinds of objects and can be satisfied in all kinds of ways" [*PhR*, 46]), then even heterosexual marriages in which one or both partners are homosexual can perform this liberating function; for extinguishing the drive in one domain will weaken it in others. Or so, perhaps and sadly, was Hegel's hope when he married at the age of forty-six.

Whatever his personal status, one thing Hegel cannot do is understand marriage in the rigidly traditional way: as an institution for passing on the human form to the next generation. For one thing, this requires that the desire from which marriage starts be stably heterosexual, which denies the true "contingency and arbitrariness of natural inclinations." Such a denial contradicts marriage's liberating mission, which is to free us from desire as it really is—not as various religious traditions would have it be. For another, there is for Hegel no "human form," for such essential forms are unchanging; what makes us human is our transformations and self-transformations. The point of marriage for him, and of his philosophical definition of it, is to facilitate this human malleability by turning creatures who are at the mercy of their physical drives into free moral agents.[29]

Conclusion

If the foregoing is correct, Hegel was the first philosopher since Heracleitus to reject atemporal truth for philosophy and (so) the first major philosopher to make the linguistic turn. Like Wittgenstein, Moore, and Austin—indeed, like Carnap, Russell, and Quine—Hegel holds that all philosophical problems are problems of language and that they can all be resolved, if at all, either by re-forming language or by understanding it better (Rorty 1967). By "understanding language better," however, Hegel does not mean laying bare the logical nature of syntax but getting better—because verified—definitions. These definitions are malleable, which in the case of philosophy means critically revisable, ways of understanding the speaking of matter; the dialectical reflections which show how the defined words came to be historically are actual cases of it. Both sides of Hegel are thus of critical importance for philosophy as it seeks its way out of its present, and longstanding, crisis. I will discuss this further in Chapter 7.

We have misunderstood Hegel by misreading him as what I have called a traditional philosopher. If Hegel were such a philosopher, he would be one of a particularly unhappy sort—for he would represent either a return to pre-Kantian metaphysics, as if Kant had never written a thing, or a hypertrophic expansion of Kantian category theory. In either case, we could safely ignore him, because in either case he would be absurd.

Now, however, we see that Hegel, not Marx or Heidegger, was the first thinker to return to Heracleitus by denying atemporal truth. It was Hegel who by doing this first pushed philosophy out of the atemporal, and so other-worldly, realms in which it had nestled for millennia and who insisted that its success or failure ultimately concerns how rigorously it deals with the here and the now. At a time when, as I suggested in the Introduction, American philosophy has been snatched from its long and happy sojourn in academic backwaters and been shoved to the center—the dead center—of every single new struggle America faces after 9/11, the lessons of Hegel—like those of the other thinkers of the return to Heracleitus—are more than salutary. Learning them is one of the very few philosophical projects that could reasonably be described as "urgent."

CHAPTER 6

THE FRAGILITY OF REASON

EARTH, ART, AND POLITICS IN HEIDEGGER

A Controversy Out of Joint

If Hegel has been dismissed for being an uncritical metaphysician or a hypertrophic Kantian, Heidegger has been excoriated for being something much worse: a Nazi. The excoriations themselves are well deserved, but their timing seems to be somewhat out of joint. As with the Great Modernism Debate, there seems to have been a strange delay—not in settling the controversy, but in beginning it. Why did Heidegger's engagement in and on behalf of the National Socialist Party of Germany not come to public light in the United States for a full fifty-six years, until the 1989 French publication of Victor Farias's *Heidegger and Nazism* (Farias 1991)? The facts were known in Germany long before then; Hans-Georg Gadamer's astonishment at the outrage ensuing upon the "revelations" of Victor Farias lay not in learning that Heidegger had been an active Nazi in 1933–34 but in learning that the French had been so totally ignorant of it (see Gadamer 1989). Nor was knowledge of Heidegger's Nazi engagement limited to his circle or to those in Freiburg, where it mostly took place. My own *Doktorvater*, the Jewish philosopher/theologian Emil Fackenheim, told me (in the late 1970s) that he heard about Heidegger's joining the Nazi Party as a nineteen-year-old student in central Germany. It was announced on the radio by a Nazi Party eager to gain the respectability Germany's greatest living philosopher could give them. The news brought Fackenheim a grim satisfaction, he told me, for if Germany's leading philosopher had become a Nazi, things couldn't possibly get any worse. The satisfaction was fleeting; five years later, Emil Fackenheim was in Sachsenhausen.

How could something so widely known in Germany in 1933–34 be so un-known across the Rhine in 1988? What, moreover, does it mean that the Americans did not know about it until the French told them?

The date of discovery is not the only thing out of joint here. In scandals like this, the usual first reaction is shock and anger, which then gives way to a more measured reaction as time goes on. This has not happened in the Heidegger controversy. In France itself, the anti-Heidegger reaction has not only lasted but grown shriller, to the point where Emmanuel Faye is now claiming that Hitler got at least some of his anti-Semitism from Heidegger.[1] The Americans, as usual, have simply divided into groups that ignore one another. One group dismisses Heidegger altogether as a *mere* Nazi, while the other takes him more "philosophically" by ignoring or explaining away the Nazi engagement. A notable few, such as Gregory Fried, struggle with the issue (Fried 2000).

One explanation for both the long denial and the present hysteria is that Heidegger's Nazi behavior is so deeply unfathomable as to fracture philosophy itself, in several directions. One is moral: if such an accomplished philosopher can give his heart and soul to the Nazi Party, what good is philosophy? Clearly it needs to be redefined, and in the most radical of ways. Simply maintaining, as some do, that the solution is to make philosophy a professional field like all the others is hardly the answer; as I noted in the Introduction, even today philosophy is not such a field, if only because it is not making the kind of progress such fields make.

A second fracture, which I have discussed elsewhere (*MO*, 1–13), is theoretical: how are we to understand the fact that one and the same person could be both a philosopher and a Nazi? When we engage this question, we find that conceptual resources are wanting. Some of the most basic and ancient of philosophical strategies, indeed, reveal themselves to be little more than comforting dodges.

The metaphysics of substance, for example, is hopelessly inadequate. On its terms, what we have is a single substrate (Heidegger) to which contradictory predicates (philosopher, Nazi) apply. The normal way to handle a contradiction like this is to temporalize it: to say that the contradictory predicates must have marked the beginning and end of a process of change. As when water in a test tube above a flame goes from being cold to hot, so Heidegger started out as a great philosopher but became a Nazi (as Habermas thinks: see Habermas 1989). But this will not work: Heidegger clearly achieved philosophical greatness in 1927, when he published *Being and Time*, and again when he published "The Origin of the Work of Art" in 1936. But he was a Nazi in between, and apparently again in 1942 when he gave the lectures that became *Hölderlin's Hymn*

"*The Ister*"—lectures which referred to the "historical uniqueness" of Nazism (Heidegger 1996, 79–80). Did he oscillate? In any case, neither the metaphysics of substance nor the kind of developmental reflection to which it gives rise gets us very far.

If we turn to the metaphysics of ousia, the dodges get more complex—but no more successful. They are more complex because now we have the notion of an intelligible essence, attempting to control the contingency and unruliness of matter. So either Heidegger was *essentially* a philosopher whose Nazi engagement was a mere *accident* (perhaps, Aristotle might say, a crazy upsurge of desire of some kind); or he was *essentially* a Nazi who by an *accident* of reception came to be viewed as a great philosopher. These are the positions of Hannah Arendt and Richard Wolin, respectively (Arendt 1971; Wolin 1990). As I have argued elsewhere (*MO*, 1–18), neither position can ultimately be sustained. Both being a philosopher and being a Nazi require absolute personal commitment; neither can be dismissed as an "accident."

It is unsurprising that something so recalcitrant to reason (even to malleable Hegelian reason) should be for so long denied or that admitting it should bring such anger. It is too late, of course, to repair the suspiciously late discovery of Heidegger's Nazi engagement. Can it possibly be time now, however, to restore a degree of normal temporality to the scandal, by beginning a more measured discussion of it? Such discussion shows us that reason itself is not only malleable, as Hegel argued, but may also be fragile—capable of being fractured.

My reasoned discussion cannot begin, however, until one crucial point has been clarified. If Heidegger joined the Nazi Party in full knowledge of what it was, then reasoned treatment is impossible; a knowing endorsement of genocidal anti-Semitism ends all discussion. My efforts here presuppose, then, that Heidegger did *not* have a clear view of what Nazism was in 1933–34. There are considerations which favor this. The times were generally confused, and in 1933–34 Hitler was still pretending to some decency as he consolidated power. And as Heidegger himself always claimed, and Hans Sluga has confirmed, his actions accorded with the run of German philosophers of the time (Sluga 1993).

Even if the Nazis in 1933–34 were not openly committed to genocide, however, they certainly were horrible people. Joining them should have been out of the question for anyone decent, however bewildered. Heidegger, and those many of his fellow philosophers who joined him in approving of the Nazis, clearly did *something* awful. The most we could say in their defense is that they were thoroughly confused, if not thoroughly evil.

From confusion to evil is a long way, and if we want to locate where Heidegger belongs on the continuum—and I believe we need to, whether we want to or not—we must first recognize that there are several intermediate stops.

"Elitism," for this purpose, is the view that some people are better than others. Whether elitism is morally objectionable or not depends, among other things, on the specific respect in which this is held to be the case. To say that some people are better basketball players than others is pretty innocuous; to say that some people are morally better than others is less so, but surely valid in some cases. One species of elitism—"nationalism"—holds that some people are better than others by virtue of belonging to a particular people or "nation"—a community which preexists its members and which is united not by personal acquaintance or the perception of a common task but by the sharing of various customs, values, and language. The appropriation of nationalism to the mechanisms, structures, and symbols of the state is what I will call "fascism." Fascism thus holds that state authority can and should both express the values of a particular national group and enforce its superiority. One species of fascism—found most fatefully in Germany—supports itself by grounding both nation and state on what it calls biological fact. This is racism but not yet Nazism: for there is an infinite distance between racist contempt for others, even if reinforced by a government at the level of the nation, and a policy of killing them. If fascism is evil, as it is, then Nazism is absolutely evil.

Elitism → nationalism → fascism → racism →. Nazism is a moral hierarchy, descending from the normally innocuous to the absolutely evil. My thesis will be that between 1933 and 1935, Heidegger went from near the bottom of this hierarchy to somewhere near the top: that from being a fascist he became a mere elitist, though of a non-innocuous sort. The signposts for this movement are the Rectoral Address of 1933 and "The Origin of the Work of Art" from 1936.

Philosophy in the Service of the Nazi State:
The Rectoral Address

The Rectoral Address, given when Heidegger assumed the rectorship of the University of Freiburg, expresses the depths of his Nazism. One of its most unusual features, when we look at it in the context of Heidegger's writings in general, is its high opinion of *Wissenschaft*, science. For the Greeks, we read, science was the "inmost determining midpoint of the entirety of Dasein in the nation-state" (*des ganzen volklich-staatlichen Daseins*; R, 12 [all translations from R are my own]).

For the Germans, science has become "the inmost necessity of Dasein," and must be made the *Grundgeschehen*, "the fundamental happening of our spiritual-national Dasein" (*R*, 13–14). The "spiritual mission" of the German people is thus to be understood as science, and vice versa (*R*, 2, 16). Science must not be split up into specialties which can be tucked away in different corners of the university but brought into unity with "all world-building powers," including nature, history, language, folk, and so forth (*R*, 13). Only then can science "create for our people its truly spiritual world" (*R*, 14). Science, in sum, is not only the defining pursuit of the German university (*R*, 10) but is the *Grundgeschehen*, the necessary founding force in history, central to the community whose world it creates.

We may ask: If science is thus basic to humanity, what is basic to science? We know the standard answer to this: science, like philosophy, is a search for truth. While individual scientists may betray this from time to time, fudging results and plagiarizing theories in quests for money, positions, and prestige, the structure of science filters this out:

> The reason that [scientific fraud] is so rare (compared with, say, corruption in politics) is that science is designed to detect deception (of one's self and others) through colleague collaboration, graduate student mentoring, peer review, experimental corroboration and results replication. The general environment of openness and honesty, though mythic in its idealized form, nonetheless exists and in the long run weeds out the cheats and exposes frauds and hoaxes, as history has demonstrated. (Shermer 2010)

Truth, as I noted in Chapter 2, can be many things. What Heidegger calls science's "primordial essence" is neither a set of sentences or propositions nor a set of methods for obtaining them. It is its "questioning stance in the midst of the whole of Being, which continually conceals itself" (*R*, 12). The "death of God" has abrogated all certainties. Since answers are no longer to be had, questioning is, so to speak, of the essence, "the highest form of knowing" (*R*, 13–14).

Heidegger has thus located himself in the philosophical space opened up for Nietzsche by Hegel, who proclaimed the death of God at the end of the *Phenomenology* (*PhS*, ¶¶ 752, 786; 455, 476). Just as for Hegel reason was not the possession of a set of successfully completed proofs or of methods for obtaining them but an ongoing dialectical activity of vocabulary adjustment, for Heidegger science is no longer primarily "theoretical" but is the highest realization of practice (*R*, 12). As a mode of practice, the questioning of science becomes a threefold service: labor service, defense service, and knowledge service (*R*, 15–16). We may therefore say that basic to science is questioning, the practice of theory. And we may ask: On what does this practice of theory rest?

First of all, on itself, on the primordial essence of science unfolding through history and now opened up to us again. But, more fatefully, it also rests upon "our" will: there does not have to be any science at all, and whether there is or not depends upon whether "we" will it (*R*, 9, 10–11, 14, 18). Who are "we"? Not a random collection of people—not even a random collection of Germans. The "we" in question is composed, we learn, of two groups: the teachers and students of the "highest school of the German people." Teacher and student are occupations created by the state, and they "belong" to the state (*R*, 9, 16, 18). Hence, the will to science is the will neither of an individual nor of a random collection of them but the will of a group of people organized in and by a state. As Heidegger sums it up, "the will which wills the essence of the German university is the will to the historical/spiritual mission of the German people insofar as it is a people which knows itself in its state" (*R*, 10).

True to German political philosophy (at least since Kant),[2] when Heidegger talks of the "university" he talks of an organ of the state; and when he speaks about the "state" he talks about organized, communal will. This will is the formative principle of the German nation, or people. Hence, when Heidegger speaks of "national state Dasein,"[3] he speaks as a fascist.

Of the three forms which service takes (which Heidegger calls "labor service," "defense service," and "knowledge service"), it should be no surprise that the central one is the *Wehrdienst*, the defense of the state; as in Plato's tale of the "city of pigs" at *Republic* 169c, the army is the middle term between subsistence labor and the fruits of higher culture. But what the army is *directly* responsible for, according to both Plato and Heidegger, is the fate of the state. So service to the army is service to the state (*R*, 15–16). The state is the true center here: it is not merely one among several necessary conditions for science but is its necessary and sufficient condition.

So far, we have a view of philosophical reason as what I call malleable. The hammer blows which reshape philosophy come not from science or general reflection on life, as for Hegel, but from the state as the expression of the people.

The role of the state thus does not exhaust itself with the notion of its being a necessary and sufficient condition for science. The state actually, it seems, directs the nature of science itself, which means that it organizes the self-knowledge of the people. The state thus assumes the position of an ousiodic form over science; and this in turn shows, I suggest, that the concept of science advanced in the Rectoral Address is incoherent. On the one hand, we saw, science has abandoned answers and regained its true nature as questioning. On the other, science is supposed to be of service to the people and the state, a "knowledge service" which requires "the hardest clarity of the highest, widest, and richest knowledge" of the people, the fate of the state, and the spiritual mission (*R*, 16). Science, in the service of the state, exhibits both the courageous obscurity of questioning and the "hardest clarity" of knowing. How can this happen?

The answer—as "The Origin of the Work of Art" will teach us—is that it cannot happen; a questioning stance is not to be combined with hard clarity, and this leads to a new question: Why does Heidegger even make this attempt to turn philosophy into state service? Is the incoherence a mere lapse, or does he gain something from it?

To see what Heidegger gains, we must remember that all science, according to the Rectoral Address, is philosophy (*R*, 11). Armed with this, we can understand what Heidegger is doing at the end of the address, where he both quotes and mistranslates Plato. I will come back to the mistranslation shortly; for the moment I want to excavate a hint made by the passage quoted itself. The sentence which stands in Plato's text just before the one Heidegger actually quotes states a question: *Tina tropon metacheirizomenē polis philosophian ou dioleitai?* It asks, "In what way may the state contain philosophy without being destroyed?" (*Republic* 497d). The whole of the Rectoral Address, at least those portions of it to which any intellectual respect at all is to be accorded, can be viewed as an attempt to answer this question of the coexistence of philosophy and the state, and thereby to legitimate philosophy in the eyes of the Nazis. The basic problem of the Rectoral Address is then how to place philosophy into the service of the Nazi state.

It seems at first that the real question is the reverse of this one: that it concerns how to place the state into the service of philosophy rather than the other way round. For what "forces" people into the state is, the Rectoral Address tells us, the "questionability of Being"—the global loss of certainty—that follows on the death of God (*R*, 16). Since that questionability cannot be overcome, it can presumably only be experienced—in the questioning proper to science. It would seem to follow that it is the need for such questioning that brings about the state. Moreover, if there are no answers, questioning must be an end in itself and so can serve no further purpose. Science, the experience of the questionability of Being, would then be the end which the state serves as a necessary means.

This view of the relation between science or philosophy and the state sounds more Aristotelian than Platonic. It is where Heidegger will eventually end up. But it is not where the Nazis are and not where he wants to go in 1933. Heidegger is, in fact, so solicitous of the state in the Rectoral Address that he cannot even translate Plato correctly. The quote from Plato at the end of the Address reads "all great things teeter" (*ta gar dē megala panta episphalē*), and as we saw above, Plato is specifically referring to the state insofar as it comes under threat from philosophy. Heidegger will not allow the state to "teeter": in his translation, it *steht im Sturm*, like a mighty but well-rooted oak; and by omitting the preceding question in Plato's text, Heidegger has obscured the fact that the tempest comes from philosophy.

Heidegger's attempt in the Rectoral Address to put philosophy into the service of the state—more precisely, of the nation organized in and by the state—has several steps. First, he identifies philosophy with "science," thus making it the essence of the university rather than a single department or faculty within it. He then grounds the university in turn on the organized public will of the national state, locates it at the center of the German "spiritual mission," and binds it to the rest of the community with the three services. None of this fascism overcomes the fact that, where Plato's philosopher-king descended into the cave armed with answers, his Heideggerian analogue comes only with questions.

What would Hitler have made of that?

Thinking in Questions

Twenty years later, the final words of "The Question Concerning Technology" (1955) maintain Heidegger's emphasis on questioning: "For questioning is the piety of thinking" (*QT*, 317). Indeed, Heidegger says right at the beginning of the essay that its point is to ask questions, not to prove a thesis or even, ultimately, to suggest one. Moreover, the questions he will be asking are in a certain sequence, that is, constitute a "way": "We would be advised . . . to pay heed to the way, and not to fix our attention on isolated sentence and topics" (*QT*, 287).

Heidegger's concept of a "way" can be viewed as his late version of what *Being and Time* called a "phenomenon."[4] Where a phenomenon was unified by Being, which gathered the stages of its gradual self-revelation together without being either one of those stages or any determinate property of the thing, so a Heideggerian way is unified not by the discipline of a theme or a thesis but by something which, like earth in "The Origin of the Work of Art" (which I will discuss shortly) does not become clear—by something which is accessible only in and as questions or what Heidegger also calls "hints."

Where a proof is a series of statements, then, Heidegger's "pious" essay is a series of questions: "We ask the 'question of technology' when we ask what it is" (QT, 288); "What is the instrumental itself? Within what do means and ends belong?" (QT, 289); "Why are there just four causes" (for Aristotle)? (QT, 290)—and so on intermittently through the essay. These questions are not, as they would be in other thinkers, orientating devices which stand outside the essay's basic argument. They constitute the main "joints" of the essay, broadly comparable to lemmas in a proof.

What Is a Question?

Given that questions are so important to Heidegger, Nazi and post-Nazi, we are entitled to ask what he thinks a "question" is. In *Being and Time*, we read that a question is, to begin with, a verbal formula, an utterance. As such, it occurs on a specific occasion: it comes from something and leads to something. What it comes from, in the first instance, is puzzlement. But we would be wrong, for Heidegger, to interpret puzzlement subjectively, as a "mere" feeling. Insofar as puzzlement is what he calls a "state of mind" (*Befindlichkeit*), it "brings-before the That of one's own thrownness [and thus] shows itself primarily in past-ness" (*BT*, 340). Puzzlement is our reaction to something that has happened in the past; and what has happened is a failure to understand. What, then, is "understanding"?

Answering this question takes us deep into *Being and Time*, according to which understanding contrasts with state of mind in that it has to do with the future. At *Being and Time* § 32, Heidegger thus calls understanding a "being-toward possibilities" (*BT*, 148). When we work out the possibilities with which a thing presents us, we "interpret" that thing: we apply to it what we already know about the world we live in, or what Heidegger calls our "fore-having." This background information is conveyed in what I will call the more or less informal "scripts" which guide us as we move through our world (*BT*, 67–71). Heidegger calls such scripts "totalities of significance" (*Bedeutungsganzen*). A script then is a sequence of patterned action such as:

1. Pick up the nail.
2. Position the nail, sharp end down, over the board.
3. Pick up the hammer with your other hand . . .

Unlike normal scripts, Heidegger's totalities of significance are usually unconscious—complexes of habits through which we move without thinking about it. Such scripts are not subjective in the sense that they are entirely in our heads; the short script above is expressed, for example, in the design and existence of such things as hammers and nails. When an individual Dasein appropriates such a script to its own current situation, it produces what Heidegger calls the *Sinn* (see *BT*, 145, 151, 161). Thus, armed with the script above, I "understand" the nail in that I see it as something I can hit with a hammer, thereby joining two boards. The *Sinn* of the nail is thus to be something-that-can-be hammered-down-to-hold-a-board-in-place. Though only clumsily expressible in English (or German), this is a quick and natural way of understanding the nail, and Heidegger calls it the "foresight" of the nail (*BT*, 150). To "understand" the nail is to see it in terms of its *Sinn*—in terms of the possibilities bestowed on it by some script or other. When worked out explicitly, this understanding becomes an interpretation (*Auslegung*).

Part of the point in calling the overall interplay of foresight and fore-having "interpreting" is suggested by Heidegger's use of the German *Vorsicht* for what I translate as "foresight"; *Vorsicht* is the German word for "caution" or "warning," and Heidegger's use of the term highlights the fact that interpretation is always fallible. What I take for a nail may be a tack, in which case its round head will likely deflect my hammer blow, and it will bend under the force of it. Or it may be a useless nail, too short to go through the board. Or it may be a defective nail, which is going to bend like a tack. In those cases, my interpretation and understanding turn out to be wrong: the nail was not "really" a nail but was something else.

The number of "something-elses" which it could be is a set not merely of alternate foresights—views of the nail itself—but of alternate categorical systems, or what Heidegger calls "pre-graspings" (*Vorgriffe*) which might be applied to it: nail/ hammer/board, tack/thumb/paper, and so forth. These pre-graspings then call in different scripts; when I actually deal with the nail, I have opted for just one of these (*BT*, 150). It is always possible that it was the wrong one.

When my foresight fails, my progress through the world is blocked. We get the famous "un-ready-to-hand" which Heidegger discusses at *Being and Time* § 16: the broken tool which brings me before all I intended to do with it and everything in my life to which that would have led. When a piece of equipment fails to function as it should, the failure snatches my scripts from the automatism of habit and brings them, often forcefully, to my awareness. It makes my world "light up." The tire becomes a flat tire and there, by the side of the road, I see the children I was going to pick up from school; I worry about how they are going to react to my lateness, which brings to mind my whole relation to them, which raises issues of the project of parenthood itself and my fitness for it. Eventually, of course, I give up these angst-ridden doubts and move to a fallback script: I phone for help. My entire world, the set of all my meaningful scripts, has not failed; I have other resources.

Now suppose that not only my foresight has failed but that *all* the pre-graspings at my disposal fail as well. The tire is not functioning, but it is some-how not a flat tire either; no categorical system or script can enable me to move ahead. I cannot move even to an alternate set of scripts, because I do not know what I am dealing with. Let us call such an incomprehensible thing an "anom-aly," with the proviso that it is not merely anomalous to this or that theory (as philosophers use the term) but to all our "theories" or possible conceptualiza-tions at once. With the recognition of such an anomaly, we get what for Hei-degger, as for Socrates, is the primary kind of question: a "what-is" question. It is not for Heidegger one which is asked about an abstraction (such as holiness in the *Euthyphro* or justice in the *Republic*) but about a concrete individual thing.

There arise on this basis a number of what we might call "metaquestions," questions about this originary what-is question.

1. Is the anomaly truly an anomaly? Have I tried all the possible scripts (or categorial systems) under which I might place it, or only the easiest and most obvious of them?

2. What exactly has failed? Did the different scripts have something in common which made them candidates for conceptualizing this thing? Is that common factor, or factors, what has failed?

3. How central is the failure? Scripts are embedded in other scripts, and a script which is an ingredient in many other scripts is more "central" to my world than something which is not. If I cannot recognize the anom-aly before me as a rat, for example, perhaps it is a possum. If I cannot recognize it even as an object, I am in much greater trouble, because a category far more central to my world has failed.

4. What are the origin and provenance of the failed conceptuality? Central categories tend to be older than peripheral ones; if I cannot recognize something as a hard drive, I am in a different position than if I cannot recognize it as a plow, and in both cases the only recourse is an histori-cal one: go back and see if there was a wrong turning in the develop-ment of the category over time.

Heidegger does not discuss these metaquestions as such, but we can see that he has produced what, in the Introduction, I said philosophy today so sorely lacked: a way, in fact a number of ways, to distinguish serious questions from adventitious ones. The serious ones, we see, involve conceptual (script) failures which are global (i.e., result from true anomalies), underlying, central, and of long provenance.[5]

In *Being and Time* § 6, Heidegger refers to the exposure of failed ontological systems as the *Destruktion*, the "destructuring" (or even the "deconstruction") of metaphysics. We can detach this project from its high ontological perspective and characterize it in a preliminary way, as follows: destructuring begins from the experience of an anomaly (in the sense just defined) and proceeds in accordance with the four metaquestions given above: (1) ascertaining the repertoire of possible interpretations, (2) isolating the common thematic of all of them, (3) understanding its centrality, and (4) understanding its historical provenance.

The first requires placing in abeyance all our accustomed and relevant ways of understanding and dealing with things. Because puzzlement, when it has even a small degree of centrality, tends to be uncomfortable (for Heidegger, the most "puzzling" thing for us is famously our own death; see *BT*, 262), we are often inclined, when one categorial system does not work, to move as quickly as possible to a similar one ("This animal *must* be a possum!"). The placing-in-abeyance of all relevant categorial systems (scripts) is thus emotionally charged—an affective version of Husserl's "scientific" brackets (for which see Husserl 1960, 60). It is what Heidegger in *Being and Time* (unfortunately) calls "resoluteness" (*Entschlossenheit*); openness and freedom are also, less tendentiously, connected with it and in his later writings become dominant:[6]

> The situation is only disclosed in a free self-resolving which is at first indeterminate, but open to determinacy. . . . This can precisely not become rigid but must understand that the resolve, in accordance with its own sense of disclosure, must be held *free and open* for the factical possibility of the moment. The certainty of the resolve means: keeping oneself free for its possible retraction. (*BT*, 307–308)

On the basis of such openness, we must then engage in an ongoing interaction with the anomaly, which, at every step, allows it to develop as what it is. Since we do not in fact know what it is, this interaction develops as a series of questions. Heidegger calls it "letting-be" as the "allowing oneself into the thing" (*Sicheinlassen auf das Seiende*): allowing it to be what it is.[7] We can also call it the formation of a Heideggerian "way."

Letting-be is what corresponds, in fragile reason, to reconciliation in malleable reason and to *karteria* in traditional/Enlightenment reason. All three are ways in which reason is deployed in bounded spaces. And all three are ways of responding to the speaking of matter: either we ignore it, with the philosophical tradition; or we reflect on it dialectically; or we let it be through a series of questions. At every step, letting-be re-asks the what-is question: each new question on a Heideggerian "way," formulated on the basis of what has been asked previously, confronts either a new anomaly or a new facet of the old anomaly. Such questioning allows the anomaly itself to suggest the next step (which is why Heidegger does not call them anomalies but "hints," *Winke*).[8] So construed, questioning is not merely the casual preliminary to answering. It is the way thinking holds itself open for future developments and, indeed, opens up the future itself, so that things are not hastily integrated into previously established scripts but allowed to be what they are—even if that utterly surprises us.

This Heidegger—at long last—is no Nazi or fascist. Indeed, if the Final Solution was an attempt to deny a future to Jews individually and collectively, then letting-be, the philosophical core of what we might call the "good Heidegger," is the exact opposite—whether he wanted it to be or not.

Letting-Be and Art

If Heidegger's praise of questioning in the Rectoral Address startled any Nazis, his praise of science there surprises many readers of his work even today. To be sure, it develops the "existential concept of science" alluded to in *Being and Time* (*BT*, 357–358). But Heidegger's normal way of referring to science is—at least after 1934—curt dismissal: "die Wissenschaft denkt nicht," from 1951; or "entsteht die Wissenschaft, vergeht das Denken," from 1946.[9] As early as 1936, in "The Origin of the Work of Art," we read:

> Science is no primordial happening of truth, but always the consolidation of a region of truth which is already open. It accomplishes this by apprehending and grounding that which shows itself to be possibly and necessarily correct in its field. When and insofar as a science surpasses correctness and reaches a truth, i.e., an essential revelation of the being as such, it is philosophy. (*OWA*, 62; my translation)

So much for the Rectoral Address's uncovering of the "primordial essence" of science. Here, science no longer questions but apprehends and grounds. It is no *Grundgeschehen* but a mere "consolidation." And it is not philosophy at all but sharply distinct from it.

What takes the place of the "science" of the Rectoral Address is art. Art, we are about to see, is everything that the "science" of the later writings is not: the first opening-up of a region of truth, the "essential revelation of the being as such," and—politically speaking, anyway—much more. We can begin by noting what the work of art will *not* be for Heidegger: an expression of "spirit," as it was (in his view) from Descartes to Hegel (see Derrida 1989, 14). Art is not to be understood in terms of the individual who creates it or of a set of "spiritual" values it is to express. It has no origin other than art itself, that is, the primordial happening of truth (*OWA*, 17, 36, 39–40, 65, 71).

Truth for Heidegger is not, as so often in the English-speaking world, the verbal capture of previously existing reality. Van Gogh's painting of shoes, of which Heidegger gives a famous discussion here, does not tell us, even imagistically, what the shoes already are as pieces of equipment (*OWA*, 36).[10] Rather, it is through the work of art that what this equipment is as equipment *first* comes to appearance for us (*erst . . . zum Vorschein kommt* [*OWA*, 36; emphasis added]). Truth for Heidegger is thus something that happens, a space or dimension in which things come to appearance (see Dahlstrom 2001, 170–174).

We can begin to understand this by noting four distinctive characteristics of the work of art's conveyance of truth. The first of these, already mentioned, is what we may call the "primal" status of the conveyance: in the work of art, something comes to appearance for us for the first time. If what the work of art conveys is truly new, it must strike us, the first time we experience it, as unique. In order for something unique to come to appearance for us, we must break with all our accustomed ways of cognizing and dealing with things: "To gain access to the work, it would be necessary to remove from it all relations to something other than itself, in order to let it stand on its own for itself alone" (*OWA*, 40). This sounds like the "placing in abeyance" of all preconceptions which was, I suggested above, part of Heidegger's earlier project of "destructuring" metaphysics. But (second) it is not, at this point, our doing; the work of art itself transports us so that in its vicinity "we were suddenly somewhere else than we usually tend to be" (*OWA*, 35).

The third distinctive characteristic of the way a work of art conveys truth needs slightly more detailed discussion. In *Being and Time*, when we use equipment, we do so in terms of what Heidegger calls a "context of significance" (and I have called a script). In this use we are not explicitly aware of the equipment; if I am watching the hammer, I will never hit the nail. What we attend to, rather, is our own movement through the script (*BT*, § 15). We can also, however, be aware of the thing independently of this context, as when we just stare at it—as we do, I noted above, with broken tools (*BT*, § 16). In *Being and Time* these two modes of encountering things yield Heidegger's most basic ontological categories, "readiness-to-hand" and "presence-at-hand," respectively. They are rigorously separate: if we are explicitly aware of something, we are not aware of the contexts of its use; if we are concerned with those contexts, we lose explicit awareness of the thing.

In "The Origin of the Work of Art," this rigorous separation is undone. As Heidegger describes the shoes in Van Gogh's painting, our awareness of them combines the two modes of encounter advanced in *Being and Time*. Unlike the person who uses the shoes (by wearing them), we are explicitly aware of them; but various facets of the shoes themselves call up the contexts of their use. The shoes themselves, as portrayed in the painting, show us that they have been worn by someone doing hard work on the soil of a wet, northern landscape (*OWA*, 33–34). The work of art, in presenting the shoes, thus calls up their script or context of significance. But if it does this for the first time, this script cannot be one with which we are already familiar. The work of art instead sets up its own script: it "belongs, as work, uniquely in the realm which is opened up by itself" (*OWA*, 41). This realm, at its widest, is itself an entire "world"—an overarching whole of meaning—and the work of art thus "sets up a world" of its own (*OWA*, 42; see also 44). The shoes thus send us a message; they are a case of the speaking of matter, resonating here through Van Gogh's painting.

It is not, I suggest, *mere* carelessness which leads Heidegger to the incorrect claim that the shoes in question belong to a peasant woman. He is attributing to Van Gogh precisely the project that was so devastatingly missing in Hegel: that of capturing the speaking of matter at the lower end of Hegel's hierarchy rather than at the top. The shoes, Heidegger is suggesting, bring a message from (literally) a downtrodden world. They do not speak with the not quite philosophically right words of a professorial colleague at the University of Berlin, as with Hegel, but speak for themselves through Van Gogh. Van Gogh might, of course, have gotten something wrong about the shoes—and Heidegger did get something wrong: the shoes famously did not belong to a peasant woman but to Van Gogh himself. But that does not change the fact that the shoes, whoever owned them, speak from an oppressed world. That is what is important—in the sense of "anti-Hegelian"—about them.

We can put Heidegger's view on how we are to hear the speaking of matter more concretely in kinesthetic terms. We circle around the painting or the sculpture; in listening to music, we resonate to motifs that have already been established and develop loose expectations about what is to come. Less corporeally, as we watch a film or read a novel, we ruminate about what has already been presented in it, gaining insights about how various things in it come together and suspicions—or questions—about where it may go. We thus understand a work of art in that we progress through it, just as we progress through contexts of significance or scripts in our daily life. The connections we find in so doing are new ones, and they do not come entirely from us; especially if others see them too, they are suggested by the work itself. The work, we may say, sets up a number of "sub-scripts" for us as we circle around it, listen to it, or read through it; it indicates to us ways in which its different parts or phases are to be related to one another. These sub-scripts are what Heidegger calls "significances" (*BT*, 87) and our encounter with the work of art is a process of coming to terms with the new significance created in it. Understanding a work of art is thus the building of a Heideggerian "way." This version of letting-be, in turn, is what Heidegger means by "preserving" the work, and the result for him here is that "the proper way to preserve the work is co-created and prescribed only and exclusively by the work" (*OWA*, 68).

But how, we may ask, is this radical newness possible? Heidegger claims, in "The Origin of the Work of Art," to be talking only about great art (*OWA*, 40); but is he even talking about that? Or is he attributing to the work of art magical properties of novelty and innovation that he himself has invented?

To see this, we must return to the beginning of the essay. I noted that Heideggerian "destructuring" begins from the failure of preconceptualities; all our ways of conceiving of the thing must be shown to be inadequate. "The Origin of the Work of Art," true to this, begins by discussing a number of ways in which things in general have been thought of in the philosophical tradition. One of these ways concerns form and matter. According to this view, which the philosophical tradition has recurrently applied not only to artworks but to everything (*OWA*, 27, 29), a thing is formed matter (*ein geformter Stoff*; *OWA*, 26); in this, "the form determines the arrangement of the matter" (*OWA*, 28): it exercises over the matter what I call "dispositive" power. The matter of the thing, like an Aristotelian housewife or slave, is better and more suitable insofar as it does not resist this; at the limit, this passivity becomes matter's total occlusion or "perishing" (*Untergehen*; *OWA*, 46).

This Aristotelian ontology, however ancient and prestigious it may be, fails to capture the work of art, which "does not cause the material to disappear, but rather causes it to come forth for the very first time" (*OWA*, 46). In a work of art, the unique qualities of its materiality—its media—are not overcome but highlighted. It is part of the business of a statue to bring forth the striations in its stone or the grains in its wood, of a painting to bring forth the colors in its pigments, of a poem to show the semantic, as well as the auditory, beauty of its words. The work of art treats matter not as something passive and receptive but as something dynamic and configurating: "The rock comes to bear and rest and so becomes rock; metals come to glitter and shimmer, colors to glow, tones to sing, the word to speak" (*OWA*, 46).

Matter so experienced should not, Heidegger goes on to say, even be called "matter"; his term for it is "earth." Since every work of art is realized in unique earth, the work is itself unique; the significances that it sets up—the sub-scripts which the work of art institutes for us as we circle around it or listen to it—thus derive their uniqueness from the earth itself in which they come to be.

Heidegger has now returned to Aristotle's hylomorphic ontology, in which matter maintains its own nature as against form; indeed, he goes so far as to call their relation one of "strife" (*OWA*, 49–50). It is this strife which gives the work of art a "resolute foundation" (*Entscheidendes*) and keeps it from being, for example, a mere play of whimsy (*OWA*, 49). True, Heidegger does not *know* that he has returned to Aristotle: he reads back into Aristotle the medieval view of matter as entirely receptive of form, which I considered in Chapter 4 (Heidegger 1998c, 183–230). More importantly, his return is critical: earth is not merely something which resists form, as matter does for Aristotle, but something whose resistance to form is the point of the whole enterprise. The form's action on the matter in a work of art is, therefore, not geared to materializing the form itself; it is supposed to bring the matter forth in its own uniqueness. It is as if an acorn, instead of using the nutrients in the soil to grow into an oak, somehow highlighted them and made them into enhanced versions of what they were before.

One aspect in which Heidegger does remain true to Aristotle's view of matter, as well as to later views of it, is that matter—or earth, for Heidegger—is inscrutable:

> [Earth] shows itself only when it remains undisclosed and unexplained. Earth thus shatters every attempt to penetrate into it. . . . The earth appears as itself only when it is perceived and preserved as that which is by nature undisclosable, that which shrinks from every disclosure and keeps itself closed up. (*OWA*, 47; my translation)

The work of art thus shows us something that science, forgetful of its origins, cannot: that the meaningful world in which we live is grounded on something entirely different, on earth—on something "not mastered, concealed, confusing" (*OWA*, 55). By disclosing this aspect of earth, the work of art not only sets up a world but also instigates *Weltzerfall*, the collapse of world, because in its newness "what went before is refuted in its [claim to] exclusive reality by the work" (*OWA*, 75). Our old ways of knowing and doing turn out to be insufficient to comprehend what we are now experiencing.

Because truth consists in the strife between world and earth, and earth is itself concealed, there always belongs to truth "the reservoir of the not-yet-revealed, the un-uncovered, in the sense of concealment" (*OWA*, 60). Earth, then, is not something that exists somewhere "out there," sending new significance which is presented in the work of art. Rather, it is futural in character: the domain of the not-yet. As such, it presents us only with—questions. These questions mark the places where the what-is question has no answer: where thought is fractured because "word breaks off" (see Heidegger 1971a). Thought, even rational thought, which is susceptible to fractures is "fragile."

The Fragility of Language

Because the work of art in the Heideggerian sense is something wholly and indeed unutterably new, we confront it without words. The successive questions that it raises ask, most fundamentally, what it is that we are experiencing: how can we formulate in our language the new significances with which the work of art is presenting us? The questions can lead us, if we do not rush to impose our accustomed ways of thinking by answering them too quickly, to new words which will designate the new meanings that have emerged for us. These new words, in turn, are not wholly our inventions. They adapt the current resources of our language in order to name significances presented to us, for the first time, by the work of art. In so doing, they are most fundamentally to be called operations of language itself: "Language, by naming beings for the first time, first brings beings to word and to appearance. Only this naming nominates beings from out of their being" (*OWA*, 73; emphasis altered).

The general picture is this: A work of art, or indeed any radically new configuration of earth, leads us to make connections we have not made before. Some of these new connections need to be put into words and shared with others. Those who respond to this need already have, as human beings, a language with a set of semantic resources, resources which have now proved inadequate; the

task is to reshape this inheritance so that it can begin to capture the new connections. The language as it already exists thus contains suggestions as to what
the new words should be, and the work of art is an encounter of language with
earth. What we regard as poetic creativity is not the spinning forth of ideas from
heads but "a drawing-up, as of water from a spring" (*OWA*, 76; my translation).

The work of art, as an entirely new constellation of meaning, thus requires
that it be experienced and talked of in new and different ways. Such speech
institutes new forms of speech, of behavior, and indeed of human relationship
(*OWA*, 66–68). It thus refutes "what went before in its exclusive reality" (*OWA*,
75).[11] It is in this way that the work of art, founded on a primal happening of
truth, is able itself to ground human community. Community of this type is essential to the work of art: "Just as a work cannot be without being created but is
essentially in need of creators, so what is created cannot itself come into being
without those who preserve it" (*OWA*, 66).

The creation/preservation of a work of art is thus intrinsically communal; it
is on our experience of the work of art that all "being-for-and-with-one-another"
is grounded (*OWA*, 67, 71).[12] Bringing together a group of people in this way,
the work of art grounds true human community; as Otto Pöggeler, citing Heidegger's then-unpublished *Contributions to Philosophy*, puts it: "If we must talk
of a 'people' at all, then this is never something given (either as race or as class),
but something that comes to be through the hearing of a common call."[13]

A community grounded on the call of a work of art is not a community
grounded on birth: it is not a race or nation. Indeed, as new and different, the
work of art tends to cut across such preexisting communities, carrying members of them away, in Heidegger's language, to unaccustomed places (see *OWA*,
35). Further, if the work of art opens up its own unique world, it is not dependent on the shared world (if any) of its audience. As Heidegger said in a Nietzsche lecture of 1937, "those who truly understand are always those who come
from afar, from their own ground and soil, who bring much with them in order
to transform much" (Heidegger 1961, 1:404). Heidegger's authentic community
begins to sound rather like Augustine's City of God, composed of those who—
wherever they find themselves in the secular cities of the world—"live by faith,"
by responding to the call of God (Augustine 1950, 3–4, 477, 534).

The hammer blows under which linguistic reason modifies itself no longer
come, in "The Origin of the Work of Art," from the state. The Nazis were hardly
interested in Heidegger's "questioning" version of science—they wanted answers,
and they already had plenty of them, in the form of pseudoscientific racial theo-

ries. Rebuffed, Heidegger abandoned science and relocated primordial questioning to art. Art so understood requires, as reflection did for Hegel, the reshaping of reason from a set of hard-and-fast propositions, "chained by adamant and steel" (*Gorgias* 509) into a set of words that is itself continually being reshaped. But for Hegel, the reshaping was a smooth development of newly defined words from older ones; for Heidegger it is more radical in two senses.

First, the work of art for Heidegger does not merely rework reason but fractures it, in that the new meanings it offers cannot be reached from the old; the "adaptation" of old words to convey new meanings is not a transparent dialectical procedure but is itself obscure. The new significances those words are supposed to capture are not worked up by means of "scientific" reflection on experience but come from a confrontation with the unfathomability of earth itself.

Second, Hegelian reflection on experience is inevitably, "in our day" (i.e., his—but ours as well), specialized. It is the fruit of a society which has organized itself to be able to carry out disciplined investigations of all aspects of life and to bring the results of those investigations to what we have seen is the "central switchyard" of philosophy. For Heidegger, preserving works of art is not the fruit of society but its ground. The struggle with earth that produces new meanings is thus not the prerogative of credentialed experts; it can reside, for example, in the day-by-day, month-by-month, year-by-year struggle of a woman with a field. It does remain, however, the prerogative of greatness: in focusing only on what he calls "great art" (*OWA*, 40), Heidegger reveals that if he is no fascist or Nazi, he is nonetheless an elitist.

We are still, then, a long way from where we want to be: equipped with philosophical tools for understanding the speaking of matter. In order to get there, to a new Enlightenment, we must make use of both Hegelian and Heideggerian modes of reason. To see why this is so and how it can work, we must return (in the next chapter) to Kant's account of imagination, already discussed in Chapter 4.

Coda: Heideggerian Art and Heidegger's Politics

The work of art is not, Heidegger tells us, the only primordial happening of truth. Another one, according to the essay, is the "deed which grounds a state" (*OWA*, 62). It seems that if science has lost its luster for Heidegger, the state has not; that instead of sharing the fate of science, the state has simply been joined on the ontological pinnacle by art.

But we must be careful. Heidegger cannot be saying that the state has the "primordial" status of a work of art; indeed, he is careful not to do so, referring not to the *Staat* but, awkwardly, to the *staatsgründende Tat*. The reason for this, I suggest, is that in order to operate like a work of art, the state would have to open up a world; and opening up a world, providing overarching new scripts and significances, is not something that any political arrangement can do. It involves, for example, setting out explicitly the "paths and relations in which birth and death, disaster and blessing, victory and disgrace, endurance and decline" give form to humanity (*OWA*, 42). And these cannot be understood as primordially grounded in—or opened up by—political structures. Consider death: if I contract cancer and die at the age of thirty, it is a tragedy no matter what political system I live under. Political systems may affect such basic happenings—they may "consolidate" some paths—but they do not first open them. Thus, when Hegel makes philosophy the outcome of a specific sort of political organization—the modern state—he relegates it to malleability as a certain sort of consolidation of what has been formulated elsewhere (*PI*, 302–304). There I think it should stay—except in Heideggerian moments.

So we must, apparently, distinguish the act which grounds a state from the consolidated state itself. The former opens up a world and the latter does not. Like science for Heidegger—a category which now implicitly includes Hegelian "science" and philosophy—the state itself takes its stand within the domain opened up by the state-founding deed. It is from there that its legitimacy must come.

The Nazi state legitimated itself as the rule of the racially superior. The fascist state legitimated itself as the expression and enforcement of the nation—the shared values and customs of the people. The democratic state legitimates itself by the individuals themselves, choosing their rulers. Other states legitimate themselves by the will of God. Can any of these principles legitimate the state for Heidegger? We cannot ask the state itself, its propagandists, or its theorists; for if the state is like science, then for the later Heidegger it is forgetful of its origins.[14] The "deed which founds a state" is not itself a state; political legitimation leads out of politics into another domain. If we are to understand this domain the way Heidegger understands art, it is a domain in which a political order is first opened up as a realm of new significance, grounded on the unique dynamism of earth.

If "legitimacy" is rationally transparent authority, then Heidegger's understanding denies full legitimacy to any institution. Indeed, in "The Origin of the Work of Art," earth, as inherently undisclosable, not only denies legitimacy *to* the state—it tends to withdraw it *from* the state; for earth, in its undisclosability, "tends always to draw the world into itself and keep it there" (*OWA*, 49). Moreover, if our response to the work of art is, like science in the Rectoral Address, a questioning stance, it is not one which somehow transforms itself into service to the state; for questioning is not obedience. The unfortunate *Wissensdienst*, the science in service to the state, of the Rectoral Address now disappears. For the questions opened up by a work of art, if indeed they go to the heart of world, call into question things more basic than the state—and with them, the state itself. The work of art is thus implacably subversive of the state (see *PI*, 140).

The distinction between the state-founding deed and the state itself yields what Otto Pöggeler tells us is the context for one of Heidegger's more infamous rectorial comments (Pöggeler 1988, 31–32). "Nicht Lehrsätze und 'Ideen' seien die Regeln eures Seins," the Freiburg student paper reported Heidegger saying to a meeting of young Nazis; "der Führer selbst und allein ist die heutige und zukünftige deutsche Wirklichkeit und ihr Gesetz."[15] The phrase "Lehrsätze und 'Ideen'" refers, we are told, to the Nazi Party program; Heidegger is trying to situate Hitler on a higher and more basic level than that on which the Nazi Party itself stands. The Führer, not the Party, embodies the "state-grounding deed" and so is the primal reality.[16]

When we look at Heidegger's Nazi commitment in terms of these levels, we see that he himself recognizes that it cannot be to the Nazi Party. What he did not see, or even want to see, is that it cannot be to Hitler either. For any political leader—even a Führer—who claims absolute justification for his policies is, like science on Heidegger's later view, forgetting the role of earth in the grounding of his world, that is, in the deed which founded his state. Heidegger's philosophy, then, is—by the time of the treatment of earth in "The Origin of the Work of Art," anyway—nonracist and antitotalitarian and so cannot be called Nazi.

Even at the lowest point of the Rectoral Address, Heidegger does not descend all the way to Nazism as I have characterized it. Racism, which, as we saw Pöggeler point out, is incompatible with Heidegger's philosophy (though not, perhaps, with Heidegger himself), does not seem to find its way into the text. While Heidegger expressed viciously anti-Semitic views at the time of his membership in the Nazi Party, as Faye and others have documented, the Rectoral Address itself does not exhibit them. Moreover, the fascism expressed in it is of an unusual type.

One wishes that dutiful Nazis such as Adolf Eichmann and Rudolf Höß had read, with any intelligence, the Nazi Heidegger: "All leadership must allow its followers their own strength. Every following, however, contains resistance within itself" (*R*, 18). The only way to derive a fascist relation of state and nation from the conceptual economy of the work of art would be, against what I have just indicated, to take the nation, as a preexistent community, to be for Heidegger the "earth" on which the state reposes. But even the nation as earth could never sanction the state as its own expression: earth is precisely what always escapes full expression and undermines whatever expression is achieved. And the state, in that case, would not enforce the earth: it would, like a work of art, struggle with it. Heidegger, then, cannot any longer conflate state and nation. He is no fascist.

Heidegger has thus rejected not only fascism but nationalism. The original human community is not the nation, still less the nation organized into a state. Rather, it is the community of preservers of works of art, called from regions that may be very disparate from one another geographically, racially, and religiously. If such a community became permanent, we may speculate, people might be born to it at later stages; it might even become a nation and organize itself as a state. But then it would no longer be primordial and would be exposed to the kind of *Weltzerfall* that art, for Heidegger, can instigate.

Merely to say of someone that he is not a Nazi, or a fascist, or a nationalist is a long way from saying he is a good person. Even if he escapes these horrors, Heidegger remains something genuinely repellent: an unequivocal elitist. Some people—a few—respond better to works of art than others; some, even fewer, are even capable of producing them.

Elitism, though never pleasant, can be innocuous. Some people play basketball better than others; only a very few would be welcome additions to, say, the Los Angeles Lakers. But Heidegger's elitism is more vicious than that, because the Lakers do not claim to be the primordial and authentic human community, providing meaning and language itself to less favored groups. That is what Heidegger's "preservers" are and do, however, and so for him some people are, somehow, better equipped to join in the primordial and authentic human community than are others. This, to be sure, is not Nazi, fascist, or nationalist. It is merely odious.

Heidegger's Nazi engagement of 1933–34 was, then, either a conscious repudiation of his own philosophical principles, or it was the reflection of defects in his earlier thought which encouraged him to Nazism. I have argued for the latter view, here and elsewhere (*PI*, 119–128; *MO*, 1–13). By 1936, when "The Origin of the Work of Art" was published, his thought had assumed stances which are, when we penetrate his prose, unmistakably anti-Nazi.

But what, for example, about the infamous remarks in the 1935 *Introduction to Metaphysics* about the "inner truth and greatness" of the Nazi movement, which Heidegger left in place in the 1953 re-edition (Heidegger 1959b, 199)? What about Karl Löwith's report that in 1936 Heidegger was still wearing his swastika button and saying that his support of Hitler was undiminished (Löwith 1986, 57–58)? What about the 1942 remarks on the "historical uniqueness" of Nazism referred to earlier? What if someone should tell me that Heidegger's lectures, pouring forth in the *Gesamtausgabe*, are chauvinistic; or that the rumors are true and the Heidegger Archive contains, in its secret recesses, reams of Nazi drivel vomited up by Heidegger in the forties, fifties, sixties, seventies? I would be horrified, as I have so often been when learning of new depths to Heidegger's treachery and sordidness. But I would not retract anything of what I have said here, concerning "The Origin of the Work of Art." For that essay is, I am persuaded, itself a primordial happening of truth. As Heidegger wrote about such happenings—amended by me:

> The more solitarily the [essay] stands on its own, the more clearly it seems to cut all ties to [its author's life] . . . the more essentially is the extraordinary thrust to the surface. . . . The truth that discloses itself in the essay can never be proved or derived from what went before. What went before [and came after] is refuted in its exclusive reality by the [essay]. (*OWA*, 66, 75)

How this relates to the Nazi Heidegger remains—a question.

CHAPTER 7

DIALECTICS, THERMODYNAMICS, AND THE END OF CRITIQUE

Philosophy's crisis, the set of widening separations I traced in the Introduction between philosophers and the larger culture, each other, and philosophy itself, stems most directly from philosophy's modern allegiance to the Enlightenment. In Chapters 2 and 3, however, I argued that it in fact has much deeper historical roots. Philosophy's investment, even today, in ancient models of being has recurrently allied it with the oppressors rather than the oppressed; and together with this has gone a view of reason itself which has kept philosophy from responding to the speaking of matter. Many of the topics I have discussed in this book—philosophical themes as diverse as Aristotelian *karteria*, Cartesian doubt, Kantian transcendentality, the Reichenbachian distinction between discovery and justification, and the Quinean omission of temporal information—have in fact served as devices for keeping philosophers from hearing the speaking of matter; there are, of course, many more. And yet such speaking is omnipresent. It comes forth not only when the world's oppressed demand to be heard but in the oppressors themselves—including philosophers—when their matter vibrates sympathetically with the sounds of the oppressed.

The only solution is to incorporate into philosophy itself precautions and techniques which allow matter to speak freely, for it cannot be heard with philosophy's usual tools. This means gaining a new and broader concept of reason. The resources now at hand for this, explored in Chapters 4, 5, and 6, are Hegelian dialectical reflection, Heideggerian questioning, and the Kantian doctrine of the imagination, which will show us how the other two can fit together.

What they fit together into is a philosophical practice which I prefer to call "reshaping" or "situating" rather than "critique" because it goes beyond merely pointing out the defects and limits of the phenomena it treats and in fact engages an activity which is far more widespread: locating ourselves in time, identifying where we have been and asking where we might go (see *RR*, 57–103). This constitutes, I suggest, a critical practice in its own right, which I will introduce by comparing it with the more familiar versions of critique that descend from Kant.

Kant, Universality, and Critique

Philosophically speaking, the twentieth century was largely a Kantian one. Kantian thought, of a sort anyway, was revived in the southern part of the German-speaking lands and in Marburg late in the nineteenth century, presenting itself successfully as an epistemologically correct alternative to the perceived metaphysical excesses of German Idealism.[1] From there, in various forms, it came to play a dominant role in Western philosophy in the twentieth century.

But it often played that role undercover. Husserl, for example, claimed that when young, "I was always very far removed from Kantianism and German Idealism." Nonetheless, his later effort to eliminate "psychologism" from philosophy in favor of an investigation of formal structures of consciousness was, as he notes in his *Logical Investigations*, Kantian in inspiration.[2] Frege, though he wrote little about Kant, helped to found analytical philosophy on the basis of an antipsychologistic gesture similar to Husserl's (see Prauss 1983). The Kantian emphasis was a lively one in subsequent continental philosophy: even Jacques Derrida, in Rodolphe Gasché's view, was a sort of "transcendental philosopher."[3] Logical positivism, too, in spite of its empiricist credentials, was on at least one essential point—the existence and limitations of a priori knowledge—thoroughly Kantian.[4] Finally, the "second generation" of Frankfurt critical theorists, in spite of its Marxist veneer, remains, as Raymond Geuss (1989) has argued, basically neo-Kantian:

> In a sense the second generation marks a return to the kind of Neo-Kantian philosophy the critical theorists of the 1930's were reacting against. . . . In the work of Habermas and his associates . . . the Kantian themes of finding a fixed universal framework for theorizing, giving firm foundations for knowledge claims of various sorts, and investigating the conditions of the possibility of various human activities, structure much of the discussion. (Geuss, 1998, 727–728)

A complete answer to the question of what these various "Kantian" strains have in common with each other would be difficult to give, and I will simply note two of their shared traits. First, they all begin, like Kant, with a gesture of dismissal which moves the philosopher from the messy, changing, and uncertain empirical world to a purer domain where philosophy can begin. Kant called this domain "transcendental," Husserl calls it "eidetic," Frege calls it "logical," Derrida (on Gasché's reading) calls it "infrastructural," and Habermas calls it the "structural presuppositions of communicative action"; but the point is to get to it, whatever it is called. The second common feature among these philosophers is that having made that opening move, they find themselves in possession of what Geuss calls a "fixed universal framework for theorizing," whether this be understood as Husserlian *eidē*, the (idealized) scientific procedures of the logical positivists, Derridean infrastructures, or the structures of communicative action which Habermas seeks to find and vindicate. They then use that knowledge as Plato used the Theory of Forms and as Aristotle used the ousia ontology: to understand and justify the world when it works according to their views and to criticize it when it does not.

A convinced pluralist (such as myself) might hold that such a widespread and little-acknowledged streak of Kantianism is not a good thing and wonder if it is not time to try, once again, to get *beyond* Kant. I will attempt this here by locating a mistake that I think all these versions of Kantianism have made and to explore what it would mean to stop making it. I will focus here on social philosophy and on the most consistent neo-Kantian currently in that field, the "second-generation" Frankfurt theorist Jürgen Habermas.

As I suggested above, all these versions of Kantianism (with the exception of Derrida, whose assignment to "Kantianism" is the most tendentious) share the view that philosophy should consist in precisely what, as Geuss notes, Adorno and other critical theorists had rejected: "a *closed* system of interconnected propositions that rested upon a purportedly *firm* foundation and claimed *universal* validity" (Geuss 1998, 727–728). "Closure," "firmness," and "universality" all point in the same direction: toward the view that philosophy rests upon something that is, or can be taken to be, permanent and unchanging. In the case of a system that is "closed" and of a foundation that is "firm," the appeal to permanence is clear. But even "universality" has today forsaken its ancient Aristotelian meaning ("predicable of many things"; *On Interpretation* 7.17a39) and, as Saul Kripke has noted for the allied notion of "a priori," come to signify something akin to "necessary" (Kripke 1980, 260–261). The necessity is usually of a rigidly Kantian type, according to which a sentence is "universally" true if it is true at all times (*CPR* B, 184) or, even more inclusively, in all possible worlds. Such "rigid universality," as I will call it, thus conveys atemporal truth claims. Adopting it for critical thought opens philosophy up to the paradoxes of Enlightenment I discussed in the Introduction.

Allen Wood has put the "situating" alternative to this in a way which brings out Kant's contrast with Hegel:

> If human self-understanding is always growing, and if the action based on it is always modifying and deepening the nature of human beings, then [we] must confess that our present self-conception is inadequate, in ways that we can never hope to repair, for deciding the good of future human beings. (Wood 1990, 34)

For Hegel, as Wood recognizes, this is an essential ethical insight; for Kant it is a counsel of despair. In Kant's view, a moral theory which cannot decide the good of future human beings is not a "moral" theory at all; its failure to apply to some people, even unborn ones, means that it does not recognize human equality. I discussed Kant's problems with such equality in the Introduction; for the moment, we can note that his espousal of it requires a moral theory which holds in exactly the same way for all human beings, including not only those alive today but those of the past and future as well. Such a moral theory must then be, in Geuss's terms, both "closed" and "firm"—or, in Kant's, it must rest upon "fully secured foundations, established forever." Only if critique is rigidly universal in this way, in fact, can it ground metaphysics as what Kant thinks it should be: a science "brought to such completion and fixity as to be in need of no further change or be subject to any augmentation by new discoveries."[5] Insofar as they remain true to this, later Kantian versions of social critique, such as that of Habermas, thus claim to offer the Big Three: systematic closure, firm foundations, and universal validity.

I do not wish to maintain that such rigid universality is always illusory; that would be self-defeating. But claiming that it applies to the foundations of critical theory itself *is*, I think, mistaken. The main problem is that in order for the various versions of such Kantian social critique to get going, two sorts of thing have to be viewed as static (if not eternal). One is the standards or norms by which we (i.e., Kantians) seek to judge practices and structures of the social world; the other is those practices and structures themselves.

The norms by which Kant's critical philosophy judges concrete historical phenomena are provided by his account of the faculties. His critical question with respect to metaphysics, for example, is whether its various practices conform to the true division of labor among the mind's cognitive powers. That division is given in turn by the a priori principles of the various faculties. These, being a priori, cannot be overthrown by new experiences and are taken to constitute a firm, closed set exhibiting rigid universality. The mind is itself a set of such necessary structures, in place for all time (see *CPR* B, 3–10, 89) and the truths of critique themselves are also necessary—that is, true for all time.

Metaphysics itself also has an unchanging nature. In the preface to the first edition of the *Critique of Pure Reason*, Kant concedes that metaphysics has taken many forms over the course of its history, ancient and modern. But all of them, we read, have been classifiable into the firm, closed opposition of dogmatism and skepticism. And this makes metaphysics, behind all its surface diversity, a single theater of "endless conflicts" (*CPR* A, viii).

The reason why metaphysics has to have an unchanging nature before Kantian critique can be applied to it is not that stability itself is problematic. It is that Kant's critical procedure involves bringing to bear a set of critical standards which, being destined to hold for all time, are formulated and legitimated without regard to the specific realities to which they are to be applied. Kant's critique of metaphysics, for example, is designed to put metaphysicians out of business forever. It is thus, of necessity, too general to be applied directly to passing practitioners such as Aristotle, Aquinas, Leibniz, and Wolff, and we do not find detailed discussions of them in Kant. Fortunately, in Kant's view, such discussions are not needed, because all metaphysicians are exponents of a single, unchanging enterprise: that of issuing cognitive claims about nonsensible entities.

Such rigid universality is more than just a goal for Kant. We saw in the Introduction, and now see again, that he believed he had actually attained it; and, indeed, the very beginning of his philosophy posits that attaining it is possible. Kant's whole doctrine of the categories, for example, begins from the supposition that a sentence such as "Every event has a cause" is *logically* distinct from one such as "Every event we have learned about up to now has had a cause."[6] The latter claims to be true everywhere for a given period of time, ending now. The former claims to be necessary, that is, true always: no rational person has ever dissented from it and none ever will. We actually do, in Kant's view, make such rigidly universal, that is, atemporally true, claims; and the principles in virtue of which we make them (the categories of the understanding) reveal the categorial apparatus of the human mind. That apparatus must therefore be in force as long as the judgments are valid, that is, for all time.

These claims ran into major trouble, and in short order. In 1801, just two years after Kant's run-in with Fichte, Schiller published his *On the Aesthetic Education of Man in a Series of Letters* (Schiller 1982). In them he raised the question of whether the cognitive faculties themselves, even if presently shared by all humans, can be anything more than the results of an historical development. Taken up by Hegel and then by Marx, Nietzsche, and Heidegger—as well as by thousands who have thought in their wake—this possibility forms the most serious challenge that Kantianism has faced, for it means that rigid universality, that is, truth for all time, cannot be achieved—even on a "transcendental" level.[7]

It is in opposition to Schiller, Hegel, Marx, Nietzsche, Heidegger, and the rest that Habermas seeks to put critical theory in possession of a "fixed, universal framework" of standards by which to judge historical phenomena.[8] His way of doing this is to claim that all utterances always claim truth, appropriateness to social norms in force, and sincerity as an expression of the speaker's state of mind. The types of communication actually present in a given society can then be evaluated as to whether they conform to these norms (see Habermas 1970). The aims and goals of Habermas's argumentation, however, change over time. In "What Is Universal Pragmatics?" (Habermas 1979), they sound standardly Kantian: the three claims (actually four, at that stage) are conditions of the possibility of speech now and forever, much as the twelve categories are for Kant conditions of the possibility of experience. Like Kant's own claims, this generated an enormous critical literature, which I will not go into here. Suffice it to say that in the later *Theory of Communicative Action* (Habermas 1984–1987), the ambitions are reduced: the universality claims are raised again but no longer with a view to actually vindicating them.

Rather, Habermas now recognizes that we are all in particular situations which condition our language and so our very thought. The whole point of critical theory is then to show us when such situations need to be transcended. The only way to do that communicatively, Habermas claims, is to raise a claim for something's holding *beyond* our current situation. As Habermas now puts it,

> the theory of communicative action aims at that moment of unconditionedness which is built into the conditions of consensus-formation by criticizable validity claims—*as claims* these transcend all spatial and temporal, all provincial limitations of the context of the moment. (Habermas 1984–1987, 2:399–400)

Without situation-transcending validity claims, we cannot get out of our "provincial limitations." This means, however, that our current context, or situation, has some degree of stability; otherwise it would pass away of its own accord, and we would not need the claims. It is not, to be sure, that Habermas thinks that social formations never change: the very title of his first path-breaking book, *Structural Transformation in the Public Sphere* (Habermas 1991), shows that he does not. Rather, the problem is that for his version of critique to work, its objects must be treatable as if they were unchanging.

In effect, Habermas has moved from the center of Kant's philosophy back to its beginning: from an approach in which temporally universal claims are (supposedly) *proven* to one in which they are merely *made*. For the earlier Habermas, "what raises us out of nature is the only thing whose nature we can know" (Habermas 1971, 314), that is, language—a suggestion which raised the hope of a critical account (in Kant's sense) of the nature of language. For the later Habermas, knowledge of "the nature of language" is not necessary; all we need do is *claim* to know it, or anything else, and the argument begins. In the earlier Habermas, the validity claims were necessary conditions of our linguistic activity, in Kant's sense of "necessary": attributable to all speakers at all times. For the later Habermas, they are practically necessary: the point of them is to get us out of our current situation by forcing us to consider what may lie beyond it. The validity claims do not lead, even indirectly, to knowledge; but they do enable us to transcend our current situation.

Kant, to be sure, holds that temporal universality claims are not only made but can sometimes be justified; Habermas has avoided that set of problems. But even as Habermas backtracks he continues, like Kant, to see critique as requiring two sorts of static entity. One is the norms by which we seek to criticize social practices and structures. These must claim, if not actually possess, temporal universality; and they must do so, we saw, because those practices and structures themselves also have a static nature in which, without the intervention of universality, we are caught. There is, Habermas thinks, no other hope.

Another Hope

Foucault, I fear, would agree with Habermas—at least in his "early" and "middle" periods, on which I focus here.[9] His answer to those who asked how he could engage in the critique of social realities without appeal to some sort of universal or necessary norm was to abjure critique altogether and to insist that his project is really one of "analysis," which has what he calls "the uncertain status of a description" (Foucault 1972, 206). When he locates himself with respect to the Kantian "critical" tradition, then, it is with reference to Kant's own sense of "critique" as "an analysis of the conditions in which certain relations of subject to object are formed or modified, insofar as they are constitutive of possible knowledge" (Foucault 1994, 4:632).

As we saw in Chapter 3, however, Foucault's a priori is not timeless but rather an "historical *a priori*" (Foucault 1972, 127) which does not assume "the existence of immobile forms" (*FR*, 78). The mutable forms of the historical a priori, because they are mutable, cannot convey fixed natures. They offer us, as we saw, "not a timeless or essential secret, but the secret that [things] have no essence or their essence was fabricated by a piecemeal fashioning from alien forms" (*FR*, 78). One accident, however, is as criticizable as another. At this point, there are no standards by which to distinguish social formations which are defective from those which are not. So the underlying problem for both Foucault and Habermas is that social formations must have a stable nature in order to be criticized. For Foucault, they would have to be nonaccidental, that is, temporally unified; they are not, so he abjures critique. For Habermas, they must have enough stability that we can be trapped in them. Accepting this, Habermas must go on and assign a stable nature to reason itself; for otherwise critique becomes no more than a passing viewpoint on a fixed reality which may well simply outlast it. Stabilizing both reason and reality, however, leads to the paradoxes of Enlightenment I discussed in the Introduction. If, however, we reject the stability of reason, then we must reject the stability of things as well; they both become, as Foucault claims, mere accidents. What, then, happens to critique?

What if there were an intellectual project which had critical potential vis-à-vis current social realities and practices but was neither critique in a Kantian sense nor Foucaldian description and was malleable enough that it did not require even the making or denial, much less the refutation or validation, of rigid universality claims?

In this chapter and the next, I will offer the outlines of such a project. The first part of such "critical" activity is dialectical, and the rest of this chapter will be spent rescuing dialectics from the distortions inflicted on it after Hegel—not so much by Marx as by Stalinist understandings of him and by the vehement rejections of those distortions on the part of philosophers opposed to Marx. The following and final chapter will introduce Heideggerian questioning as a necessary complement to dialectics and briefly discuss one kind of reality upon which such critical activity can profitably be directed: public language. The account of questioning will rely on the discussion of Heidegger in Chapter 6, and the account of dialectics on the view of Hegel put forth in Chapter 5. The way the two can be combined will draw on the discussion of Kantian imagination in Chapter 4.

Rescuing dialectics begins from the plain fact that, contrary to Habermas, universality claims are not necessary in order for us to transcend our current historical situation. Consider in this regard the second law of thermodynamics, which postulates the inexorable increase of entropy in an isolated system. When the system in question is the entire universe, this results eventually either in heat death or in some sort of cosmic collapse brought about by gravitational pull. In either case, all structures disappear, including social structures. Capitalism (and socialism), patriarchy (and matriarchy), racism (and humanism), theocracy (and democracy)—indeed all the social evils (and goods) we find around us—are therefore doomed.

Those who have fought international capitalism for the last 150 years need not despair, then. In the long run, it will disappear. Not only that: it is already marching toward its doom, as each new event increases entropy in the universe of which that economic system is a part. Generally speaking, then, transcending "provincial limitations" is hardly a problem that needs universal claims to solve it. If you don't like your current situation, all you have to do is wait around. Eventually it will pass away—or you will.

Which will happen first we do not know from the second law of thermodynamics; it is too general to tell us. It merely says that the entropy in the system will increase, that is, that information and structure will be lost. In order to identify which structures will be lost first and what intermediate structures will replace them on the road to absolute entropy, we would need the familiar accoutrements of scientific explanation: initial conditions and covering laws.

I am advancing these considerations not as giving us a metaphor for or analogy to critical theory but as indicating a relevant fact for it. For it changes the basic game. The point is no longer somehow to introduce change into a static system which, without intervention, will simply remain as it is; for nothing *simply* remains as it is. The point now is to find and administer changes that are already underway. This, in fact, is how Marx sees the situation; in the passage I quoted in Chapter 5 and will quote again below, he urges us to take the "transient nature" of capitalism into account—its "inevitable breaking up." This does not mean adopting the kind of vulgar Heracleitean view of social reality I identified in that chapter, according to which reality is in constant flux in all respects. But it does mean recognizing that *panta ta politika rhei*: all social structures will pass away, and probably long before the universe reaches heat death or cosmic collapse.

But that may not be nearly soon enough. The second law of thermodynamics is perfectly consistent with the idea that social structures and practices, which are not isolated systems, can import energy from elsewhere and buy themselves stability for long periods of time. Enrique Dussel has argued that modern capitalism does exactly this—by providing itself with generation after generation of new workers and by exploiting new parts of the planet.[10] But the argument's burden has nonetheless changed. Social systems are, after all, at bottom physical systems; and it has to be shown, in the face of the universal move toward entropy, that a given social system is able to import energy from elsewhere. Even when such a burden has been discharged, the borrowing will, like all physical things, have to end at some point, and I think we are entitled to assume at least the following: that any social structure or practice, even if not changing in all respects, is at any time likely to be changing in some respect. The first problem of "critique" is to find out where.

The Kantian version of critical theory as developed in the second generation of the Frankfurt School—that is, primarily by Habermas—is not geared to this. It can tell us, for example, that patriarchy is evil because it denies women the chance to speak. But that very judgment presupposes the stability of patriarchy: if patriarchy were changing and dynamic, it would be too slippery to evaluate, or even (contrary to Foucault) to describe. Or at least (for, I insist, I am not a vulgar Heracleitean) those parts of it that are changing and dynamic would be too slippery. The proper tool to cope with this is not "critique" in a Kantian sense but dialectics.

What Is Dialectics, Really?

Few concepts in philosophy have been as elusive and fraught as the nature of dialectics. In Plato's *Philebus*, dialectics is a gift of the gods and the source of the highest knowledge (*Philebus* 16c, 57e). For Aristotle, it is arguing not from first principles but merely from received opinions (see *Metaphysics* 2.1.995b23). Kant brutally reduces this to the dissimulation of ignorance (*CPR* B, 85–86). Hegel, Marx, and many others add to the conceptual stew, and it is unsurprising that by the beginning of the 1980s, Jaako Hintikka, at a symposium on Hegelian dialectics and formal logic, counted over twenty different senses given to "dialectics" by the participants alone (Hintikka 1981, 109–110). Let us return to the classics, and to Marx's definition of "dialectics" as thinking which

> regards every historically developed social form as in fluid movement, and
> hence takes into account its transient nature not less than its momentary exis-

tence; . . . it lets nothing impose upon it, and is in its essence critical and revolutionary. (Marx 1906, 26)

That is the sense in which I intend "dialectics" here (and one in which its alliance with thermodynamics becomes evident). True, Marx himself fell short of it, since he anchored dialectics in class struggle. This led him to take the physical layout of the modern factory as an unchanging point around which revolutions would swirl and to miss the diversity of people needing liberation, of mechanisms of oppression, and of strategies for liberation. But his characterization here moves dialectics away from some of the more absurd portrayals that have been given of it.[11] For dialectics conceived in Marx's way, ~p follows p not logically but in time. On the level of the universe, this means merely that all nontrivial sentences will become untrue—if not upon heat death or cosmic collapse, when there will be nothing to refer to, then sometime before.

But what does it mean to see something concrete as being "in time"? Plato suggested the answer (at *Theaetetus* 152d). Something which is changing is moving from a state in which certain sentences are true of it to one in which their contraries (*enantia*) are true: from "x is hot" to "x is not-hot."[12] While that transition is underway, the thing in question is in an intermediate state in which either contrary can with equal warrant be asserted or denied of it. Thus, if something is moving from being hot to being not-hot, we can equally well say that it is both hot and not-hot, since its state has aspects of both; or that it is neither hot nor not-hot, since in fact it is neither. If we say the former, we produce a dialectical contradiction; if we say the latter, we generate what I call an "anomaly."[13]

This does not mean that intermediate predicates—for example, "warm"—which cover a range of states between contrary states are not possible. These can, of course, be used to describe something which is in transition from one opposite state to the other, though they do not capture the direction of the transition (to say that something is "warm" is not to say that it is growing colder). My point here is not that the entity in transition cannot be described at all but that one or more properties first assigned to it do not continue to hold.

I am not here ascribing to things themselves anything strange or illogical, for dialectical contradiction and anomaly do not inhere directly in things. They are relative to the predicates available in the language with which we are trying to describe them. Nonetheless, it is difficult to imagine an actual language which contains predicates for two adjacent states of a thing in transition—no less difficult, in fact, than imagining an adjacent rational number. The dialecti-cal fun begins when we accept this and try to describe states that differ but are almost adjacent—which means that since our descriptions themselves take up a bit of time, we must say that one and the same thing at one and the same time (the time taken by our utterance) is both hot and not-hot.

Hegel enjoys this sort of thing rather too much, but the critical project I am advancing does not. It begins merely with the fact that any social reality is in time. It will eventually pass out of existence altogether and in the meantime is likely to be, to some degree and in some places, unstable. To locate the instabili-ties dialectically, we look to see where we cannot describe it without contradic-tion. To say, as Hegel does, that "alle Dinge sind an sich selbst widersprüchlich" is just to say that all things are in time, are changing.[14]

Neither the theory nor the practice of such instability is particularly new. Consider the sort of patriarch who, for various reasons, speaks with the women whose humanity he would deny. In this behavior he contradicts himself, be-cause we humans, as what Aristotle called *zōia logon echonta*, animals possess-ing speech, by definition cannot "speak" with nonhumans. And so a patriarch's talking with the women to whom he denies the status of humanity and there-fore the possession of speech is the weak point of his domination of them, the place where it can be attacked by women who persist in showing him the error of his ways. (Aristotle's conception of *karteria*, discussed in Chapter 3, was ap-parently designed to cope with women who do this: they shall not be listened to). Martin Luther King Jr., of course, did something similar for the entire United States, pointing out that it could not meaningfully advocate freedom and equality while denying them to some of its own citizens. And no nation, said Abraham Lincoln in a speech I will discuss presently, can survive "half slave and half free."

But such weak spots need not be internal to a social structure or practice; they may occur between a social structure and a larger society. To carry my earlier relevant fact over into an overt analogy: entropy can be staved off only in nonisolated systems, systems which can maintain their structure by tak-ing in energy from the surrounding environment. It is therefore unthinkable that there could ever have existed just one patriarchal household, a single slave plantation, or a unique factory.[15] Such individual structures survived by im-porting energy, not merely from the women, slaves, and workers inside them but from other structures of their kind. A dialectical contradiction in the case of a nonisolated system would occur when it acts in such a way as to cut off its own energy supply: by allowing slaves or women to be educated, for example, or simply by laying waste to the environment. When a system can be described equally well as dependent on the social or natural environment and as destructive of it, the contradiction is obvious.

Let us now assume that we have before us a case of such dialectical contradiction within a social formation of some sort. This is an indication that the formation is unstable, and indeed that it is already in transition to something else. In accordance with the aspirations of what we might call thermodynamically inspired critique, we want to manage this transition, which means that we have to understand it. How do we do so?

We have to understand no fewer than four sorts of things. Three of these are relevant facts about the transition itself. First, we need to identify the contradiction as precisely as possible. Second, we need to ascertain the initial state from which the transition began. And third we need to understand the state to which it is heading—or, in Aristotelian terms, we need to understand the *meson*, the contradictory "middle" state; the *archē*, or the beginning; and the *telos*, the end toward which a process is headed (Aristotle, *Poetics* 7.1450b27–33). The final piece of knowledge we need is not of social facts but of our own desires: we need to understand not only where things are going but where we want them to go. Moreover, if our understanding of this is to deserve the name of "critique," we need to understand why we want them to go there. Once we have determined these things, we can move from critique to deliberation: to the issue of what we can do now to bend the transition to our desired result. And from there we can pass to action.

The "House Divided" Speech: A Case of Dialectical Reflection

Let me look at this more concretely by turning to one of the most important socially critical utterances ever made by an American: Abraham Lincoln's "House Divided" speech of June 16, 1858.[16] The crucial words of that speech, known (one hopes) to every American schoolchild, are: "I believe that this government cannot endure, permanently half slave and half free."

These words are often glossed by Americans as "a nation cannot endure half slave and half free," but Lincoln is not uttering disconnected generalities; he is identifying a contradiction with precision, and it is in the American government. On the one hand, Congress has passed, and President Franklin Pierce has signed, what Lincoln calls the "Nebraska Bill," known today as the Kansas-Nebraska Act (1854). This act, in the name of popular sovereignty, gave to the people in the new state of Nebraska the right to decide whether or not slavery would be allowed in the state. It thus abrogated the Missouri Compromise of 1820, according to which Nebraska had to enter the Union as a free state. Lincoln sees it as a contradiction—a division in the house—because "popular sovereignty," the right of the people to decide to allow slavery, has come to mean taking sovereignty away from the people as a whole and giving it to just some of the people. The result is an instability in the government:

> I do not expect the Union to be *dissolved*—I do not expect the house to *fall*—but I *do* expect it will cease to be divided.
>
> It will become *all* one thing or *all* the other.

The next step, I suggested, is to ascertain the *archē*, the beginning of the process of transition. It matters greatly whether the current situation of being "half slave, half free" comes from a condition of being entirely free or entirely slave, or something else in between. Here, however, is a difficulty, for the beginning of an historical process cannot be fixed definitively. Aristotle had in fact claimed that there is no such thing as the beginning of a physical change, since that moment would have to be adjacent to the last moment before the change began; since time is infinitely divisible, no moment is adjacent to any other (*Physics* 6.5.236a10–28). This means that to speak of the "beginning" of a change is always to some degree arbitrary: it is we who take something as the beginning of a change, a fact which Aristotle honors with his frequent expressions *archēn lambanesthai* or *archēn poiein*, to "take" or "make" a beginning.[17]

The beginning of slavery in the United States, true to the above, cannot be located with precision. Slavery was a fluid status in the early colonies; the first slaves to arrive from Africa were often treated as indentured servants and allowed, for example, to buy their freedom. Though the United States had long been divided into "half slave and half free," Lincoln somewhat arbitrarily traces the division in the government back only to 1854 and the passing of the "Nebraska Bill."

At the beginning of 1854, progress against slavery had reached the point where "the new year . . . found slavery excluded from more than half the States by State Constitutions, and from most of the national territory by congressional prohibition." This was not a static condition but one stage in a process by which slavery, which was not only evil but irrational, was withering away. As such, it would generate a reaction; for those who supported slavery were being forced to defend it ever more desperately. Having "taken" this beginning, Lincoln proceeds to recapitulate the steps which have led to the current situation. We can recapitulate his recapitulation as follows:

1. The Nebraska Bill is passed, allowing the settlers, in the name of "popular sovereignty," to permit slavery in the new state.

2. While the bill is being debated, an amendment is offered to declare explicitly that the people of the territory may exclude slavery. This seems to be a mere statement of what was already clearly implicit in the notion of popular sovereignty, but is nonetheless voted down by the bill's supporters.

3. At about this time, the Dred Scott case is taken up by the Supreme Court. Consideration of it is deferred, however, until after the presidential election of 1856.

4. The election is won by James Buchanan with less than 50 percent of the vote in a three-way race with John C. Fremont and Millard Fillmore.

5. President Pierce (who has been denied renomination by the Democratic Party) then gives a speech applauding the election of his fellow Democrat.

6. Instead of coming to a decision on Dred Scott, the Supreme Court, under the direction of seventy-nine-year-old Chief Justice Roger B. Taney, orders that the case be reargued.

7. The decision, one of the most disastrous in the history of world law, is finally announced just two days after Buchanan's inauguration. It is far more sweeping than the case requires and is in fact a last-ditch attempt not merely to rescue slavery in the South but to force it upon the rest of the Union.

8. At that point, Buchanan and the Democrats suddenly drop their talk of "popular sovereignty" and rely instead on the Dred Scott decision to bring slavery to Nebraska. Among them is the "reputed author" of the Nebraska Bill itself, who thus praises his own handiwork's undoing.

The official narrative of these events is that there is no narrative, that these are merely a "dark and mysterious" series of unrelated incidents. Lincoln sees it differently. His next step after recounting the events is to call attention to a number of what I call anomalies, and he brings this out in a barrage of questions:

Why was the amendment, expressly declaring the right of the people, voted down? . . . Why was the court decision held up? Why even a Senator's individual

opinion withheld, till after the presidential election? . . . Why the outgoing Pres-
ident's felicitation on the indorsement [*sic*]? Why the delay of a re-argument?
Why the incoming President's advance exhortation in favor of the decision? . . .
And why the hasty after-indorsement of the decision by the President and others?

The various steps of Lincoln's narrative go on to reconceive these anomalies
as a series of contradictions (the relation of anomalies to contradictions will be
discussed in the next chapter): an appeal to popular sovereignty, which in fact
abrogates it (1); an innocuous amendment which is nonetheless voted down
(2); a Supreme Court case which is taken up and not taken up (3, 6); an election
which is won but not won (4); a speech praising the Democrats by a man who
has suffered their rejection (5); a Supreme Court decision on Dred Scott which
is not a decision on Dred Scott, being of much wider scope (7); and a sudden
decision by the framers of the Nebraska Bill that it is not their handiwork after
all but something to be forgotten (8).

These, Lincoln says, do not officially appear as a connected narrative at all;
rather, the sequence of events is "dark and mysterious." What he offers, by way of
illumination, is what I call a dialectical reflection on the entire series of events,
claiming that they were no innocent set of unrelated occurrences but stages
in a conscious plan to introduce slavery into Nebraska against the will of the
American people. "Popular sovereignty," to begin with, was a mere feint aimed
at giving populist cover to the introduction of slavery: "the Nebraska doctrine,
or what is left of it, is to educate and mold public opinion, at least Northern
public opinion, not to care whether slavery is voted down or voted up."

Invoking popular sovereignty was merely a ploy to open up the public mind
to the idea that introducing slavery in Nebraska was, somehow, an exercise
in democracy. This would in turn make the Dred Scott decision, which was
already underway, more politically palatable: it prepared what Lincoln calls a
"niche" for it in popular opinion. But when real democracy became an issue—
in the amendment to the Nebraska Bill—it was voted down because "the adoption of it would have spoiled the niche for the Dred Scott decision." With the
bill passed and the Dred Scott decision on the way, the next step was to get a
proslavery president elected before the decision was announced, for announc-
ing the decision prior to the election "would have damaged the perfectly free
argument upon which the election was to be carried." When the president was
elected with only a minority of the votes, however, it was decided to delay an-
nouncing the Dred Scott decision until he actually took office. Once that happened there was no reason for delay; the decision was speedily announced, and

those who had been in on the plot loudly abandoned their earlier support for the Nebraska Bill.

Lincoln's reconstruction presents the succession of events as a step-by-step plan to make Nebraska (whose northern boundary was to be the Canadian border) a slave state—and following that, the rest of the country. Lincoln reports as fact the various events in that sequence; but his claim that the story they tell is one of a conscious plot is a reconstruction and cannot be known with certainty. What he claims for it is the virtue of coherence over time, that is, of retrospective or teleological unity:

> We cannot absolutely know that all these exact adaptations are the result of pre-concert. But when we see a lot of framed timbers, different portions of which we know have been gotten out at different times and places, and by different workmen—Stephen [Douglas], Franklin [Pierce], Roger [Taney], and James [Buchanan], for instance—and when we see these timbers joined together, and see they exactly matte the frame of a house or a mill, all the tenons and mortices exactly fitting, and all the lengths and proportions of the different pieces exactly adapted to their respective places, and not a piece too many or too few—not omitting even scaffolding—or, if a single piece be lacking, we see the place in the frame exactly fitted and prepared yet to bring such piece in—in such a case we find it impossible not to believe that Stephen and Franklin and Roger and James all understood one another from the beginning and all worked upon a common plan or draft drawn up before the first blow was struck.

The story ends with a nation on the brink, awaiting

> another Supreme Court decision declaring that the Constitution of the United States does not permit a State to exclude slavery from its limits. And this may especially be expected if the doctrine of "care not whether slavery be voted down or voted up," shall gain upon the public mind sufficiently to give promise that such a decision can be maintained when made. . . . Such a decision is all that slavery now lacks of being alike lawful in all the States.

Lincoln thus begins by locating the points of instability in a social structure or practice, the places where description breaks down: the government's support for a popular sovereignty which is in fact the destruction of popular sovereignty. He then finds other such instabilities, a whole string of them, in fact. These are the places where the structure and practices of slavery are already in transition. He then orders these points of instability into a story which leads to a nation which is all slave. He has constructed his narrative according to the basic moves of what I have elsewhere (*CW*, 143–148) called Hegel's "historical dialectics."

The introduction to the *Phenomenology* (*PhS* ¶¶ 73–89; 46–57), where Hegel discusses the method of his undertaking, suggests three further ways in which Lincoln's narrative has Hegelian norms. First, he makes a provisional beginning. The beginning, then, is not a beginning, any more than is a "certainty" in the *Phenomenology*; it is a modification of specific circumstances, just as the Nebraska Bill modified the Missouri Compromise, but it is "taken as" a beginning.

Lincoln's story is then constructed as a series of instabilities—no fewer, we saw, than eight of them. These are of two kinds. One is the points of incoherence to the official story which lead Lincoln to construct his account; I will discuss these further in a moment. The other is the difficulties encountered by the plot itself: the suggested amendment to the Nebraska Bill and the minority election of 1858.

Second, to be a "determinate negation," the new stage in the *Phenomenology* must resolve only the problem at hand; if it solves others as well, it is generic rather than determinate. Similarly for the plotters, as Lincoln reflects on them: each stage is crafted only to move the plot along to the next. Thus, when the amendment arises, it is voted down; when the election fails, the announcement of the Dred Scott decision is delayed. Once it is announced, former supporters of the Nebraska Bill line up loudly to defend it. And so on.

Finally, the *Phenomenology* issues in the Absolute. I argued in Chapter 5 that in virtue of the malleability of reason for Hegel, this is merely the current state of things, as reflected in language. For Lincoln, the concluding language is still outstanding: the coming Supreme Court decision.

Lincoln and Hegel v. Habermas

Lincoln's critical practice does not fit easily under standard neo-Kantian views of critical theory. It does not bring a reality conceived as static up against norms conceived as universal; it cannot afford to do so, because slavery—like everything historical—is not static. It is both withering and growing, and so radically mutating. Lincoln's critical enterprise is founded on that fact and so is of the kind I call "dialectical reflection." Its aim is not to introduce change into a static society but to locate and manage changes which are already underway in it. What role do universality claims play in it?

In Habermas's version of Kantian critique, they can play two roles. The first, we saw, is to serve as invitations, to get the process of situation transcendence going. In that respect, Lincoln has no need of them; situation transcendence is already underway, with a vengeance. This, I have suggested, reflects a general fact of history—that it is part of the nature of historical situations to transcend themselves. From this point of view, Lincoln does not need to argue that slavery is *always* wrong, though by this time he clearly believes that. He needs only to claim that the plot he has reconstructed is moving the entire nation to slavery. The nation is thus in the contradictory situation of being "half slave and half free."

There is, however, another way to retain a role for rigid universality claims. We seek not merely to locate and understand transitions underway but to manage their direction and velocity. Where do we want the changes to go? How fast? Can anything less than universal standards guide us here? Might not universal standards still be required, in other words, to *manage* the changes that are underway? Merely locating contradictions will not help us here, because contradiction is an empirical indicator and not a moral or political one: it does not indicate something which is evil and needs to be overcome but merely a point of instability.

Broadly speaking, there are two ways to oppose the claim that our critical standards must be universal, one more radical than the other. The less radical way is to claim, as Alasdair MacIntyre does, that our standards should not be universal (MacIntyre 1984, passim). The more radical way is to say, with Geuss (Geuss 1981, 66–67), that it does not even matter whether our standards are universal or not and refuse even to begin the argument over whether they should be.

I will take the radical route. Let us suppose that we think the way out of the patriarchal contradiction I mentioned above would be for men to stop dominating women and to continue speaking to them, rather than merely not listening to them and ordering them around. This claim can be argued by appealing to the sort of society each course of affairs would produce. Do we want a society of peremptory men and unheard women, or a society of egalitarian communication?

Notice, first, that we are arguing about societies here, not standards or norms. This is what Lincoln does, and it strikes me as a plausible thing to do; talk about "the kind of society we want" is very common (though rarely dialectical). But it is a significant change and should be argued for (if only briefly). The argument takes us back to Kant.

For Kant in the *Groundwork of the Metaphysics of Morals*, moral deliberation involves deciding whether to adopt a "maxim": a rule for one's own conduct in a particular situation (*AA*, 4:400–401). The first two formulations of the moral law, which deal with such cases, use "maxim" in the singular, as if every act has a single maxim. (The third formulation, which universalizes moral obligation to all rational beings, refers to "maxims" collectively—but does not deny that in each case there will be a single maxim: *AA*, 4:401 421, 432). True to this, Habermas's model of critical discourse tends to restrict it to examining just one norm at a time: he defines practical discourse as "the medium in which we can hypothetically test whether *a* norm of action . . . can be impartially justified."[18] This talk of testing the legitimacy of an isolated norm is not merely adventitious but is, I suggest, itself an artifact of universalism. If a norm claims universal validity, then it claims to be valid independent of particular circumstances, including the circumstance that other norms hold or do not. If it is universally true that I ought not to steal, then it is true irrespective of whether I also ought not to murder (even though both may in fact follow from some higher principle). But if a norm cannot claim that sort of universal validity, then its validity is parasitic on other things, probably including the other norms in force in its world.

But norms do not merely coexist, of course, in a given society: they either cohere in what Hegel called a "system of ethical life" (Hegel 1979) or they conflict with one another. We may take it that whether one norm agrees or conflicts with other norms in its society is relevant to its legitimacy, and it follows that no norm can be judged alone: one must always look to the way it relates to other norms in its society. Forcing second daughters to become nuns would, today, be a shameful violation of their rights; in certain medieval societies, it may have been the only way to save them from abjectly inferior status in an older sister's household. Thus, slavery for Lincoln is not an isolated norm. Since many Americans oppose it, its introduction throughout the Union will disunify the nation (as, in the event, did its abolition). It will also perpetuate the rule of liars (like "Stephen," "Franklin," "Roger," and "James" above). Lincoln's argument thus appeals not only to freedom but to unity and honesty. This is what enables him to give the situation in January 1854 his qualified endorsement: true, slavery was still in force throughout the South; but under the rule of such liars as the president, the chief justice, and leading congressmen, what do you expect?

Once we start looking at norms in the context of other norms and historical developments, the question of whether they are universal or not becomes a distraction. That freedom is a universal value, whether for all human beings or for all time, is irrelevant when the country is ruled by liars; indeed, when the country is so ruled, what good is it for individuals to be juridically free? This shift from judging individual norms separately to evaluating whole sets of them

at once has an air of plausibility. It maintains that the critical evaluation of social norms must include looking at broader contexts which universalism tends
to deny and often making trade-offs among norms. But where does it get us?
How do we decide which sort of society we want? Must we not judge societies,
or sets of norms, by some set of universal criteria?

The first place it gets us is to fallibilism. If norms can be brought before the
bar of discursive critique one by one, there is perhaps some hope of reaching
a definitive judgment on at least some of them. But if they confront reason
only as parts of networks of norms, our certitude diminishes: how can we be
sure that we have fully spelled out the normative context of a given practice
or action? When fallibilism arrives, then, rigid universality departs. To claim
universal validity for a set of norms would be to claim that its members are
the norms that should govern all societies. Suppose, for example, that we have
found some points of instability in our society and have decided upon the direction in which to move the transitions already underway, so that we know,
in general terms, what we want our next society to look like (in Lincoln's case,
honest, unified, and free). Our moral affinity to that next society may have any
of a variety of sources—reasoned argumentation, emotion, convenience, compromise with each other. What would be the point of arguing that the standards by which we decided upon that particular next society were universal?

The only thing gained by that would be the knowledge that, once we had
reached that state of affairs, further change would be unnecessary: that the next
society would, in respect of those norms at least, be the last society. And who
would be so glum and foolish as to want to claim that? What, in fact, is the
point of arguing about the last society at all? What we want to decide upon, in
any given case, is the next society: where we go from here. Where we go from
that society, if anywhere, is most reasonably left until we are there and have
experienced it.

Indeed, one important characteristic of the most desirable next society
cannot in fact be universal, and that is its reachability from this society, from
here. A society in which all women were accorded full equal rights and rewards
would be "more superior" to the medieval society I mentioned above than is
our current world; but you can't get there from there. (It is far from sure that
you can get there from here!) Considerations of practical viability are obviously
essential to political action; their absence from critical theory vitiates it. Introducing them into such theory renders it malleable, in one way or another; I am
exploring one of those ways here.

Finally, universal norms, if they can be rationally justified, are something with which all rational beings must agree. This means that we can argue with those opposed to our position and convince them to join with us. This seems to be the point of Habermas's argument, referred to above, that the norms of communicative action are presupposed by every speech act and so must be assented to by all who speak—including, for example, Nazis. It is not, however, a concern for Lincoln:

> Our cause, then, must be intrusted to [sic], and conducted by, its own undoubted friends—those whose hands are free, whose hearts are in the work—who do care for the result. Two years ago the Republicans of the nation mustered over thirteen hundred thousand strong. We did this under the single impulse of resistance to a common danger, with every external circumstance against us. Of strange, discordant, and even hostile elements, we gathered from the four winds, and formed and fought the battle through, under the constant hot fire of a disciplined, proud, and pampered enemy. Did we brave all them to falter now?—now, when that same enemy is wavering, dissevered, and belligerent? The result is not doubtful. We shall not fail—if we stand firm, we shall not fail. Wise counsels may accelerate, or mistakes delay it, but, sooner or later, the victory is sure to come.

Lincoln is not concerned to argue with Stephen, Franklin, Roger, James, and the rest. This is presumably because they (like Nazis) are liars, and you can't argue with a liar. Whether liars are "rational" in some Kantian sense or not, they are speakers; and they have power. Lincoln wants to talk to those with whom he can work—those with "heart," who "care." In this respect, his position is akin to the Platonic one I mentioned in Chapter 2: critical dialogue is possible only with those who are favorably disposed on an affective level. The favorable disposition in question is, for Lincoln, freed from the erotic basis it had in Plato and probably owes more to Christian *agapē* than to anything classically Greek (see Nygren 1982); but the principle is the same.

Habermas's approach, based on Kant's, directs us away from consideration of the dynamism of social reality and of the interaction of norms with each other in particular situations and toward an unrealistic model in which unrealistically stable institutions and practices confront unchanging norms one by one. It thus becomes a distraction from work—a critical theory which destroys critical practice. This is confirmed by the fact that in the over forty years since it was first systematically advanced in *Knowledge and Human Interests*, the

Habermasian approach has not resulted in much actual social criticism. Habermas himself recognizes this and is untroubled by it: "Communicative reason . . . does not itself supply any substantive orientation for managing practical tasks—it is neither informative nor immediately practical" (Habermas 1998, 5). Habermas thus does not believe it is the job of his normative theory—the theory which makes the universality claims I have criticized in this chapter—to provide concrete guidance. But what, then, is the point of calling that normative theory "critical theory"?

Conclusion

Let me draw all this together into a practice of social/ethical critique:

> First, places are found where a given structure or institution cannot be unequivocally described. These are its points of instability.
>
> Second, these instabilities are defined in terms of the particular conceptual oppositions which both do and do not apply to them.
>
> Third, directions of change are established by comparing these sites with previous states of the structure or institution, including previous points of instability.
>
> Fourth, the norms which govern these points of instability are formulated and located within the normative network which supports them.
>
> Fifth, we try to see what would be the best normative network to move to next.

This final step would involve, among other things, a series of thought experiments which (a) took the identified change to its maximum and (b) asked what sort of points of instability were to be found there. In this way, a second normative network would be formulated. Some of the standards by which it is compared with the first one, the one actually in force, might extend beyond just those two and might even be standards by which all normative networks could be judged; but that question would not arise, being irrelevant.

Such reflection is a normatively developed case of the speaking of matter. Like a speech at Boston AA, it recapitulates a series of events which, in the first instance, seem to have no connection. Crucial to the success of this stage of the reflection, as we see from Boston AA, is that the various events be recapitulated accurately—that the description be independent of any guiding expectations about where the exercise is going to lead. If Lincoln's description of the various events he describes—from the passage of the Kansas-Nebraska Act to its sudden dropping by its own supporters—were in any way guided by the view that they are going to turn out to have been stages in a plot, then Lincoln's account could be dismissed as biased. His own analogy with framed timbers would fail because the "timbers" were not in fact framed; only his descriptions of them were.[19] At the end of the recapitulation, a concept is found ("plot to extend slavery to the entire Union"). But the concept leaves the final situation open: just as speeches at Boston AA end with the alternative "AA or death," so Lincoln's speech ends at a Bottom: slave nation or free.

Lincoln has not merely *listened* to the speaking of matter in someone else, then; his own discourse is an instance of it. This does not mean that it is bereft of sophisticated conceptual resources. It does mean that at a certain stage of the discourse, Lincoln has "checked his brain at the door": he has allowed the events he describes to send their own message. To put this somewhat differently: the actual events of the narrative Lincoln has formulated stand to his sophisticated recounting of them as the bulk of the *Phenomenology* stands to its brief recapitulation in its final chapter, and to the way that the events of an addict's life stand to his recapitulation of his Disease at Boston AA.

In a context of critical practice, the pull to universal standards is suspect in many ways. As Schiller's influential reaction to Kant shows, no set of such standards has ever won universal acceptance. Hegel called Kant's efforts at it "quite unphilosophic" (Hegel 1892, 3:439), and even Habermas, we saw, has cut back his claims. Moreover, the pull raises us too high to have much content, leading to widespread diversions of critical energy from real issues to abstract ones.

Fortunately, the desire for such standards in the case of Habermas rests upon a mistaken presumption: that social realities, in order to be objects of critique, must be taken as intrinsically static. Once that has been seen not to be the case, a different model for social critique—the "situating" model of dialectical reflection—recommends itself. Like neo-Kantian critical theory, dialectical reflection allows us to argue rationally about the nature of a better society. Unlike such critical theory, it does not claim an unconvincing universal validity for the norms to which such argument appeals. Operating on a concrete yet situation-transcending level, it gives specific guidance of a kind rarely attempted by neo-Kantian critical theorists.

But is there some aspect of Habermasian critique that cannot be accomplished by dialectical reflection? I think there is one—but that it is not worth accomplishing. Consider the practice of female circumcision. No one with whom I (for one) am going to talk seriously would defend it. According to my account of dialectical reflection, the mere fact that some members of the socie-ties where it is in force find it to be repugnant would constitute a contradiction. For a social norm is supposed to be in force everywhere within a society, and one that is seriously challenged by those to whom it applies is not "in force" everywhere. So any time a norm comes under serious challenge within its own society, so to speak, we have a contradiction and my model can kick in. What remains to the good offices of Habermas's variety of critique, then, can only be a practice which is evil but which no one opposes. In which case, however, it is useless to oppose it from outside.[20]

Kantian social critique, as developed by Habermas, thus relies on false pre-suppositions to obtain unconvincing results which allow it, at best, to attempt the useless. It can be replaced by dialectical reflection without serious loss, and when that happens we will have moved—once again—beyond Kant. This time, we make our move with the malleability of reason standing in for the meta-physical pretensions of German Idealism, and so (I hope) for good.

CHAPTER 8

CRITICAL PRACTICE
AND PUBLIC LANGUAGE

THE ROLE OF PHILOSOPHY

Dialectical Reflection as Narrative

Two tasks remain: to complete my account of critical or situating methods and
to offer some observations on the kind of object to which those methods may
apply. The reason the discussion of methods is still incomplete is that dialectical
reflection, as introduced in the last chapter, cannot stand on its own. The problem has to do with a certain kind of reification to which it is intrinsically prone.
To reify something is, of course, to make a "thing" of it; and in this connection,
it is important to keep separate two strands in philosophy's traditional notion
of a "thing." These need only a vague statement here: a "thing" exists independently of us, and it is something which we must accept. The two do not always
go together. The human immunodeficiency virus is something whose existence
we must accept, but it is not something that exists independently of us. The
average winter temperature in Minneapolis exists independently of us, but it is
not something everyone has to accept: at least some people can move to Miami.

Narratives, dialectical and other, are not independent of us, for their unity
is our doing: even Aristotle, as we saw in Chapter 7, thought that natural
processes have no beginnings, which means that narratives are indebted to
us even as they get underway. Most people today, after ousia's eviction from
nature, probably agree that narratives also have no intrinsic ends: processes
underway do not prescribe their own conclusions. Moreover, the dialectical
transitions which make up their middles, and which turn a series of isolated
events into a narrative, are also, to some extent, the narrator's doing; for if their

nature were given, so would be the conclusion to which they lead. An honest narrative thus presents itself not as the report of a set of facts but as the articulation of a perspective. When such a perspective is offered without alternatives, as in a novel, it becomes something that the hearer has to accept. Think of the safeguards in place, for example, to keep any contemporary reader from changing the plot of *Les miserables*. They range from ethical to legal to typographical to epistemological.

Viewing a narrative as a "thing" in this way thus brings us to a problem of what we may call historical honesty: I should never claim that the story I am telling actually happened as I am telling it. It also confronts a problem of what could be called novelistic authoritarianism: as a novelist, I must say that even though my story is fictional, you (Dear Reader) must accept it. Encounter it as you will, as intelligently or unreflectively as you like; but do not try to change it.

Unlike fictional narratives, which end with their characters in some new place or other, narratives of an historical or political sort often claim to end with us, in our current situation. One purpose of such narratives, then, is to define that situation: to suggest to us which of its components have come about accidentally (and so cannot be narrated) and which are to be considered as the outcome of longer developments. Lincoln's narrative in the "House Divided" speech has such a purpose: to show that the passage of the Kansas-Nebraska Act and the Dred Scott decision are not, as the official story has it, merely random and unrelated events but stages in an ongoing plot to make the United States into a slave-holding country.

The "Heresy" of Mononarrativism

To tell just one story, even a dialectical one, about how we got where we are then means to present just one definition of our current situation. Once that definition is accepted as the only account of where we are, its necessity gets read back into the story of how we got here, which then becomes the only possible story—and so becomes, inevitably, something that must really have happened (see *RR*, 86–89). My name for the overall heresy is "mononarrativism": the idea that it is ever the case that just one story can be constructed from a sequence of historical facts (see *RR*, 78–83).

Only . . . mononarrativism (unlike the Christian heresy of monophysitism, which is a variant of it) is not really a heresy—it is orthodoxy. It goes back, like so many things philosophical, to Aristotle, for whom only one basic story is to be told about (say) an oak: that of how it grew from an acorn.

Mononarrativism thus seems to be connected with a species of teleology, and it is Aristotle who explains how this works. No one, in his view, can determine the *archē* of a process of physical change, since, as we saw in the previous chapter, it does not exist. The same is not, however, true of its *telos* (*Physics* 6.5.236a10–7). The end of a process of change for Aristotle must exist if anything at all is to reach *entelecheia*, the plenary presence of form in matter which provides what I called, in Chapter 2, "partial intelligibility." Since natural processes have no beginnings, it must be their ends which individuate them; until a process reaches its end, we do not have "a" process at all. In order to individuate a process, which includes enabling us to distinguish it from other processes, a *telos* for Aristotle must itself be unequivocally determinate; otherwise, the process it individuated would be indistinct. The *telos* is thus an immanent, determinate unifying factor, and as such is nothing other than the ousiodic form of the being whose coming-to-be we are narrating.[1] This means that it was there all along, unifying the process from within in the manner of the kind of historical unity that Foucault attributes to Hegel. Once we have a determinate *telos* functioning as the unifying factor in a process, it is but a short step from "everything led to this final state" to "everything *had* to lead to this final state." The entire story is then reified, not merely in the sense that we have to accept it as something that actually happened but in the sense that it *could not* have happened differently.

In the mid-twentieth century, Marxism was often accused of falling into precisely this kind of thing. Marx and Engels had brought a vast amount of empirical material together into a narrative of unrivaled organization and comprehensiveness; their narrative of the evolution of the means of production from hunter-gatherers to capitalists and proletarians has still, even today, not been equaled with regard to such narrative values as comprehensiveness and rational transparency (for which see *CW*, 116–118). But Marx and Engels offered that one narrative alone, and they made no effort to indicate its scope—in particular, to show that it subordinated the kinds of oppression inflicted upon women, people of color, and people of unconventional gender.[2] The view that our situation is defined mainly, if not entirely, by the oppression of workers thus became, in its own many ways, oppressive.

It is not only Marxism that suffered this fate; it happens recurrently. The history of the United States, we read, is the story of expanding freedom, *and not* one of lies told to Native Americans. The French Revolution was a battle for *liberté*, *égalité*, and *fraternité*, *and not* a struggle for wealth and power. Farther back, the Persian Wars were fought for Hellenic identity against a foreign invader, *and not* to preserve the privileged positions of the Greek upper classes; and so on and so forth. Lapses into mononarrativism in Western culture alone have been recurrent enough to call forth what Lucius Outlaw calls "deliberately disruptive" counterdiscourses such as Afrocentrism, "intended to interrupt the continuation of the supposedly progressive 'evolutionary flow' of Reason embodied in the historical development of the peoples of Western Europe and their American descendents" (Outlaw 1996b, 100).

The way out of mononarrativism begins when we see that interruptions of this sort are just as "natural" as the processes they interrupt. Indeed, most if not all *telē* are not inherent in the process they end, as they are for Aristotle, but are instead the products of outside intervention. The intervention, at minimum, consists in taking one phase of a process as its final phase, ignoring subsequent events or assigning them to other processes. It may also, if we are mononarrativists, require some interpretive management of the earlier phases, which must be seen as leading up to this one.

There are, to be sure, occasions when we need to set a determinate *telos* to an historical process—for example, when we decide to move from understanding to deliberation (and thence to action). For in order to act in concert, we need an accepted definition of where we are: we need an unequivocal, and so mutually understood, statement of what recent developments have led to. What we are agreeing on then includes the narrative of how we got to this point, and in that sense the narrative is accepted over its rivals. But it is one thing to accept a narrative as leading to a clear and useful definition of the present situation and another to say that it provides the only story that can be told from the relevant facts. Mononarrativism means allowing the acceptance, and so the accepted *telos*, to be more than provisional.

Mononarrativism in the "House Divided" Speech

Lincoln's "House Divided" speech suffers from this. The end of his historical narrative is the time of his speaking, with both government and nation divided and on the brink of becoming wholly slave. At that point, the conceptual uncertainties to which we have seen him refer stop:

> The result is not doubtful. We shall not fail—if we stand firm, we shall not fail. Wise counsels may accelerate, or mistakes delay it, but, sooner or later, the victory is sure to come.

The suspension I noted in the previous chapter, in which Lincoln's story ends with the "nation on the brink," awaiting a further Supreme Court decision that will open the entire country to slavery, is (unlike the Bottom of Boston AA) only temporary. In the long run, the only doubts concern the possible behavior of Stephen A. Douglas if he is reelected to the Senate. The way to eliminate those doubts and have a sure path to a future of freedom is to elect Lincoln. Lincoln suddenly veers, here, from defining the overall situation to frying his own fish—and the speech, as an example of dialectical reflection, gets into trouble, for Lincoln's *telos* is not as secure as he takes it to be. He has left out one very important factor in his account of the situation at the end of the speech. It is not, to be sure, one he could have foreseen; but he could have allowed for it, by asking the right question.

The factor I have in mind is the powerful effect of the speech itself. As Derrida writes in "Signature Event Context," no one can control the "iteration" of his words (Derrida 1977). As far as Lincoln's text itself goes, the only effect that the "House Divided" speech is going to have is to get Illinoisans to vote for Lincoln. But that its effects could be limited in such a way is at best questionable. The metaphor of the "house divided" between slave and free is both extremely vivid and further empowered by its New Testament origins (at Matthew 12:25). It helped set the agenda for the ensuing Lincoln-Douglas debates. Indeed, Douglas brought it up, to great effect, in the first of these:

> In his speech at Springfield to the Convention which nominated him for the Senate, [Lincoln] said: . . .
>
>> "A house divided against itself cannot stand." I believe this government cannot endure permanently half slave and half free. . . . Either the opponents of slavery will arrest the further spread of it, and place it where the public mind shall rest in the belief that it is in the course of ultimate extinction, or its advocates will push it forward till it shall become alike lawful in all the States,—old as well as new, North as well as South.
>
> ["Good," "Good," and cheers.]
>
> I am delighted to hear you Black Republicans say "good." I have no doubt that doctrine expresses your sentiments.[3]

Douglas's iteration of Lincoln's words had an effect directly opposite to Lincoln's intentions. Merely citing (at notable length) the metaphor of the "house divided" provokes audible praise from the African Americans in the audience, which enables Douglas to jeer at them and turn white listeners against them.

Lincoln's speech, like a Heideggerian work of art, has thus increased the distance between white and black; in Heidegger's unfortunately apposite words, quoted in Chapter 6, it has caused "colors to glow"—indeed, to ignite. Lincoln's national reputation, established both by the "House Divided" speech itself and the debates with Douglas for which it set the tone, was such that his mere election was the signal for the South to secede. By the time he actually took office, seven states had done so.

Lincoln thus fails, at the end of his speech, to recognize that the situation is not as he has defined it because his own words have changed things. In addition to the three possibilities he mentions—the impossible continuation of the division and its resolution into either fully slave or fully free—there is the alternative of a prolonged and gruesome war. By 1858, of course, Lincoln, like many others, could fully foresee the possibility of war, and the reasons why he does not bring it up in his speech are obvious. What he can hardly have seen fully is the role of his own speech itself in helping to bring it about. To understand this, and to correct the reifying tendencies of dialectical critique, we need to turn to Heidegger.

Questioning Our Narratives

The first, abstract step out of mononarrativism is simply to recognize that even the end of an historical or political narrative, to say nothing of a fictional one, is our own doing. It is not somehow present in it from the beginning. But we must also be able to fill this in concretely, and there are two different paths to doing so. One is to show that the *telos* is in itself unclear: that the story ends not with an achievement of completion but with *in*completion, which can only mean with a suspension among a number of alternative possibilities (i.e., in some version of what Boston AA calls the Bottom). The other is to show that the series of events which led to this *telos* is not exhausted by that—that there are resources, in the facts themselves, for assigning a different *telos* (as when we say that the facts of American expansionism led not to liberty but to white ownership from "sea to shining sea"). Both are cases of the Heideggerian project of *Destruktion* that I discussed in Chapter 6.

This brings us to a peculiar looseness between Hegelian dialectical reflection and Heideggerian questioning. I noted in Chapter 4 that reflective judgment, the search for a concept, takes two forms: that of the beautiful, in which a "harmonious" form indicates that a concept can be found, and that of the sublime, in which the disharmony of the form indicates that a concept will not be forthcoming. The kind of concept which emerges from the former kind of judgment is for Kant the concept of a *telos*: a concept of the end not of the object but of the search itself, which is then "projected" back onto the object (*CJ*, 211, 256, 264). What emerges from the latter kind of judgment is not a *telos* or even a concept but something like an ongoing "vibration" between being repelled by the "abyssal" thing we find to be sublime and being attracted by its conformity to reason's law (*CJ*, 258).

Kant's inability to distinguish the beautiful from the sublime, which I discussed in Chapter 4, means that any set of sensory givens can be recapitulated in either way. This corresponds to the fact, noted in Chapter 7, that we can understand something in transition from A to B in two ways: as both A and B ("contradiction") or as neither ("anomaly").

Dialectical contradictions, we now see, belong under the heading of the beautiful. In them, each of two opposed concepts applies equally well to an object. Since such a situation is unstable, it points beyond itself, to a completion which can be conceived in terms of these two concepts—in terms either of one of them alone, as suggested by Lincoln's certainty that the United States will be either slave or free, or in terms of a critical hybrid of both, as in Hegelian "sublation."

But if we can take the contradictory Hegelian road of both/and, we can also take the anomalous Heideggerian road of neither/nor. Any dialectical contradiction can also be seen as an anomaly, and vice versa: if I can say that "hot" and "not-hot" apply equally well to my cooling tea, I can say that both apply equally poorly. This opens the way for the Heideggerian questioning of any narrative, for it means that whether to take a particular stage in a narrative as a contradiction or as an anomaly is up to us. Lincoln's narrative of the conspiracy to introduce slavery into the whole United States points to this, for as we saw in the previous chapter, it presents several of its stages in the form of questions. Only in the context of the developed narrative are they reshaped as dialectical contradictions rather than as anomalies—when Lincoln substitutes the Hegelian "both/and" for the Heideggerian "neither/nor." His narrative thus takes the Hegelian road and ends, finally, with a United States which will be entirely and unequivocally free. But what if Lincoln had chosen the other road—the Heideggerian path of neither/nor? What if the questions he asked in the course of the speech were not given ready (if contradictory) answers? What if he had continued the questions all the way to the speech's end, instead of closing on a certainty?

To assert that something is neither A nor B does not tell us what it is and so does not tell us in what direction to move on from it. Maintaining the Heideggerian road through the entirety of his speech—treating each and every stage of his narrative as a "neither/nor" rather than a "both/and"—would not, to be sure, leave Lincoln with the mere series of random incidents that constitutes the "official story." For the questions he asks could then be construed as forming a path, which (in the manner of Heidegger) would then be held together by something yet unknown. If Lincoln had applied Heideggerian questioning throughout his narrative, then, it would have become a Heideggerian way: a series of questionable stages united by something that never clearly comes forth. Lincoln does not do this, clearly, because such a series of mystifications is not a basis for action—that is, for voting.

Heideggerian letting-be may be a valid ethical stance, from time to time, but it is of little use when we must, in concert, come to action. That, I take it, is why so many efforts to find a basis for politics in Heidegger, or indeed in his postmodern successors such as Foucault and Derrida—efforts which began so disastrously with Heidegger himself—have ended in frustration.[4]

That Lincoln cannot completely destructure his narrative by questioning its various stages does not mean that he cannot destructure part of it; and the part which needs destructuring, I suggest, is the end. Such destructuring could have come about if Lincoln had considered the possible effects of the speech itself. Instead of ending with the certitude that freedom will prevail, he might have ended with questions such as: "And so, my friends, for what is the United States waiting now? For a Supreme Court decision which will take us all the way into slavery? Or for my words here, which if taken to heart can avert that—but perhaps at the cost of exacerbating tensions to the point of war?"

The context of the speech did not allow for such uncertainties. The "House Divided" speech cannot itself be "half-slave and half free"; it comes down, as it must, totally on the side of freedom (and of Lincoln's election). Yet it inspires the proslavery forces. This leads to a sort of paradox. If we take the speech as an intervention on the side of freedom, then we must admit that it strengthened proslavery forces and so was an intervention on the side of slavery. If we take it to be an unintended intervention on behalf of slavery, then we must admit that it eventually contributed to freedom, through the terrible war which it helped provoke.

Questioning and Reflection

In order not to be reified, political narrative—as a product of dialectical reflection—needs to be questioned at its end; otherwise the end assumes the unequivocal status of an Aristotelian *telos*. The anomalies existing between the end and the two kinds of reality with which it must deal—the earlier stages of the narrative which it ends and the current situation the narrative is to define—must be brought forward: the "both-ands" of dialectical reflection need to be shown equally as anomalous "neither-nors." We do this by highlighting their questionability.

Questioning the end of the narrative itself means subtracting from it the unequivocal determinacy of the *telos* and leaving it with the openness of a question—in some version of the Bottom of the speaking of matter in Boston AA. The speaking of matter, being at most only partially conceptual, can thus be recapitulated as a series of contradictions, a series of anomalies, or as a mixture of both—but it cannot end in the ousiodic power of a *telos*.

Questioning the relation of the narrative's end to its earlier stages will include questioning those earlier stages as well—to see if they have been entirely subsumed into the narrative. To the extent that such a stage is exhausted by the way it moves the narrative along, we may say it is a dialectical contradiction; to the extent that it is something over and above that, it is anomalous to the narrative.

We can see how this works by considering Cynthia Willett's discussion of the autobiographies of Frederick Douglass's 1845 *Narrative of the Life of Frederick Douglass, an American Slave*, the earliest of Douglass's autobiographies. On the one hand, Douglass's valorization of resistance on the part of the individual slave (exemplified in his own encounter with the slave breaker Edward Covey),[5] stands as an anomaly to Hegel's narrative, in the *Phenomenology*, of a bondsman who escapes his master by elevating himself ironically to the Stoic domain of the pure intellect (*MESM*, 142; *PhS*, ¶ 197; 119–121). It also stands, we may note, as an anomaly to Marx's narrative of revolution, according to which individuals' acts of resistance signify only when they are taken up by others, igniting mass movements. For Douglass, by contrast, the individual's resistance gains importance because of what it does for that individual: "For Douglass the oppressed establishes an identity as a person through the act of rebellion" (*MESM*, 148). Indeed, Douglass's valorization of individual resistance runs counter to the general view of the entire philosophical tradition, which (as we saw in Chapter 2) is at pains to deny agency to both slaves and women. Thus, Willett concludes, "By introducing a strong concept of individual agency into a dialectical narrative of social freedom, Douglass transforms the meaning of freedom in the West" (*MESM*, 151).

Such a transformation is no small thing. But it is consonant with the kind of unequivocal *telos* that Lincoln tries to bring to his narrative: the *telos* of Douglass's story would then be Douglass himself, having attained his own freedom, writing his memoirs in Boston while awaiting the liberation of African Americans in general. While Douglass does end his *Narrative* in this way, however, that is not (so to speak) the whole story. He goes on to append a clarification of his previous critical remarks on religion. Christianity as it has figured in his narrative is not the same as Christianity in the rest of the world: "Between the Christianity of this land, and the Christianity of Christ, I recognize the widest possible difference" (*NFD*, 97).

Christianity now appears as twofold. On the one hand, we have the Christianity of the masters, which provides "religious sanction and support" for their cruelty and is "part and parcel of the gross fraud" (*NFD*, 52, 66). On the other hand, we have the Christianity of the slaves, which is deeply felt and inspiring but, since they cannot read, uninformed: the local slaves need to be taught, by Douglass himself, to "read the will of God" (*NFD*, 71). Christianity is thus both liberating and enslaving, both lettered and unlettered. "Christianity proper," that is, Christianity outside the system of slavery, is anomalous to both: like the Christianity of the slaves it is morally salvific, and like that of the masters it is literate—a liberating encounter with the word of God. Douglass's discussion at the end of his *Narrative* thus implicitly raises the question of how "the pure, peaceable, and impartial Christianity of Christ" could have become the "corrupt, slave-holding, women-whipping, cradle-plundering, partial and corrupt Christianity of this land" (*NFD*, 97). The question is not explicitly asked, let alone answered; but Douglass's discussion is enough to show the reader that other kinds of Christianity are possible.

A second destructuring by Douglass of his own narrative comes not at the end but in what Willett calls a "brief and crucial discussion" of slave songs in chapter 2 (*MESM*, 156). These songs, Douglass says, capture the essence of slavery, not merely in their words but in their very sound: "The thought that came up, came out—if not in the word, in the sound; and as frequently in the one as in the other" (*NFD*, 23).

The end of Douglass's narrative cannot be an unequivocal realization of freedom because freedom, in Willett's words, is "originally a music" (*MESM*, 156); and the music, one form of the speaking of matter, is not over when Douglass writes "those songs still follow me" (*NFD*, 24). Douglass thus achieves, at the end of his narrative, what Lincoln did not at the end of the

"House Divided" speech: a conclusion which is not presented in the form of an unequivocal and inevitable *telos* but one which opens onto the uncertainties of the future—of African Americans, of American Christianity, and of freedom itself.

Dialectics and destructuring are, from the point of view of traditional Enlightenment reason, irrational; for such reason, contradictions are there to be resolved and questions are there to be answered. Traditional reason has problems with processes, with developments underway; that is why, as I observed in the Introduction, Enlightenment becomes paradoxical when placed into time.

Though foreign to traditional philosophy, dialectical reflection and Heideggerian questioning are not new to today's continental philosophers. The problem is that they have always been explored separately. Most such philosophers are in either the Hegelian or the Heideggerian vein, and few attempt to deal with both thinkers.[6] If we stay with Hegel and avoid Heidegger, however, we are prone to misunderstand Hegel by reading the final stage of Hegel's dialectical reconstruction of history as the *telos* of the whole development and then to see that development as necessary. Such reading encourages what might be called the "hyperdeterministic" tenor of Hegel's thought: the general feeling one has from it, not that there is only one way forward from here but that there is no way forward at all.[7] Generalizing this beyond Hegel leads us to the orthodoxy of mononarrativism.

Heidegger has replaced Hegel's optimistic account of history as a learning process with a view of it as a series of discontinuous yet increasingly gloomy "epochs of Being." If we stay with Heidegger and avoid Hegel, we are prone to misunderstand Heidegger by seeing his meticulous fracturing of reason to be an unbridled fragmenting of it. Post-Heideggerian philosophy, particularly in its French dispensation, is subject to this. It has no vigorous sense of the past as something built—much less as something built with good reasons. Thus, Derrida, Foucault, and Lyotard all begin from unified historical discourses— metaphysics, epistemes, and metanarratives—and seek to undo them. Lyotard's *The Postmodern Condition* is a good example. He defines postmodernity as the suspicion of metanarratives—of the grand stories, including Hegel's, of the triumph of freedom and knowledge. Lyotard never tells us where metanarratives come from or how they are constituted, but he does admit that they may be necessary:

> It is not inconceivable that the recourse to narrative is inevitable, at least to the extent that the language game of science desires its statements to be true but

does not have the resources to legitimate their truth on its own. If this is the case, it is necessary to admit an irreducible need for history. (Lyotard 1984, 28)

Ordinary narratives are not suspect in this way but "are legitimated by the simple fact that they do what they do" (Lyotard 1984, 23). Each such narrative is legitimated on its own terms alone. Once we abandon metanarratives and become "postmodern," we are left with a fragmented plurality of narratives construed as mutually incommensurable "language games" (Lyotard 1984, 43; 1985, 22, 51).

Continental philosophy, I believe, is the only approach which has the conceptual resources needed to bring philosophy out of its current crisis. But to realize that promise, it must be seen as two things which need to become a third. In its current state, it represents the *disjecta membra* of a larger, still unbroached project—the post-Kantian critical practice whose basic methods I have sketched here. Since this practice, being post-Kantian, is non-Kantian, I prefer to call the pursuit of it not "critical" but "situating." It goes beyond simply pointing out what is defective in the human world and is a general procedure for orienting ourselves as material beings in time. I will give an account of a noncritical example, from Hegel, below.

Conducted within the context of dialectical reflection, destructuring serves to "fracture" the narratives such reflection constructs by showing that the words in which they are couched do not come to rest in the definitive plenitude of a *telos* but open out onto new meanings as the narrative moves on. Within such a context, the destructuring questions are directed toward stages in that narrative (particularly the final stage). Taken outside it, destructuring risks becoming a general fragmenting.

Civic Language

It remains to discuss the kinds of realities on which situating activity can be directed. While the domain of application of any set of methods is best left to be discovered by actual use, some points can be made briefly in general terms. Since Heidegger, in this approach, is useful mainly as a check on Hegelian reification, my remarks will be keyed to Hegel.

One important aspect of Douglass's narrative of his progress toward freedom is his concern with language. Learning to read and write is a major component of that liberation, but spoken language also figures importantly as Douglass moves from not knowing the meaning of the word "abolition" to discovering his ability to speak before white people (*NFD*, 43, 96). Though freedom may be expressed in many ways, musically as well as verbally, it—by definition—is never silenced. Thus, as Michael Goldhaber writes, "language is perhaps the quintessential public good":

> Without the free flow of words, indeed, there can be no public. It is only because in public discourse meanings are continually in flux, always open to new shadings and redefinitions, regardless of what quarter they come from, that society can navigate the continual changes it itself undergoes and still retain any semblance of communal coherence, even the minimal sort needed for a functioning market." (Goldhaber 2000, 328)

In order to negotiate this mutating social phenomenon, reason must become both malleable and fragile. Only so can it assist in the ongoing modifications of language which yield new words.

Without language, everything would be private—-and nothing would be property, because we would not be human. As Aristotle put it:

> Now, that humans are more of a political animal than bees or any other "social" animals is evident. . . . Whereas mere voice signifies merely pleasure and pain, and is therefore found in other animals (for their nature attains to the perception of pleasure and pain and the signifying of these to one another, and no farther) the power of speech works to set forth the expedient and inexpedient, and therefore likewise the just and the unjust. (*Politics* 1.2.1253a, 7–15)

Language is public in two senses. First and more generally, it is a "public good" in that it is something everyone has the right (and the need) to use. In that sense, all language is public, and there is no such thing as a "private language" (a point I discussed in Chapter 1). Second and more specifically, language can be public in that it is used (like the speeches in Boston AA) to address whole communities, that is, is used politically. Such "civic language," as I will call it, corresponds to what Kant, in "What Is Enlightenment?," called the "public use of reason" (*AA*, 8:37–38). It includes political language, as in Lincoln's speech, but also things like literature, journalism, and scholarly publication. Certain aspects of how language functions as a public good can, I think, be more easily seen by looking to such speech, and I will key my treatment here to it.

How does civic language function? What norms does it come under? To a degree, the answers seem obvious. We want our language, like other public goods, to be able to fulfill its purpose, which means capacious enough for people to express whatever they want to express in it; and we want it to be accessible to all. How can these desiderata be defined more precisely, and what justifies them? There are, in short, lots of philosophical issues about civic language, language which addresses entire communities as a public good; but if one looks close at hand, to the classic figures of Anglo-American philosophy of language, disappointment looms.

Even in the *Philosophical Investigations*, for example, Wittgenstein understands language primarily through its use in private encounters. From the famous example of one worker calling "slab" to another, with which the book opens, almost all of his examples of language use are from the private sphere: political, literary, and other public types of language are simply not dealt with. This makes good sense in terms of Wittgenstein's therapeutic project, for the incursions of metaphysical essentialism into the more intimate uses of language are surely among its most damaging effects. But it should also be understood as a result of the atrophy of public discourse in the Vienna of Wittgenstein's formative years—in other words, as a philosophical effect with political causes (Toulmin and Janik 1973). In any case, the result is that there is, apparently, no complete philosophy of language in the *Investigations*. Such a project is not even broached.

If we cross the Atlantic we find that W. V. O. Quine—no marginal figure—keys his entire philosophy of language to what he calls the "language of the marketplace" (Quine 1960, 234, 272). This is language composed of utterances in which we assume no more about our interlocutors than that they go by the most general rules of interpretation that our culture contains. What attracts Quine to such language is, of course, that the role of specific rules of interpretation, including those that are based on background knowledge, is reduced. As a speaker of English, for example, I have specific rules for understanding the utterances of someone I know to be a Catholic priest, and they are very different from my equally specific rules for understanding the speech of a lawyer or a professional football player. The "language of the marketplace" as Quine defines it retains only a minimal role for such background knowledge and so lacks nonlogical norms, leaving logic largely in control of the field (see *CW*, 270–275).

The absence of such background information also, however, renders this kind of speech relatively rare (except in marketplaces). Quine's counter to this in the passages cited is that the language of the marketplace should be the primary object of philosophical study because its minimal reliance on nonlogical norms renders it basic to other, more complex forms of language. So, just as science starts but does not end with physics, so philosophy of language should start with the language of the marketplace. Other forms of speech are merely complications of it.

But how do we know that other forms of speech are merely complications of the language of the marketplace unless we have already studied them? Quine's approach may, in fact, be like trying to understand human thought processes by looking to someone with only minimal brain function: the basic functions are there but contribute little to understanding the higher ones. Indeed, what if civic language, addressing whole communities, were the basic kind and language used in private encounters were merely a truncated, and so distorted, version of it? Wouldn't a multipronged approach be better?

Documentation of absence is a tiresome activity, and I will only discuss one further case of inattention to civic language. Donald Davidson came of age not in Central Europe but in a Red-hunting America where the atrophy of public discourse was comparable in scope to that in Wittgenstein's Vienna, and I think his philosophy shows effects of this.[8] In "A Nice Derangement of Epitaphs," which is perhaps where Davidson most effectively instates the social embeddedness of language (see *CW*, 267–269), language is once again understood solely through its operations in private encounters, the least intimate of which are ordering coffee and giving directions to a taxi driver (Davidson 1986, 443).[9]

Against this background, Robert Brandom's *Making It Explicit* is an important step forward. Here, as in my *Poetic Interaction*, the meaning of an utterance is itself social, produced through a cooperative endeavor. It consists, for Brandom, in the set of other sentences to which, in the view of the hearers, the speaker is committed in virtue of that utterance. As an interpersonal achievement, meaning is public from the start. But Brandom still has problems defining what the meaning of an utterance is. If you tell me "Don't hit yourself on the desk" and I swerve to avoid it as I walk out, is my action part of the meaning of your sentence? Brandom wants to deny that it is: the meaning of a sentence is reached by a process of "material inference," and in his view of inference Brandom thus retains what he calls the "pragmatic priority of the propositional": "propositions are what can serve as premises and conclusions of inferences" (Brandom 1994, xiv, 82; see also Brandom 2000, 3). The meaning of a sentence is thus a set of propositions. While meanings are produced by a cooperative endeavor, the results of that endeavor are still, as beliefs, located within the individual. Civic language thus continues to elude the analytical net.

Just why this is so remains unclear. For Brandom, it seems to be motivated by a desire to make language something reliably distinct from other things—an ambition which, if Brandom's, would run counter to Wittgenstein's later insight, discussed in Chapter 5, that an utterance is a move in a language game and therefore entirely bound up with forms of life. Once we remove it, we can say that the "meaning" of an utterance is simply what normally happens after that utterance. This view of meaning leads us back to speech which is not merely public in the sense that it is not the private language of an individual, but civic in the sense that its words can, and often do, have effects on the behavior of entire communities.

Language has always been an important topic for philosophers. However, as Richard Rorty has argued, at a certain point philosophy's concern with language was transformed. Instead of being one topic among others, language swallowed philosophy, in the sense that it came to be accepted that "all philosophical problems are problems which may be solved (or dissolved) either by reforming language, or by understanding more about the language we presently use" (Rorty 1967, 3). The "revolution" is undeniable; Rorty, however, misdates it. The earliest text in his anthology *The Linguistic Turn* is from 1931. In fact, the first thinker to take the view Rorty formulates was the German philosopher Johann Georg Hamann, and he stated it in 1784.[10]

There is an entire tradition of philosophy of language among German-language thinkers, moving from Hamann all the way to Fritz Mauthner, against whom Wittgenstein defines himself in the *Tractatus* (¶ 40031). It is not an easy tradition to disengage, because it tends to be buried under reams of talk about God and Being and various Absolutes, or about the Will to Power, or about the "Spirit of a people."[11] I will offer here only a few observations gleaned from it.

The first point evidenced in this tradition, whose greatest practitioner, in my opinion, was Hegel, is that civic language is not merely a continuation of private interchanges such as those of the marketplace (Quine) or even the workplace (Wittgenstein). The second is that civic language itself exhibits various types and takes different forms, including (to use Hegel's typology) not merely politics and science but art and religion as well. It is to these latter two that the German thinkers tend most productively to key their accounts of language. (They talk little about empirical science, and when they talk about political language it tends to be quite unsavory.)[12]

The third point to be made about this tradition is, perhaps, clear from its relative neglect of scientific language: the German thinkers do not accord truth the kind of role that it has in much of the more recent analytical philosophy of language. That is, they do not view truth telling to be the fundamental linguistic activity (any more than does the later Wittgenstein);[13] they are more interested in what language expresses and how it ties people together than with how it makes claims about reality. This is in contrast to Davidson and others, for whom meaning is reducible to truth and for whom the most basic form of linguistic behavior—the one which underlies all uses of language—is to hold something for true (see *CW*, 250–277).

Consider what Hegel has to say, in *Lectures on the Philosophy of Religion*, concerning God. The existence of God "in Himself," that is, as a being in his own right, distinct from the world he created—in other words, the single issue that everybody thinks is absolutely basic to religion—is dismissed as of no concern at all; the only topic worth philosophical treatment is God as he relates to us, that is, religion itself (Hegel 1984, 1:115–116). Hence Hegel does not write a theology but a philosophy of religion. He clearly does not care, philosophically, whether the term "God" "refers" or not; what he is interested in is how the idea of God organizes our behavior, that is, in religion. Here, there is obviously an enormous wealth of material (and Hegel's accounts of the philosophy of religion fill three very thick volumes, though with a lot of repetition). One practical effect of the concept of God, in Hegel's view, is that God is supposed to be (a) the source of all moral value, and (b) powerful enough to be able to operate without intermediaries. The effect of belief in this sort of being (independently of whether that being actually exists) is that any entity, no matter how lowly, is capable of standing in direct contact with the source of all moral value—and had better be treated as such. This, Hegel thinks, is especially significant with regard to human beings, and so he thinks that the concept of God, as it has evolved through the millennia down to his own version of Lutheranism, is responsible for any concept of universal humanity and so makes possible all attempts to liberate humans as such (see, e.g., Hegel 1984, 3:109).

As this example shows, history is essential to understanding civic language, if only because the consequences of using a word in civic discourse can be historical.[14] But even noncivic language is always understood historically. Any word we use, in whatever interpersonal context we use it, must, for better or worse, be true to its history. How else will other people understand it? If I use the word "victory," for example, I am expecting that other people know what I mean—and what they know is what the term has meant up to now. If I change the meaning of the word by using it in some new way, as poets often do, then I cannot hope to be immediately understood. In order to use and evaluate words, then, we must turn to their histories. The need for words in civic language to be true to their histories is why the most basic form of language for Heidegger—the upsurge of new words in poetry—is restricted to small groups, to those people who have actually experienced a given work of art. Only later can such speech become truly civic—when many people have read or heard the poem, for example, or when people who have not hear those who have using a word in new ways and adopt it themselves.

One way in which public language differs crucially from the language of private encounters—a way which I am tempted to regard as a way to define the notion of civic language itself—is that in civic speech a hearer cannot ask the speaker what she means by a given utterance. Much greater precision is therefore demanded of such speech: if I am just chatting with you and say something you do not understand, you can simply ask me what I meant. If I am delivering a speech, writing a play, or writing a book, my words must convey their meanings without the hearers having to ask. Indeed, in such cases asking after the author's intention is almost senseless.

As we saw in Chapter 5, Hegel attempts to meet these demands for precision, in his philosophical system, by defining the various meanings a given word has and arranging them in such a way that more complex meanings are built out of simpler ones in a step-by-step fashion. When in his logic he treats of "cause," he begins with the simplest form of cause—one which is not distinct from its effect, as when we say that a football team is larger than a basketball team *because* it has more players on it. He then moves to cases in which cause is distinct from effect, the kind of cases discussed by contemporary science. And he ends with the very complex cases in which part A of a thing affects part B, which in turn affects part A, making A both distinct from and not distinct from its effects (see *SL*, 558–569).

On this view of Hegel's thought, he is very much concerned with language as a public good. As I put it in Chapter 5, he hopes to help ordinary people talk to the learned, and the learned to talk to one another. His step-by-step method, for example, assures that all the different meanings of a word will be brought up, defined, and arranged in the system: the system will, in my earlier word, be capacious. Since the definitions will be precise, the terms defined will be usable in public discourse. And Hegel even tries to guarantee accessibility, by making the development of the system entirely immanent. Each term is defined *only* by terms which themselves have been defined in the system, so that if I have followed its development to a certain point—even if I do not speak German—I will know the terms which define that particular term and will know the definitions of those terms as well.

Of course, there are some large problems with this procedure, and I will mention three of them. First, Hegel's vision of "accessibility" does not exactly work. I have said that the system is accessible in that any human being, from any culture, who has followed the development to a given point will know the terms which define whatever term is under discussion at that point. But nobody ever in fact follows that development, so Hegel's discourse became a self-enclosed language—and Hegel himself became perhaps the most misunderstood philosopher in history.

Second: If philosophy is a defining and arranging of words, where do those words come from? After all, the system cannot be more capacious, it would seem, than the language which it is trying to comprehend. (Actually it can, but not by much.) The short answer to this is, from all walks of life. But as we saw in Chapter 5, Hegel positions philosophy at the top of a hierarchy: in the modern world, philosophy is parasitical, so to speak, on the specialized discourses of science. When we look back beyond modernity to history as a whole, a different discourse is more responsible for our words than others, and it is to that discourse that philosophy turns most—namely, poetry:

> The chief task of poetry is to bring before our minds the powers governing spiritual life [in Hegel's sense of "spiritual"] . . . the all-encompassing realm of human ideas, deeds, actions and fates, the bustle of life in this world, and the divine rule of the universe. Thus poetry has been and still is the most universal and widespread teacher of the human race. (Hegel 1975a, 972)

In fact, many scientific words (most famously, perhaps, "quark"[15]) have backgrounds in poetry, literature, and religion. Hegel takes account of this in his system, often to the puzzlement of readers. What does it mean, for example, to say that light is the "self" of matter, as Hegel does in his *Philosophy of Nature* (Hegel 1970b, 87)? It means, among other things, that Hegel is trying to accommodate not merely the science of his day but the religious illuminationism of Augustine and others, according to which light was the boundary between the physical and intellectual worlds and constituted the relation between God and created beings.

Not all words come from poetry; many come from science and religion. The account of the word "God" which I mentioned earlier could not, for Hegel, have come from poetry, because poetry, like art in general, is for him elitist: it concerns appearances, and some things are better looking than others (McCumber 1984). The idea that any human being, no matter how ugly or repulsive, is in direct contact with the source of all moral value is not merely unpoetic but antipoetic; as such, it is religious.

The third and final problem is this: even if a community has followed Hegel and understands the words in its civic speech as he has tried to define them, problems would remain. Which of the several meanings of "cause" that Hegel discusses, for example, might a given speaker intend on a given occasion? It seems that we still have a choice, though this time it is among several meanings of the term, each of which has been clearly defined.

Since we do have a choice, civic speech as Hegel understands it becomes oriented to freedom rather than solely to truth: a given utterance will not have a meaning until we decide one for it, presumably by choosing among the alternatives which Hegel himself has prepared for us. Or we could leave the term, and the meaning, undefined, with several of the alternatives in play. In both cases, we are forced to act freely (see *PI*, 418). This emancipatory dimension of language is more evident in civic than in private language, at least to the extent that in the case of civic speech, we cannot ask the speaker what she meant.

Hegel's way of caring for civic language is like setting up and maintaining a public park—designing and building it so that it will have the facilities that people need and want to use, designing new equipment when necessary, and making the whole thing accessible to everyone. It is they, however, who actually decide how they are going to use it. There is also the issue of maintaining the equipment already in place, that is, guarding language against misuse. Goldhaber, in the essay referred to, is concerned with misuse in the form of encroachments upon civic language in the form of copyrighting of various words and phrases, fixing what should be a common labor of development into words and phrases that cannot be changed because we (the people) do not "own" them. There is another sort of problem which I want to discuss a bit here, and that is the misuse of words.

Once we have a well-defined set of words for public (or private) discourse, we can tell if someone is using them with meanings which differ from those and so are ill formed. Hegel's main example concerns the term "state." As I noted in Chapter 5, part of the definition of "state" in the *Philosophy of Right* is that a "state" gives equal rights to all its citizens. A government which does not do this—Hegel's example is the "states" of eastern Europe which did not give civil rights to Jews—has no right to call itself a "state" (see Hegel 1975a,

208, 210–211). If it does, then it is abusing systematically defined language—and philosophers should point that out.[16]

The norms I have adumbrated here for public language obviously hold, though perhaps less stringently, for language in general. It seems from them that the requirements for an effective civic language concern its vocabulary more than its syntax and have to do with three things: past, present, and future.

The *past* of a word is the history which has formed it. This history is essential to its being a word at all. Since one can only understand a word in terms of what one has learned in the past about its meaning, a word without a history is not a word. If I start talking about "bluptharps," for example, I am not using an English word because "bluptharp" has no past in the English language. In order to use a word effectively, then, I have to know something about its history—and since the histories of words are not transparent, knowing the histories means investigating complicities and connections which lie far below the surface (as Heidegger shows repeatedly). The Greek word for intellect, *nous*, is related to the English "nose": the intellect was originally a sort of intellectual "sniffer" which did not undertake inferences but, as in Aristotle, apprehended universals (see *De anima*, 3.5, 3.6).

The *future* of a word is the actions which use of it on a given occasion will trigger in those present (including the speaker). Ethnic slurs are obvious examples of words which trigger all kinds of things which another word, referring to the same person, would not. But there are many other examples, such as the way the word "God," as used in Christianity, has triggered everything from crusades to campaigns for social justice. Lincoln's words about a "house divided" had futures he could hardly imagine.

And the *present* of a word is the interplay of clarity and ambiguity of its use on a given occasion: Do we know what it means? Or are we free to come up with a meaning for it?

Philosophers have looked at all these things, of course, but as I suggested in Chapter 1, I think they should do a lot more looking and a lot more systematically, and I think they should pay a lot more attention to civic language when they do. For our language is an important part of our infrastructure—indeed, it is the fundamental part, without which we would have no other infrastructure. And there is reason to think our linguistic infrastructure, like the rest of it, is in pretty bad shape; I have given examples elsewhere (*TD*, 102–103). The fact is that, as Hegel put it, words are the "net" in which all our thinking is caught (Hegel 1892, 1:57); and, as Wittgenstein showed, we will not work free of the entrapments until we understand them.

Hegel on Marriage and Its History

I will conclude this discussion of critical practice in philosophy with a second look at Hegel's view of marriage and family, this time to show how he falls into the same trap as Lincoln—and how the resources are at hand to rescue him. Like Lincoln's "House Divided" speech, Hegel's treatment of marriage in the *Philosophy of Right* presents a masterful dialectical recapitulation, here of the history of marriage, showing how its current shape emerges from a rational past. And, like Lincoln, he fails to see anomalies in his own account. His account of modern marriage is thus not critical of it; rather, it situates such marriage as the outcome of an historical process, and—perhaps against Hegel's wishes—shows how that process must be carried further.

In Hegel's general account of "ethical life" in the *Philosophy of Right*, one function of the community is to determine whether or not a given individual act was a case of some recognized social practice or not. Finding people guilty of crimes is one way of doing this, since things like murder and burglary count as social practices; but another, happier one comes when the community "recognizes and confirms" a marriage by certifying that the ceremony which launches it was a valid one (*PhR*, 204–205). Only when recognized in this way does the marriage become a really existing ethical bond; prior to that, a loving relationship has no sanction beyond the sentiments of the partners. Thus, my beloved and I can stand up in front of someone and sincerely recite all kinds of vows; but until the community in general agrees that our actions constitute a marriage ceremony, we are not married. Marriage is thus a case of civic speech in which the meaning of that speech is what the community says it is, rather than what I intend by my utterance.

Like everything else in the modern world, the institution of marriage is the outcome of a painfully long process of trial and error. Hegel does not attempt a full history of the different forms marriage has taken down through the millennia the way he does for art, religion, and philosophy but confines his discussion to "remarks" and "supplements" in the *Philosophy of Right* and the lectures for which it was a handbook. Placing what he says on a time line shows, however, that there has been a learning process in which a number of alternative structures of marriage have been left behind.

The most primitive view of marriage sees it in animalistic terms, as strictly a sexual relation (*PhR*, 200–201). This, says Hegel, is not marriage at all but concubinage: a permanent arrangement for satisfying the sexual drive. It is presumably the male whose sexual drive is being satisfied, and as an institution which relegates one person to satisfying the desires of another person on a permanent basis, concubinage bears a strong resemblance to slavery in the *Phenomenology of Spirit* (*PhS*, ¶¶ 178–196; 111–119).

The next level would be exogamous marriage, which at least deserves to be called "marriage" because it is, as it were, half in and half out of the natural world. It and its opposite, endogamous marriage, come into being when whether or not someone is closely related to you becomes relevant to whether you are to marry them. To make this distinction at all is to opt for exogamy, because marrying within your family is both naturally and ethically counterproductive. It is naturally disfavored because it results in weakened offspring (*PhR*, 208), but it is also ethically deficient. This is because, in line with Hegel's discussion of the *Antigone* in the *Phenomenology* (*PhS*, ¶¶ 446–463; 267–278), members of a family are defined against one another not as individually distinct personalities but in terms of roles they have played from birth (*PhR*, 207).[17]

The distinction between endogamy and exogamy, and the preference for the latter, are thus at once both natural and ethical. When the distinction is made, we can view marriage as a relationship not merely between individuals but between bloodlines or houses; and here, too, we find a distinction between what is natural and what is ethical (*PhR*, 202). Some parents, especially in cultures where women are "held in little esteem," arrange marriages for their children without consulting them. The result of this is that the child remains defined as a child, playing the natural and abstract role assigned by the family: "The girl wants only to find *a* husband, and the man wants only to find *a* wife" (*PhR*, 202).

Others adopt an approach Hegel identifies as "more ethical": they introduce their children to the prospective mates, but if mutual attraction does not develop, they go no further (*PhR*, 201–202). The decision not to go further, however, belongs to the parents alone.

These two forms of arranged marriage are opposed not merely to concubinage but to views of marriage in the modern world, where individuals have rights against their families. In that context, marriage becomes a matter of individual commitment, and there are two main ways in which it can be understood. One of these is as exclusively grounded in being in love. This approach can, as with Friedrich von Schlegel, go so far as to deny that the community has any ethical role in a marriage at all, even one limited to recognizing it in a ceremony (*PhR*, 205).

The individual can also abandon sentiment altogether and view marriage in the cold terms of individual rationality: as a contract. This view gives marriage social recognition, but it is based on the image of the contracting individual as a self-sufficient unit whose basic nature never changes (*PhR*, 203). It thus denies the very nature of marriage as the free self-surrender of individuality; Kant's adoption of it was "disgraceful" and "crude" (*PhR*, 105, 201).

Marriage in the modern world is thus for Hegel grounded in feelings and the free commitment of individuals—but of individuals who are radically self-transforming, not the kind of fixed individuals who enter into contracts. As such, marriage is not a contract to perform specified services at a later date but an agreement to transform yourself. The partners "consent to constitute a single person and to give up their natural and individual personalities within this union" (*PhR*, 201). This is their liberation—from the animalistic selfishness and contingency of natural desire:

> The natural drive is reduced to the modality of a moment of nature which is destined to be extinguished in its very satisfaction, while the spiritual bond asserts its rights as the substantial factor. (*PhR*, 202)

This form of marriage, then, is the outcome of a history in which other arrangements have been tried and have failed. Only it isn't; history has not led to the state Hegel describes, and we see this in his thought itself—in the ghastly remarks on women at §§ 165–166 of the *Philosophy of Right*. Though Hegel did not see himself as a despiser of women (see *PhR*, 202), modern marriage in his view *rightly* relegates women to the domain of the family and *rightly* denies that they have the mental capacity for action outside the household. These views are clearly at variance with the egalitarian nature of marriage as complete ethical self-surrender (and implicit, moreover, in Hegel's rejection of polygamy).[18] Hegel's philosophical narrative thus needs to be destructured, and he himself (however unwillingly) begins that process.

Hegel's task, at least as I see it, is to comprehend the German language as it has been historically shaped. That language, we see, contains two different discourses on marriage: one according to which it is a mutual self-surrender and another according to which it is an instrument of oppression.[19] Hegel never attempts to bring these two discourses together and never even acknowledges their incompatibility. How deeply embedded in his philosophy are they?

An important consideration here is that Hegel's vilification of women is dialectically misplaced. Marriage, like all of ethical life, is a movement from the natural to the ethical such that the latter comes to predominate; that is what makes it "ethical." In keeping with this, Hegel ought to begin with his account of the "natural determinacy of the two sexes" (*PhR*, 206), before going on to show how this is overcome in marriage. Instead, the discussion of the natural determinacy comes *after* the discussion of ethical substantiality, with the result that—for women—biology suddenly reappears to become destiny. The discussion is festooned with general references to "rationality" and "concrete unity"—the former being too abstract to justify anything, the latter being a misapplication, for the concrete unity of two things precludes the dominance of one of them; the point is central to Hegel's culminating account of "reconciliation" in the *Phenomenology* (401–409), which I discussed briefly in Chapter 5 (and at *PI*, 60–62). The odious views on women at §§ 165–166 of the *Philosophy of Right* are thus dialectically ill founded; they are not stages in the overall development but what I would call anomalous to it.

Like Lincoln, then, Hegel does not take the Heideggerian step of questioning the end of his own narrative; perhaps we should not expect him to do so, a century before the publication of *Being and Time*. But he has provided the basis for such questioning, with the dialectical anomaly of his remarks on the incapacities of women. His account of marriage testifies, in spite of Hegel himself, to new directions which must be taken on our path to full humanity—and to the new words which had to come forth to articulate, eventually, what Friedan called the "problem with no name."

EPILOGUE

In history, things always hide other things. What is hidden may be less important than the fact that it is hidden and also less important than what is hiding it. This is as true of the history of philosophy as of any other kind. Consider the variety of screens we have explored here:

1. Philosophy's overall status as an obsession with ousia has been hidden by the view of it as a search for truth.

2. The role of form in Aristotle as dominating a resistant matter has been hidden by medieval readings of him whose appeals to a creator-God prohibit any such resistance and so any such domination.

3. The importance of tolerance and intolerance to Aristotle's metaphysics has been hidden by views of ontology as a purely theoretical enterprise unrelated to human conduct.

4. Kant the opponent of equality has been hidden by his own paeans to it.

5. Kant's subversion of the Enlightenment in his account of imagination has been hidden by his embrace of it in his accounts of will and the understanding.

6. Hegel's Heracleitean side has been hidden by the myths of his Kantian or pre-Kantian derivation.

7. The questioning, careful Heidegger has been hidden by the reality of the Nazi Heidegger.

These screens are discursive realities, each of which has its own dynamics. Sometimes the screens are put up by the philosopher himself, intentionally (as with Kant [4, 5]) or via blunder and coercion, as with Heidegger (7). Sometimes they are raised by later philosophers, as when the medievals misread Aristotle and the moderns misread Hegel (2, 6). Sometimes the screen is simply an overly strong distinction that philosophers make, such as that between practical and theoretical undertakings (1, 3), sometimes through their tendency to absolutize certain notions, such as truth and God (1, 2). Just as a doctor must know how to cure many different kinds of ailments, then, so the historian of philosophy must be ready to deal with many different kinds of occlusion. Add to those mentioned such standard things as mistranslations (see *CW*, 290–291); the partial availability of texts (as with Hegel's *Philosophy of Right*, an important version of which was discovered in Indiana in 1969);[1] and just our human desire to have the people we write about be nice people (as with the British Empiricists and the slave trade), and the screens proliferate beyond counting.

An archeologist who uncovers a potsherd may be justified in scrubbing away the dirt that covered it; dirt is dirt. But the many screens which stand between us and the history of philosophy are multifarious and important, and it would be irresponsible to present the results without the search. Nonetheless, it is perhaps allowable, here at the end, to give a short summary of where we have arrived, without reviving issues of how we got there.

Only for metaphysicians is matter silent. In fact, it sends us messages all the time. But its speaking cannot be heard in the usual ways, because to hear it we must always chime in. Changes in the pressure of the atmosphere surrounding our bodies lead to changes in our own tissues, and these atmospheric changes perpetuate themselves when our bodies vibrate.

We distinguish vibrations from punctual changes—an ongoing rhythm from a single handclap, or a sudden accident from a message—by recapitulation. Recapitulation in turn pushes us toward a meaning, toward a formulation of what it is that unifies the various things being recapitulated. For unless such a formulation is at least possible, we do not know what to recapitulate: we cannot distinguish what belongs to a given series of sounds from what does not.

Each successive component of such a series differs, to be sure, from its predecessors; perfect repetition is impossible. Coming after what is taken as the beginning of the series, all its other members are measured by that beginning; when this ceases to be the case, and recapitulation takes a new beginning, we have a new series.

As far as similarity is concerned, the recapitulation moves forward as a series which progressively distances itself from the beginning and so is *malleable*. In its limit case, such a progression is continuous, that is, each member differs from the preceding one in only one respect. I call such a limit case "dialectical," and when a recapitulation of the speaking of matter approximates to this I call it "dialectical reflection." A rule or concept can be specified for this, though only when the series ends; for if the various members of the series were distancing themselves from the beginning, they were assimilating themselves to what we take as its final state. The rule retrospectively assigns to each component its place in the series, according to the inversely variant degrees of its resemblances to the beginning and to the end.

When an intermediate member is considered as differing from the preceding one, however, the series is *fractured*. It cannot be recapitulated as a unity, for there is no progressive distancing from the beginning and so no progressive approximation to an end—and no way, finally, to tell why any member is where it is; no rule for the progression can be given. Our confrontation with something for which there is no explanation is, most basically, a questioning one, and we therefore end such a series in a question (or several). I call such questioning confrontation "destructuring."

Dialectical reflection and destructuring are the two ways in which philosophy can chime in with the speaking of matter and so with some of the most important voices of our time: the insurgent discourses of those who, up until the middle of the last century, were so brutally silenced.

Philosophy must learn to hear the speaking of matter. The only alternative is to flee back into its traditional repertoire of concepts, the repertoire given unparalleled formulation in Enlightenment thought: truth, justice, reason, existence, and the like. That core repertoire exists today in two ways: as explicit in philosophy and as implicit in other discursive practices. In both cases, it is walled off from all other concepts by its supposedly non-empirical origins, ordered by argument and definition, and capable of reproducing itself in the minds of succeeding generations. It is an intellectual version of ousia, the schema of oppression that philosophers since Aristotle have helped foist on the world. (And first of all on themselves.)

If that schema of oppression is philosophy's core, then philosophy is better off without its core. Abandoning it means bringing dialectical reflection into the heart of reason itself, so that its various rules and procedures—the "laws" of being, of beauty, of justice, even of logic—are understood to be not timeless truths but merely the most recent stages in a long sequence of such rules and procedures; it means seeing reason itself as historically malleable. It also means destructuring reason: seeing it as recurrently susceptible to fracture and mystery.

Philosophy's current crisis, the widening gaps between it and the world at large, other discourses, and its own practitioners, is thus the expression of an underlying and ancient structural dilemma. Institutional measures such as opening more philosophy departments in diverse locales, hiring people of diverse ethnicities, starting new and more "relevant" journals, raising philosophers' salaries and awarding them fellowships—even, most utopian of all, getting analysts and continentals to talk meaningfully to each other—will not solve this underlying problem. Such measures, to be sure, are laudable and necessary. But even if carried through, they would only palliate the underlying issue, which concerns not who does philosophy, or where, or what philosophers think about, but what philosophy itself has always been and must not be.

To fix this core dilemma so that the crisis does not reappear in some new guise, philosophers must begin hearing. recapitulating, and propagating the speaking of matter. This means throwing off the stubbornness (*karteria*) with which they have tolerated matter's speech, as well as the anger with which they have on occasion sought to extirpate it, and embracing instead the stances of dialectical reconciliation and destructuring letting-be.

Placing yourself repeatedly into the same experiential stance counts as addiction: I am "addicted" in this sense when it does not matter if I am at work or a wedding, driving a car or making love, because *I am always high*. Philosophy's relation to its timeless repertoire is, I suggest, similar to this; and like all addictions, it is unsustainable. For as time goes by, there come to be more and more experiences which the addicted party simply does not have. As these multiply, their pressure on the addict—the pressure of an unlived life—increases, and the addiction becomes stronger. His tolerance for the addictive Substance, which is actually the means for "tolerating" everything else, grows. The inadequacy of that Substance (here, ousia) gradually becomes more and more evident, at least to others. Eventually, the pressure of the increasing number of things with which the addict cannot deal pulls him into crisis, and he loses his final faith, the faith in addiction itself. His Disease becomes evident to him as well, and he hits Bottom.

Philosophy, I believe (and if I had written a Preface to this book, here would have been its burden), is finally beginning to recognize, at the hands of feminists, race theorists, queer theorists, and others, where it stands: at the crossroads between the speaking of matter—or death.

> And when he came back to, he was flat on his back on the beach in the freezing sand, and it was raining out of a low sky, and the *tide* was way out. (*IJ*, 981; emphasis added)

REFERENCE MATTER

NOTES

INTRODUCTION

1. Cf. Bellow's self-defense at Bellow 1994. For a discussion of the original, see Taylor 1994, 42.

2. According to the relevant web pages, philosophers have gotten six MacArthur "genius" grants, compared to thirteen each in literary studies and in the history and philosophy of science, and of those six only one—Thomas Scanlon—can be considered a mainstream American philosopher. Those who win Guggenheims tend to be in ethics and social philosophy, rather than the "core areas" of metaphysics and epistemology. See http://www.macfound.org/site/c.lkLXJ8MQKrH/b.1139453/k.B938/Search_All_Fellows .htm; http://www.gf.org/fellows/all/ (retrieved September 30, 2010).

3. http://www.insidehighered.com/views/2010/04/05/stanley (retrieved June 24, 2010).

4. http://apaonline.org/ (consulted June 21, 2010). Bad as this was, it was not nearly as bad as what happened just after the crisis of 1989, between 1992 and 1996, when according to the *New York Times*, about four hundred American philosophy departments were closed or amalgamated (Cropper 1997).

5. Cf. Plato, *Republic* 379e5.

6. Wielenberg actually does this; his interests lie in the important intersection of humanism and theology: see http://dpuadweb.depauw.edu/ewielenberg_web/ (retrieved March 21, 2012). The question is why he doesn't see it necessary to describe his work in that way.

7. Indeed, this may already be happening: anecdotes suggest that one reason philosophers win fewer fellowships is that the evaluations of their projects by other philosophers are increasingly hostile.

8. The text of the letter is available at Derrida 1995, 419–421.

9. It has now been conveniently replaced by the so-called Argument to Improper Authority, since citing authorities is crucial to academic reasoning these days; see Walton 1995. From this point of view as well, the Open Letter is fallacious—not in appealing to authority but in taking authority to be lodged among those employed in "leading departments."

10. As any number of people can testify, anything written by an American continental philosopher which is not an exposition of some European philosopher is guaranteed to be impact free.

11. Habermas and Hegel will be considered later in this book. For an introduction to object-oriented philosophy, see Meillassoux, Badiou, and Brassier 2010.

12. Among the main examples are the interviews with Jacques Derrida and Jürgen Habermas in Borradori 2004; also cf. Appiah 2007; Bernstein 2006; Borradori 2004; Butler 2006; Margolis 2005; and Rockmore, Margolis, and Marsoobian 2005.

13. Hobbes, Locke, and Berkeley were heavily invested in the slave trade. On the complicities of their philosophy in the colonial project, see Mills 1997 and Bracken 1973.

14. See Knobe and Nichols 2008, 3–14, and Bryant, Harman, and Srnicek 2011, 1–18, for details; both anthologies are highly instructive.

15. Gay 1977, 20–21; Kant, "Conjectural Beginning of Universal History," at *AA*, 8:29–30.

16. See Herman 2001, 1–15.

17. Kant, "Of National Characteristics, so far as They Depend upon the Distinct Feeling of the Beautiful and Sublime," in Kant, *Observations on the Feeling of the Beautiful and the Sublime*, at *AA*, 2:255. For Kant's later racism, see Eze 1995. Eze points out (201) that in the last work that Kant edited, *Anthropology from a Pragmatic Point of View*, he incorporated some of his precritical writings, though not this particular passage. For a succinct account of Kant's views on women, see *SC*, 168–173.

18. See Outlaw 1996b, esp. 146–151. For further insight on this entire section, see Outlaw 1996d.

19. On Kant's polemical practices in general, see also Saner 1973, 108–213.

20. "Open Letter on Fichte's *Wissenschaftslehre*," August 7, 1799, cited after Kant 1967, 254. This contrasts sadly with Kant's generalized recognition of fallibility when, in "What Is Enlightenment?," he says that no generation can bind future generations to any dogma (*AA*, 8:38–39).

21. Cf. Kant, *The Metaphysics of Morals*, at *AA*, 6:277.

22. Quine 1987, 209; see the discussion in Golumbia 1999.

23. The literature is vast; for first steps into it, see Hedrick 2008 and Golumbia 1999.

24. For an account of tragic *hamartia* as the presence in the soul of too much of something good, see McCumber 1988.

25. Sally Sedgwick, Presidential Address, meeting of the Central Division of the American Philosophical Association, 2010, MS.

26. The term "queer" seems to me to be associated primarily with gay and lesbian theorists, though it is increasingly accommodating transgender thought; as will be evident from the rest of the book, however, I am no expert on these discourses.

27. http://leiterreports.typepad.com/blog/2010/10/more-peculiarities-of-the-nrc-rankings-the-more-women-and-minorities-the-worse-the-program.html (retrieved October 11, 2010).

CHAPTER 1

1. For a history of the controversy, see Hoyningen-Huene 1987.

2. An example is the 1887 Michelson-Morley experiment regarding the speed of light, in which the unexpected movement (or lack of movement) of the interferometer led eventually to the special theory of relativity. For a classic account of it, see Shankland 1964.

3. Shoshana Felman has illuminated this issue for the speaking body in Felman 2003. My concern here is with the speaking of matter; the main difference is that matter as such is not packaged into discrete bodies. Its speaking is therefore not localized in the way that a body's is, and so it cannot seduce or perform.

4. The phenomenon of sympathetic vibration has been submitted to a number of loose, New Age interpretations. For a more straightforward account, see Ronald Lewcock et al., "Acoustics," in Grove Music Online, Oxford Music Online, http://www.oxfordmusic online.com/subscriber/article/grove/music/00134pg1 (accessed October 9, 2010).

5. See Hume 1896, 317–320; see also Morrow 1923. For the dominance of visual metaphors in modern philosophy, see the essays in Levin 1993.

6. The very existence of art testifies both to the broad nature of the speaking of matter and to its intersubjective character. There were many artists painting landscapes in the south of France in the second half of the nineteenth century; but the landscapes that presented themselves to Cézanne and Van Gogh, their "loyal and disciplined" though decidedly unscientific spokespersons, presented messages that the others did not—and we know this only because it is they, and not the others, who reached an audience.

7. For this role of the will, see *MO*, 121–124, 139–140.

8. "We are a residue of what we have said to one another" (Derrida 1987, 7).

9. Gately finds his Bottom at the end of the novel, watching the horrible murder of his friend Fackelmann. The two in fact find their Bottoms together, in a mutual act of sympathy which consists in taking every drug they can get their hands on. They then go their separate ways, Fackelmann to die and Gately to AA; in the final words of Plato's *Apology*, "which is better, no one knows but God."

10. It also shares, for example, features that Enrique Dussel attributes to Latin American "base communities," in which isolated individuals, coming together outside hegemonic structures, recognize in themselves "their own means to raise their consciousness" (Dussel 2003c, 150–151).

11. See Ströker 1993, 146–159, 226–229; Lawlor 2002, 47–48.

12. Or "judgment of taste"; the differences are not important here.

13. For aesthetic form in the *Critique of Judgment*, see Pillow 2000, 44–53. There is also a second requirement: if the conceptual realm is not to be a "useless duplication" of the empirical, we want to have fewer concepts than there are entities; and this requires us to assume that the universe is sufficiently well organized that the object in question comes under a relatively small number of yet-to-be-discovered general concepts and laws. This latter assumption is about the "form" of the universe itself and is not entailed by empirical givens. It is, the *Critique* argues, a basic principle of reflective judgment and gives such judgment heuristic value (*CJ*, 183–185).

14. *Angesinnet*, not *postuliert*; *CJ*, 216. See also *CJ*, 212–216, 237, 284–285.

15. Kant expresses this more forcefully in his unpublished material, through such observations as "the beautiful form seems only to be for society," "when we are alone we never attend to the beautiful," and "all solitary eccentrics have no taste." See Guyer 1982, 41.

16. Wittgenstein 1958, §§ 256–270, 91–95.

17. Not all encounters between oppressors and oppressed can count as cases of the speaking of matter, and sometimes encounters which are not are mistaken for encounters which are. The 1524 exchange between Aztec *tlamatinime* (philosophers) and twelve Franciscan friars to which Dussel refers in *Beyond Philosophy* was, he points out, a dialogue between two highly sophisticated philosophical traditions—but the Franciscans were less well educated than their Aztec counterparts, failed to recognize this, and thought they were speaking to unlettered peasants; see Dussel 2003b, passim, esp. 169.

18. For a sensitive broaching of this issue, see Butler 1997, 1–13.

19. The writer is male.

20. The distinction between original and sympathetic vibration, transposed to an intellectual level, gains relevance for "standpoint" epistemologies. The question it raises is not that of whether women, people of color, queers, and other disprivileged groups have knowledge which is unattainable by privileged subjects (such as white males), which may well be the case, but whether there are certain kinds of knowledge that they are going to attain *first*. Persistent failures on the part of the privileged to understand the disprivileged may often be understood as limit cases of this in which the privileged do not *let* themselves understand. See Alcoff 2000 and the nuanced treatment of standpoint epistemologies in Harding 1986, esp. 136–162, 243–251. For a classic anthology of writings on standpoint epistemology, see Harding and Hintikka 1983.

21. See Wallace's interview with Larry McCaffery (Wallace n.d.) at http://www .dalkeyarchive.com/book/?fa=customcontent&GCOI=15647100621780&extrasfile=A09 F8296%2DB0D0%2DB086%2DB6A350F4F59FD1F7%2Ehtml.

22. Cf. Aristotle, *Physics* 2.7.198a24–25, 2.8.199a30–33; *Metaphysics* 5.4.1015a10, etc.

23. See my *Time and Philosophy*, chapter 1.

CHAPTER 2

1. See the essays collected in Williams 2006.

2. See Rorty's obituary in the *Washington Post*, June 11, 2007.

3. For a fuller account of the French developments, see Gutting 2003.

4. Hobbes 1991, 370. For a general summary of Hobbes's reduction of Aristotle's cosmos to the "rigid unity of geometrical science," see Bernhardt 1989.

5. Descartes's recurrent use of the language and thought of Aristotle and his successors, the Scholastics, is documented in Gilson 1930, 1979.

6. Hume 1896, 415. For the equation of character with passion, see McIntyre 1990, 200–201.

7. *CPR* B, 119. Kant's debt to Leibniz is at its apex in his discussion, in the *Groundwork of the Metaphysics of Morals*, of the Kingdom of Ends, which is a clear reformulation, from a critical or subjectivized perspective, of the "Kingdom of Wisdom" discussed at Leibniz, "Specimen dynamicum" (Leibniz 1969, 442); see also Leibniz, *Monadology* (Leibniz 1969, 643–653, esp. §§ 85–90).

8. Plato, *Euthyphro* 6e.

9. Quine 1959, xi; for a more recent affirmation of this view, see Quine 1990, 77 (in conjunction, of course, with the book's title—*Pursuit of Truth*).

10. As I noted in the Introduction, Quine himself takes it in that direction.

11. *BT*, 214–215; Tarski 1943–44, esp. 343; see also *CW*, 74–75.

12. Augustine 1954, 177; Anselm 2000, 164.

13. The association of error with movement is captured in the Latin word "errare," which originally meant "to wander."

14. See Proclus, *In Timaeo* 2:287, 3–5, cited at Beierwaltes 1965, 129; but also see 337–338. See also Moutsopoulos 1982.

15. Aquinas, *Summa theologica*, pt. 1, ques. 16, art. 2, cited from Aquinas 1945, 1:170–171.

16. Benedict de Spinoza, *Ethics* I.A.6, II.P.34, in Spinoza 1985, 410, 472–473.

17. See *MO* for an extended argument.

18. The reference to "rule" here is no accident: as we will see in Chapter 3, ousia is intimately connected, from the very beginning, with domination (*kratia*); its political complicities are as obvious and unsavory as its metaphysical origins.

19. When violence is directed against all and only members of a defined group, as in the Holocaust, it is not random; such undertakings must be planned and clearly constitute an attempt to order a society by eliminating some of its members.

20. As Mary Louise Gill puts it, "The Aristotelian cosmos is a world of tension and commotion—ordered and preserved by form, disordered by matter" (Gill 1989, 242).

21. See the discussion of Augustine at *MR*, 28–33.

22. For the complex situation in Plato, see Okin 1979, 51–70.

23. As Rousseau put it, "If someone torments me in one place, what will prevent me from going elsewhere?" (Rousseau 1987, 58).

24. For this criterion of the "natural" in Aristotle, see *Physics* 2.8.198b35–36; *On the Heavens* 3.2.301a8–9; *Prior Analytics* 1.2 25a14–15, 1.13 32b18–20, 1.15 35b14–15; etc. Aristotle puts the epistemological aspiration very clearly at *NE* 6.3.1139b19–23: "We all suppose that what we know is not even capable of being otherwise. . . . Therefore the object of scientific knowledge is of necessity. Therefore it is eternal."

25. Reason also, of course, governs our interaction with the world outside our minds, in that moral action for Kant is performed freely and so from reason alone.

26. Descartes, *Principles of Philosophy*, at *DOe*, 8A:22–24, 34–39; see also *MO*, 120–125.

27. See Quine 1960, 26–79; 1953b, passim; Plato, *Phaedrus* 263a–b.

28. Aristotle thought the *chōrismos* was central to Plato; postmodernists such as Derrida ignore it. See *MO*, 97–101.

29. Aristotle, *Politics* 1.13.1260a13–15; Beauvoir 1952, xxxvi.

30. Hence, what Robert Piercey (2009) calls the "historical thesis" about philosophy—the thesis that we cannot do philosophy without doing history of philosophy—is an attempt to define philosophy, and in so doing to place people like Quine outside it. Piercey's claim that in order to accept the historical thesis we must accept the view that truth is found in history would in any case be beside my point: what can be found there, I have argued, is ousia.

CHAPTER 3

1. For Kant, of course, reason was just such an atemporal cause, operating as will; but—of course—in his view we cannot, strictly speaking, "know" this.

2. Indeed, the *Phenomenology of Spirit* concludes with a far mightier death than our own, that of God. See McCumber 2000b.

3. I will criticize this reading in Chapter 5, but for now those criticisms are beside the point.

4. Foucault's own deployment of his critical perspective, guided by his instatement of historical rupture as the *single* basic category for understanding history, ran into problems which, I have argued, become evident when we try to imagine what he might have said about the Holocaust. See McCumber 1998.

5. The concepts of being and presence have special status within metaphysics, as is indicated by the tendency of philosophers to conflate them. Even the two thinkers who have most relentlessly interrogated them, Heidegger and Derrida, do not consistently keep them apart. See *PF*, 35–36, for a fuller discussion.

6. Separability and self-accordance are related at *Metaphysics* 5.18: while in most senses to exist "in accordance with self" is to have an essence, it can in one sense be said that any property a thing has when it is considered as existing by itself, separately, from other things, it has "according to itself."

7. To take this out of the language of "separability" and put it in the more perspicuous vocabulary of "being in" or "inhering" (*eggignesthai*) found at *Categories* 1.1a22–23: If property φ inheres in some ousia S in that it is incapable of existence apart from S; and if S and some other ousia S" are capable of existence apart from one another; then φ cannot inhere in both S and S", for then S could go out of existence and φ would still exist, which would mean that φ is capable of existence apart from S, is separable from it, and so cannot have inhered in it.

8. For a similar critique of the metaphysics of substance from the point of view of race, see Outlaw 1996a. Outlaw's reflections on the limits of European conceptions of humanity and rationality here are particularly instructive.

9. See Deleuze 1994; Derrida 1977; Kierkegaard 1964.

10. See Graham 1987; for a more detailed account of ousia in Aristotle, see *MO*, 21–70.

11. See Aristotle, *Metaphysics* 9.7.1049a23–26.

12. Aristotle, *Physics* 2.1.193b8, 2.2.194b13, 2.7.198a26, 3.2.202a11; *Metaphysics* 7.7.1032a25, 7.8.1033b32, 9.8.1049b24–25, 12.4.1070a8, 12.4.1070a28–29, 12.4.1070b31, 12.4.1070b34, 14.5.1092a17.

13. Aristotle's whole account of the knowing soul is structured by the association of form and knowability: see *MO*, 48–56. For an equation of ousia with *logos* itself, see *Metaphysics* 7.10.1035b27–28, 7.15.1039b20–21. To know an individual thing is to know the form in it.

14. Derrida 1974, 270; see also Derrida 1978c, 102.

15. The Greeks in fact had two words for "moon": *selēnē*, which was commonly used, and *mēnē*, which was reserved for sacred uses. That the name *katamēnia* is com-

pounded from the latter reveals the frighteningly mysterious nature of menstruation for the Greeks.

16. Aristotle's Greek does not in fact refer explicitly to "man," but it has masculine adjectives which do the job.

17. In general terms: "The lower always exists for the sake of the higher, and the higher is that which has a rational principle" (*Politics* 7.14.1333a21–23). In the unhindered man, this can go so far that the desire takes over the whole person, driving out reason altogether (*NE* 3.13.1119b7–11).

18. *NE* 6.2.1139b4–5; see also *PI*, 225–226.

19. *NE* 8.3.1156b1–3, 9.5.1167a3–12, 9.12.1171b29–30.

20. *Eudemian Ethics* 2.10.1225b30; *NE* 7.1.1145a36, 7.1.1145b8.

21. W. W. Fortenbaugh (1977) has argued that the lack of "authority" (*kyrios*) Aristotle here imputes to woman's reason resides first in its inability to control her own emotions—in my terms, to dispose of the ethical matter of her life.

22. Also see *Physics* 4.8.215a1, 5.6.230a29–30; *Metaphysics* 5.5.1015a26–28, etc.

23. With (perhaps) certain exceptions such as true friendship, which fulfills our rational nature; see *PI*, 232–234.

24. *Metaphysics* 12.10.1076a4; quoted from Homer, *Iliad* 2.204.

25. *Politics* 1.13.1260a13–15.

26. I will ignore the issue of children here, restricting myself to the oppression of adults.

27. *On the Generation of Animals* 4.3.767b8–768a9; the entire chapter is relevant here.

28. See the Vatican document *Persona Humana*, § 8, at http://www.vatican.va/roman_curia/congregations/cfaith/documents/rc_con_cfaith_doc_19751229_persona-humana_en.html; and *The Catechism of the Catholic Church*, §§ 2357–2359, at http://www.vatican.va/archive/catechism/p3s2c2a6.htm (both retrieved July 9, 2010).

29. Sophocles 1902, ll. 490, 680; my translation.

CHAPTER 4

1. See Pippin's remarks about Derrida at Pippin 1991, 161; see also Laura Hengehold, "Subject, Postmodern Critique of," in E. Craig (ed.), *Routledge Encyclopedia of Philosophy* (London: Routledge, 1998); retrieved May 25, 2011, from http://www.rep.routledge.com/article/DE023.

2. Gill 1989, 166; see also 212–214, 77–82, for an account of the nature and status of the elements. Also see Haring 1956–57, 310 (emphasis added): "[The elements] can be taken up into more determinate beings. . . . They become limited, pervaded, and oriented by the nature of the whole containing them. . . . Within wholes, they are in the *dominion* of something other." And finally, Witt 1989, 120.

3. For which, see Gill 1989, 242.

4. So constituted, God as ousia "is" the human situation: "an potius non essem, si non essem in te?" (Augustine 1988, 1.4).

5. For further detail, see *MO*, 71–85.

6. For a brief (and devastating) account of this involvement, see Bracken 1973.

7. Descartes, "Letter to More," August 1629, at *DOe*, 5:401; see also Hatfield 1979, 131.

8. Garber 1992, 116; see also *MO*, 116–120.

9. An idea which, Joseph Needham notes, was never even comprehensible to people as sophisticated as the Chinese; Needham 1969, 302, quoted and discussed at *SSI*, 45.

10. See Descartes, "Letter to Elizabeth," September 1646, at *DOe*, 4:485–492.

11. See *RC*, 13, 19–31, and passim.

12. Aristotle also knew about the power of certain illusions. "Even when persons are in excellent health, and know the facts of the case perfectly well, the sun nevertheless appears to them to be only a foot wide" (*De somniis* 458b).

13. The answer turns out to be the matter of the sensory organs: *De somniis* 460a–b.

14. On the primacy of the will in Descartes, see also Schouls 1994, 172–176.

15. Also see Descartes, *Meditations* 3, passim, at *DOe*, 8:34–52.

16. *Meditations* 4 argues that the only reason we have to think that the objects of our knowledge, which are ideas in us, correspond to realities outside us is that God tells us so, and he is no liar.

17. See Descartes, *Principles of Philosophy* 1:24, at *DOe*, 8A:14. The whole approach of *Meditations* 4 to the question of error moves from the consideration of God's nature to that of our own: see *DOe*, 7:54.

18. Kant, *Prolegomena to Any Future Metaphysics*, at *AA*, 4:260. Hume's skeptical treatment of the notion of causality blocked reasoning back from the universe or anything in it to God as its cause; see *CPrR*, 51.

19. Kant, *The Metaphysics of Morals*, at *AA* 6:218–222. For more on Kant's view of legislation, see *PI*, 277–282.

20. *CPrR*, 21 and passim; see also *Groundwork of the Metaphysics of Morals*, at *AA*, 4:15, 19.

21. This problematic is explored in Deleuze 1984.

22. *CJ*, 179–181; see also *CPR* B, 670–697.

23. Meerbote 1982, 79; see also Pillow 2000, 44–53, 17–123, passim.

24. On this, see *PF*, 20–33, 110–123.

25. Derrida 1974, 158; see also 35, 44–65; and Derrida 1981a, 35, 103.

26. Derrida 1981a, 344; see also 328.

27. This is the pedagogical intention which Derrida, for example, ascribes to Hegel's *Encyclopedia*; Derrida 1981a, 46–47.

28. Derrida 1981a, 6–7; Derrida 1974, 157–159.

CHAPTER 5

1. For statements of these positions, see Hartmann 1972; Pinkard 1988; and Pippin 1989.

2. See Mure 1940, passim. More recently, Tom Rockmore has demonstrated the centrality of Descartes, rather than Kant, to Hegel's epistemology: Rockmore 1986, 141–158.

3. And, I have argued elsewhere, of British Empiricism: see McCumber 2002, passim.

4. See Kirk and Raven 1960, 184; see also Hegel's comments at *HWe*, 18:322/281.

5. *HWe*, 18:330; this passage is not in the English translation. Hegel's account of Heracleitus is accurate on this point: see Kirk and Raven 1960, 185. For Cratylus, see Kirk and Raven 1960, 197–198.

6. Most strenuously at *Metaphysics* 1.9.

7. As I maintain in Chapter 4 and, at greater length, elsewhere: see *MO*, 105–202.

8. *BT*, 2–4; also see Heidegger 1998f, passim.

9. Hegel himself claimed that he finished it to the sound of the cannonades of the Battle of Jena. For doubts about this, see Pinkard 2000, 228–229.

10. Those who, like Habermas, uncritically accept Heidegger's view that Hegel is *merely* a "philosopher of consciousness" should take note of this. See Habermas 1990; for Heidegger's views on Hegel, see Heidegger 1975b, 105, 176, 178–179, 216, 218; Heidegger 2002b; Heidegger 1969, 68–73.

11. Cf. McCumber 2011, ch. 2.

12. The particular was already present in sense-certainty—first as the "night" which named the Now (*PhS*, ¶ 95; 60). But its presence could not be recognized or exploited because, for complex reasons, to do so would be to introduce mediation. Everything in "Sense-Certainty," however, is—as we are repeatedly told in that section—supposed to be strictly immediate.

13. Most famously, perhaps, when the book rejects the death of the battlers because it would be a case of abstract negation rather than the determinate kind; *PhS*, ¶ 188; 114–115.

14. Hegel was well aware of his own limitations. Already in the preface to the *Phenomenology*, he had claimed to hear at the door "the feet of those who will carry you out" (*PhS*, ¶ 71; 44).

15. This in spite of the fact that much of the mountainous literature on the *Phenomenology* consists largely in surmising various truth claims it might be making and then trying to explain why anybody would ever make them.

16. This is Hegel's doctrine of "determinate negation," for which see *CW*, 148–149.

17. *SL*, 53. As Hegel puts it in the *Philosophy of Mind*, § 462: "The *name* is thus the *thing* as it is present and valid in the *realm of representation*. . . . *Reproductive* memory has and cognizes the thing in the name and with the thing the name. . . . The name as the existence of content in the intelligence is the *externality* of that content within it"; Hegel 1971, 219, my translation.

18. I have argued this point in much greater detail in *CW*.

19. As definitions of the absolute, *SL*, 74, 137; as definitions of God, *SL*, 78.

20. For more on this, see *CW*, passim.

21. For which in Heracleitus, see Kirk and Raven 1960, 189–196.

22. See the summaries of the ways in which Hegel changed his way of organizing the world's religions in what became his *Lectures on the Philosophy of Religion* from 1824 to 1831 at Hoffheimer 2005, 203–206.

23. See Hardimon 1994; and *PI*, 59–62.

24. For a penetrating account of this, see Comay 2011, 119–131.

25. Hegel calls this process *Erinnerung*, recollection or interiorization; Terry Pinkard, in an illuminating discussion, calls it "idealization" (Pinkard 1988, 104–108).

26. Mills provides a trenchant statement of such disparity in the African American folk aphorism which forms the epigraph to *RC*: "When white people say 'justice,' they really mean 'just us.'"

27. John Findlay's notes to *PhS* uncover many of these vague references to external realities.

28. See my *Hegel's Mature Critique of Kant: Issues in the Later Writings* (Stanford University Press, 2013).

29. Hegel's criticism of contract views of marriage, such as Kant's, is that they presuppose the stability of the parties to them; *PhR*, ¶ 163.

CHAPTER 6

1. Faye 2005. For reviews, see Meyer 2005 and Kirsch 2010.

2. See Kant, *The Conflict of the Faculties*, at *AA*, 7:5–116.

3. *Volklich-staatliches Dasein*, *R*, 12; see also 16. And see Pöggeler 1988, 31.

4. For discussions of the concept of "way" in Heidegger's thought, see *PI*, 107–108, 145–153; and *MO*, 235–246.

5. This presumably is why Heidegger was so good at locating himself with respect to the history of philosophy, as we saw Strawson note at the beginning of the previous chapter.

6. For example, in Heidegger 1998d. For Heidegger on resoluteness, see *PI*, 124–128.

7. Heidegger 1998d, 143–144; see also Heidegger 1959a, passim.

8. For Heidegger's treatment of hints, see *PI*, 153, 157.

9. "Science does not think"; "when science arises, thinking passes away"(Heidegger 1968, 134; Heidegger 1998b, 269).

10. Heidegger's concept of "truth" as an event has nothing to do with such notions as sentences and propositions and has in common with those views of truth only that truth is what we are seeking, the object of our investigation; see Dahlstrom 2001, 21.

11. For an account of Afrocentric discourse as such a refutation, see Asante 1987, 6–9, 16.

12. On this, see Pöggeler 1985, 28, 42n, 44, 62; see also Pöggeler 1988, 19–20, 32, 44; and Löwith 1986, 40.

13. Pöggeler 1988, 44–45. See Heidegger 1989, 319.

14. For a reliable account of Heidegger's views on science, see Kockelmans 1984, 209–225.

15. "Do not make 'theorems' and 'ideas' the rules of your Being; the Führer himself, and he alone, is today's and tomorrow's German reality and its law."

16. To say that Heidegger is distanced from Nazism in 1933–34 by his *admiration* for Hitler exemplifies the kind of absurdity in which discussion of Heidegger, and not only of his Nazism, repeatedly lands us. But Heidegger's perversely misplaced admiration does not invalidate the distinction of levels itself. The Philadelphia Constitutional Convention is not the American state: it opened up a whole new order; the state does not.

CHAPTER 7

1. On the revival of Kantianism, see Wiley 1987.

2. Husserl, letter to Marvin Farber, n.d., quoted at Farber 1943, 17; Husserl 1970, 57, 92.

3. Gasché 1986; see also Rorty 1991, 119–128.

4. Hence Alasdair MacIntyre could characterize analytical philosophy in general as a "reformulation" of Kantianism in response to empiricist challenges rather than a genuine empiricism: MacIntyre 1984, 266; see also Stuart Barnett, "Introduction," in Barnett 1998, 7–10, 295 n.18. The logical positivists, however, took a priori knowledge to be analytical; they denied Kant's "synthetic a priori."

5. Kant, *Prolegomena to Any Future Metaphysics*, at *AA*, 4:366. The science Kant is speaking of is in fact his reformed version of metaphysics, whose limits are drawn by critique. If the limits are unchanging, so must be that which draws them; see *AA*, 4:263.

6. See Kant, *Prolegomena to Any Future Metaphysics*, at *AA*, 4:298–300.

7. As I have argued elsewhere, it was Schiller's approach, not Kant's, which led Germany to the greatest string of philosophical innovations since the Greeks; see Mc-Cumber 2011, 23.

8. Though Habermas's view of history as a set of "learning processes" seems to place him on Hegelian/Schillerian terrain, it does not. Habermas uses the view that modernity is the outcome of a long history as support for his account of the three validity claims, but the account is to be adopted independently of that. Moreover, the validity claims are not supposed to be provisional outcomes but valid for all time—including the future, about which Hegel and Schiller can say nothing. For further discussion, see *PF*, 91–96, 102–104.

9. For the periodization of Foucault's work and a critique of the unfortunate emphasis on his later works, see Nealon 2008.

10. See Dussel's discussion of the "limits" to modernity (Dussel 2003d, esp. 68–70). Dussel's basic view, restated in my terms, is as follows: Modernity has pushed its ousiodic boundaries to the edge of nature and now encounters resistance from three directions. Matter, turned into debris, can no longer be ordered by the economic system—waste cannot be exploited. Labor is turned into "superfluous humanity," that is, the boundaries of the society are redrawn so as to exclude large numbers of people whose labor power is without value (as in Young's concept of "marginalization," discussed in Chapter 2). And initiative—the expansion of the system beyond its boundaries—is blocked because the population on its peripheries—Africans, Asians, and Latin Americans—show an "indomitable will to survive." Thus, the first limit shows that modernity is losing dispositive power; the second, that it can no longer set its own boundaries; and the third, that its initiative is stymied.

11. Such as that of Karl Popper, according to which it asserts contradictions, and anything you like can follow from a contradiction (Popper 1965). Or of those many who seek to "rescue" Marx from thermodynamic extinction by taking him to postulate underlying and unchanging laws of history such as the necessary movement from thesis to antithesis to synthesis.

12. Or, in slightly more modern format, "not (x is hot)." The difference is important, but not here.

13. An anomaly in this sense differs from what is conventionally called a dialectical "antithesis." Both terms indicate failures of subsumption, but in the case of a dialectical antithesis the failed subsumption is under a description of the initial state, which is presumed to be static, and says that the phenomenon in question can be subsumed equally well under both the description of that state and the description of its opposite: "x is not-cold" is the antithesis to "x is cold." An anomaly indicates a failure to subsume under *either* the thesis or the antithesis: x is neither cold nor not-cold.

14. "All things are contradictory in themselves" (*SL*, 439). I depart from Hegel in that for him contradiction is, as Charles Taylor notes (Taylor 1979, 43–46), the source or root of all movement, while for me it is an indication of movement or change. Hegel has systematic reasons for his claim which anchor it in his metaphysics. I will not go into those reasons here, since I am anchoring dialectics in thermodynamics.

15. If my potential employer pressures me into signing a contract, the contract is invalid; but if the entire economic system does the same, its validity is unimpeachable.

16. This speech is available in many places on the Web; I am using http://showcase .netins.net/web/creative/lincoln/speeches/house.htm (consulted July 22, 2010).

17. On these locutions, which Aristotle often uses of his own investigations, see Bonitz 1961, 111; on the general issue, see also *RR*, 138–140.

18. Habermas 1984–1987, 1:19 (emphasis added); see also 1:25.

19. I am not claiming that, as a matter of fact, Lincoln was not guided in his recapitulation of the events by his view that they constituted a plot. My claim is that it lies in the nature of his "argument" itself that such guidance should be minimized.

20. See the article on attempts to outlaw female circumcision in the *Economist*, February 13, 1999, 45–46.

CHAPTER 8

1. For the equivalence of *eidos* and *telos* in Aristotle, see *Physics* 2.8.199a31–32; see also *Physics* 2.7.198a24; *Metaphysics* 8.4.1044a35–1044b1.

2. See Hartmann 1979.

3. http://www.milestonedocuments.com/documents/full-text/stephen-a-douglass -first-speech-of-the-lincoln-douglas-debates/ (retrieved July 28, 2010; brackets in original).

4. As Derrida asks in *The Politics of Friendship* (Derrida 1997): "What politics could still be founded on this friendship which exceeds the measure of man . . . ? Would it still be a politics?" (294). He asks, but does not answer.

5. Douglass, *NFD*, 54–66; see *MO*, 187–189.

6. Among these we may mention Dahlstrom (2008) and Kolb (1991).

7. See Hegel's discussion of the fading of the world into gray on gray in the preface to the *Philosophy of Right* (*PhR*, 23).

8. For the general background in the United States at that time as it affected philosophy, see *TD*, passim.

9. Davidson's inattention to public language can be traced back through his writing to a startling example in his early essay "True to the Facts" (1969). There (as I noted at *CW*, 274), the first example given of a true sentence is "French is the official language

of Mauritius." This is in fact false. English is the official language of Mauritius, though for a long time the island's elite conducted its private affairs and business in French (Davidson 1984, 38).

10. In his *Metacritique on the Purism of Pure Reason*; see Hamann 2007, 205–218.

11. The best introduction in English is Cloeren 1988.

12. Heidegger did not originate this unsavoriness. An earlier example is Fichte's *Addresses to the German Nation* (Fichte 2009), which is largely a recapitulation of the worst features of Herder's linguistic philosophy (for which see Herder 2000, 33–164) and views language as the binding force of a people. Fichte goes beyond Herder in claiming that the better the language, the better the people. His onward course from that point is sadly predictable.

13. Even Brandom implicitly instates truth telling as the basic function of language, when he takes the view that the meaning of a sentence is the set of propositions to whose truth its speaker is committed.

14. Looking to the histories of words in this way is, like civic language itself, foreign to most contemporary philosophy of language; when Wittgenstein, for example, replaces the question of what a word "means" with the question of how it is used, he refers only to the effects it has as a move within a language-game—not to any effects on history itself: Wittgenstein 1958, passim.

15. The word "quark" legendarily was taken from James Joyce's *Finnegans Wake*: "Three quarks for Muster Mark" (Joyce 2000, 383).

16. Similarly for the United States in 1967, when Secretary of Defense Robert McNamara was asked by Congress if we were "winning" the war in Vietnam. He responded by saying that North Vietnam was not getting as many soldiers back as it was sending south. The definition of "victory" on which this traded was, to say the least, bizarre.

17. In the *Phenomenology*'s discussion, the familial roles are husband/wife, mother/father, son/daughter, and sister/brother. In lectures given in 1819–20 on the philosophy of right, Hegel also points out that the gift of oneself to one's spouse cannot be totally free if the two are related by blood, for then it merely confirms an already-shared identity: Hegel 1983, 140.

18. See *PhR*, 207. On this egalitarianism in the context of Hegel's denigration of women, see Williams 1997, 224.

19. This duplicity is not new in Hegel's time; it reflects what Carole Pateman calls "the great contradiction and paradox of slavery: that the master must at once affirm and deny the humanity of the slave" (*SC*, 72). Hegel himself calls attention to this paradox—but only in the case of slavery—at *PhR*, 27.

EPILOGUE

1. See the editor's notes in Hegel 1983, 297–302.

REFERENCES

Alcoff, Linda Martín. 2000. "On Judging Epistemic Reliability: Is Social Identity Relevant?" In *Women of Color and Philosophy*, edited by Naomi Zack, 235–262. Oxford: Blackwell.

Anselm, Saint. 2000. *De veritate*. In *Complete Philosophical and Theological Treatises of Anselm of Canterbury*, translated by Jasper Hopkins and Herbert Richardson, 163–190. Minneapolis: Arthur J. Banning.

Appiah, Kwame Anthony. 2007. *Cosmopolitanism: Ethics in a World of Strangers*. New York: W. W. Norton.

Aquinas, St. Thomas. 1945. *Basic Writings of St. Thomas Aquinas*. Edited by Anton C. Pegis. 2 vols. New York: Random House.

———. 1949. *On Being and Essence*. Translated by Armand Maurer. Toronto: Pontifical Institute of Medieval Studies.

Arendt, Hannah. 1958. *The Human Condition*. Chicago: University of Chicago Press.

———. 1971. "Martin Heidegger at 80." *New York Review of Books*, October 21.

Asante, Molefi. 1987. *The Afrocentric Idea*. Philadelphia: Temple University Press.

Augustine, Saint. 1950. *The City of God*. Translated by Marcus Dodd, DD, et al. New York: Random House.

———. 1954. *Soliloquien*. Edited by Hanspeter Müller. Bern: Benteli.

———. 1988. *Confessions*. Translated by William Watts. 2 vols. Cambridge, MA: Harvard University Press (Loeb Classical Library).

Barnett, Stuart, ed. 1998. *Hegel after Derrida*. London: Routledge.

Beauvoir, Simone de. 1952. *The Second Sex*. Edited and translated by H. M. Parshley. New York: Knopf.

Beierwaltes, Werner. 1965. *Proklos: Grundzüge seiner Metaphysik*. Frankfurt: Klostermann.

Bellow, Saul. 1994. "Papuans and Zulus." Op-ed, *New York Times Book Review*, March 10.

Bernhardt, Jean. 1989. "L'Aristotelisme et la pensée de Hobbes." In *Thomas Hobbes: De la métaphysique à la politique*, edited by Maartin Bertman and Michel Malherbe, 9–15. Paris: Jean Vrin.

Bernstein, Richard J. 2006. *The Abuse of Evil: The Corruption of Politics and Religion since 9/11*. Malden, MA: Polity Press.

Bonitz, Hermann. 1961. *Index Aristotelicus*. Berlin: Walter de Gruyter.

Borradori, Giovanna. 2004. *Philosophy in a Time of Terror*. Chicago: University of Chicago Press.

Bracken, Harry. 1973. "Essence, Accident, and Race." *Hermenathena* 116:81–96.

Brandom, Robert. 1994. *Making It Explicit*. Cambridge, MA: Harvard University Press.

———. 2000. *Articulating Reasons: An Introduction to Inferentialism*. Cambridge, MA: Harvard University Press.

Bryant, Levi, Graham Harman, and Nick Srnicek, eds. 2011. *The Speculative Turn: Continental Materialism and Realism*. Melbourne: re.press.

Butler, Judith. 1990. *Gender Trouble*. London: Routledge.

———. 1997. *Excitable Speech*. London: Routledge.

———. 2006. *Precarious Life*. London: Verso.

Cloeren, Hermann J. 1988. *Language and Thought: German Approaches to Analytic Philosophy in the 18th and 19th Centuries*. Berlin: Walter de Gruyter.

Cohen, Avner, and Marcelo Dascal, eds. 1989. *The Institution of Philosophy: A Discipline in Crisis?* La Salle, IL: Open Court.

Cohen, Ted, and Paul Guyer, eds. 1982. *Essays in Kant's Aesthetics*. Chicago: University of Chicago Press.

Comay, Rebecca. 2011. *Mourning Sickness*. Stanford, CA: Stanford University Press.

Cropper, Carol Marie. 1997. "Philosophers Find the Degree Pays Off in Life and Work." *New York Times*, December 26.

Cudd, Ann E. 2006. *Analyzing Oppression*. Oxford: Oxford University Press.

Dahlstrom, Daniel. 2001. *Heidegger's Concept of Truth*. Cambridge: Cambridge University Press.

———. 2008. *Philosophical Legacies: Essays on the Thought of Kant, Hegel, and Their Contemporaries*. Washington, DC: Catholic University of America Press.

Darwin, Charles. 2008. *On the Origin of Species*. Rev. ed. Edited by Gillian Beer. Oxford: Oxford University Press.

Davidson, Donald. 1984. "True to the Facts." In *Inquiries into Truth and Interpretation*, 43–54. Oxford: Clarendon.

———. 1986. "A Nice Derangement of Epitaphs." In *Truth and Interpretation: Perspectives on the Philosophy of Donald Davidson*, edited by Ernest LePore, 433–446. Oxford: Blackwell.

Deleuze, Gilles. 1984. *Kant's Critical Philosophy*. Translated by Hugh Tomlinson and Barbara Habberjam. Minneapolis: University of Minnesota Press.

———. 1994. *Difference and Repetition*. Translated by Paul Patton. London: Athlone.

Derrida, Jacques. 1973. "Differance." In *Speech and Phenomena*, translated by David B. Allison, 129–159. Evanston, IL: Northwestern University Press.

———. 1974. *Of Grammatology*. Translated by Gayatri Chakravorty Spivak. Baltimore: Johns Hopkins University Press.

———. 1977. "Signature Event Context." *Glyph* 1:172–197.

———. 1978a. "Force and Signification." In Derrida 1978d, 3–30.

———. 1978b. "Structure, Sign and Play in the Discourse of the Human Sciences." In Derrida 1978d, 278–293.

——. 1978c. "Violence and Metaphysics: An Essay on the Thought of Emmanuel Lévinas." In Derrida 1978d, 79–153.

——. 1978d. *Writing and Difference*. Translated by Alan Bass. Chicago: University of Chicago Press.

——. 1981a. *Dissemination*. Translated by Barbara Johnson. Chicago: University of Chicago Press.

——. 1981b. *Positions*. Translated by Alan Bass. Chicago: University of Chicago Press.

——. 1982a. *Margins of Philosophy*. Translated by Alan Bass. Chicago: University of Chicago Press.

——. 1982b. "The Pit and the Pyramid: Introduction to Hegel's Semiology." In Derrida 1982a, 69–108.

——. 1982c. "The Supplement of Copula: Philosophy before Linguistics." In Derrida 1982a, 175–205.

——. 1987. *The Post Card*. Translated by Alan Bass. Chicago: University of Chicago Press.

——. 1989. *Of Spirit: Heidegger and the Question*. Translated by Geoffrey Bennington and Rachel Bowlby. Chicago: University of Chicago Press.

——. 1990. "Heidegger's Silence." In *Martin Heidegger and National Socialism*, edited by Günther Neske and Emil Kettering, 145–148. New York: Paragon House.

——. 1995. *Points*. Edited by Elisabeth Weber. Translated by Peggy Kamuf et al. Stanford, CA: Stanford University Press.

——. 1997. *The Politics of Friendship*. Translated by George Collins. London: Verso.

Descartes, René. 1897–1910. *Oeuvres de Descartes*. Edited by Charles Adam and Paul Tannery. 12 vols. Paris: Cerf.

di Giovanni, George, and H. S. Harris, ed. and trans. 1985. *Between Kant and Hegel*. Albany: SUNY Press.

Douglas, Stephen A. 1858. "Speech." http://www.milestonedocuments.com/documents/full-text/stephen-a-douglass-first-speech-of-the-lincoln-douglas-debates/.

Douglass, Frederick A. 1994. *Narrative of the Life of Frederick Douglass, an American Slave*. In *Autobiographies*, 3–102. New York: Library of America.

Dubois, W. E. B. 1969. *The Souls of Black Folk*. New York: New American Library.

Dussel, Enrique. 2003a. *Beyond Philosophy: Ethics, History, Marxism, and Liberation Theology*. Edited by Eduardo Mendieta. Oxford: Rowman & Littlefield.

——. 2003b. "The 1994 Maya Rebellion in Chiapas." In Dussel 2003a, 167–183.

——. 2003c. "Theology and Economy." In Dussel 2003a, 149–165.

——. 2003d. "The 'World System." In Dussel 2003a, 53–81.

Eze, Emmanuel. 1995. "The Color of Reason: The Idea of 'Race' in Kant's Anthropology." In *Anthropology and the German Enlightenment*, edited by Katherine Faull, 200–241. Lewisburg, PA: Bucknell University Press.

Farber, Marvin. 1943. *The Foundation of Phenomenology*. Albany: SUNY Press.

Farias, Victor. 1991. *Heidegger and Nazism*. Philadelphia: Temple University Press.

Faye, Emmanuel. 2005. *Heidegger, l'introduction du nazisme dans la philosophie*. Paris: Albin Michel.

Felman, Shoshana. 2003. *The Scandal of the Speaking Body*. Stanford, CA: Stanford University Press.

Ferry, Luc, and Alain Renaut. 1990. *French Philosophy of the Sixties*. Translated by Mary H. S. Cattani. Amherst: University of Massachusetts Press.

Fichte, Johann Gottlieb. 2009. *Addresses to the German Nation*. Edited by Gregory Moore. Cambridge: Cambridge University Press.

Fine, Arthur. 1986. *The Shaky Game: Einstein, Realism, and the Quantum Theory*. Chicago: University of Chicago Press.

Fiske, Edward B. 1981. "Analysts Win Battle in War of Philosophy." *New York Times*, January 6.

Fortenbaugh, W. W. 1977. "Aristotle on Slaves and Women." In *Articles on Aristotle*, edited by Jonathan Barnes, Malcolm Schofield, and Richard Sorabji, vol. 4, 135–139. London: Duckworth.

Foucault, Michel. 1972. *The Archeology of Knowledge*. Translated by A. M. Sheridan Smith. New York: Pantheon.

———. 1976. *Histoire de la sexualité*. Vol. 1, *La volonté de savoir*. Paris: Gallimard.

———. 1977. *Language, Counter-Memory, Practice*. Translated by Daniel F. Bouchard and Sherry Simon. Ithaca, NY: Cornell University Press.

———. 1984. "Nietzsche, Genealogy, History." In *The Foucault Reader*, edited by Paul Rabinow, 76–100. New York: Pantheon.

———. 1994. *Dits et écrits*. Edited by Daniel Defort et al. 4 vols. Paris: Gallimard.

Fried, Gregory. 2000. *Heidegger's Polemos: From Being to Politics*. New Haven, CT: Yale University Press.

Friedan, Betty. 2001. *The Feminine Mystique*. New York: W. W. Norton.

Frye, Marilyn. 2005. "Oppression." In *Feminist Theory: A Philosophical Anthology*, edited by Ann E. Cudd and Robin O. Andreasen, 84–90. Oxford: Blackwell.

Gadamer, Hans-Georg. 1989. "Back from Syracuse." *Critical Inquiry* 15:427–430.

Garber, Daniel. 1992. *Descartes' Metaphysical Physics*. Chicago: University of Chicago Press.

Gasché, Rodolphe. 1986. *The Tain of the Mirror*. Cambridge, MA: Harvard University Press.

Gay, Peter. 1977. *The Enlightenment*. Vol. 1, *The Rise of Modern Paganism*. New York: W. W. Norton.

Geuss, Raymond. 1981. *The Idea of a Critical Theory: Habermas and the Frankfurt School*. Cambridge: Cambridge University Press.

———. 1998. "Critical Theory." In *The Routledge Encyclopedia of Philosophy*, edited by Edward Craig, 10 vols., 2:722–728. London: Routledge.

Gill, Mary Louise. 1989. *Aristotle on Substance: The Paradox of Unity*. Princeton, NJ: Princeton University Press.

Gilson, Étienne. 1930. *Études sur le rôle de la pensée médiévale dans la formation du système cartésien*. Paris: Jean Vrin.

———. 1956. *The Christian Philosophy of St. Thomas Aquinas*. Translated by L. K. Shook. New York: Random House.

————. 1979. *Index scolastico-cartésien*. 2nd ed. Paris: Jean Vrin.

Glock, Hans-Johann. 2008. *What Is Analytical Philosophy?* Cambridge: Cambridge University Press.

Goldhaber, Michael H. 2000. "Language as a Public Good under Threat: The Private Ownership of Brand Names." In *In Defense of Public Goods*, edited by Anatole Anton, Milton Fisk, and Nancy Holmstrom, 323–344. Boulder, CO: Westview Press.

Golumbia, David. 1999. "Quine, Derrida, and the Question of Philosophy." *Philosophical Forum* 30:163–186.

Graham, Daniel. 1987. *Aristotle's Two Systems*. Oxford: Clarendon.

Gutting, Gary. 2003. "Thomas Kuhn and French Philosophy of Science." In *Thomas Kuhn*, edited by Thomas Nickles, 45–64. Cambridge: Cambridge University Press.

Guyer, Paul. 1982. "Pleasure and Society in Kant's Theory of Taste." In Cohen and Guyer 1982, 21–54.

Habermas, Jürgen. 1970. "On Systematically Distorted Communication." *Inquiry* 13:205–218.

————. 1971. *Knowledge and Human Interests*. Translated by Jeremy J. Shapiro. Boston: Beacon Press.

————. 1979. "What Is Universal Pragmatics?" In *Communication and the Evolution of Society*, translated by Thomas McCarthy, 1–68. Boston: Beacon Press.

————. 1981. "Modernity vs. Postmodernity." *New German Critique* 22:3–14.

————. 1983. "Modernity: An Incomplete Project." In *The Anti-aesthetic*, edited by Hal Foster, 3–15. Port Townsend, WA: Bay Press.

————. 1984–1987. *The Theory of Communicative Action*. Translated by Thomas McCarthy. 2 vols. Boston: Beacon Press.

————. 1989. "Work and Weltanschauung: The Heidegger Controversy from a German Perspective." *Critical Inquiry* 15:431–456.

————. 1990. *The Philosophical Discourse of Modernity*. Translated by Thomas McCarthy. Cambridge, MA: MIT Press.

————. 1991. *Structural Transformation in the Public Sphere*. Translated by Thomas Burger. Cambridge, MA: MIT Press.

————. 1998. *Between Facts and Norms*. Translated by William Rehg. Cambridge, MA: MIT Press.

Hamann, J. G. 2007. *Writings on Philosophy and Language*. Edited and translated by Kenneth Haynes. Cambridge: Cambridge University Press.

Hardimon, Michael O. 1994. *Hegel's Social Philosophy: The Project of Reconciliation*. Cambridge: Cambridge University Press.

Harding, Sandra. 1986. *The Science Question in Feminism*. Ithaca, NY: Cornell University Press.

————. 2006. *Science and Social Inequality*. Urbana: University of Illinois Press.

Harding, Sandra, and Merrill Hintikka, eds. 1983. *Discovering Reality: Feminist Perspectives in Epistemology, Metaphysics, Methodology and Philosophy of Science*. Dordrecht: D. Reidel.

Haring, Ellen Stone. 1956–57. "Substantial Form in *Metaphysics* Z, II." *Review of Metaphysics* 10:482–501.

Hartmann, Heidi I. 1979. "The Unhappy Marriage of Marxism and Feminism: Towards a More Progressive Union." *Capital & Class* 3; http://cnc.sagepub.com/content/3/2/1 (retrieved June 3, 2011).

Hartmann, Klaus. 1972. "Hegel: A Non-metaphysical View." In *Hegel: A Collection of Critical Essays*, edited by Alasdair MacIntyre, 101–124. Garden City, NY: Anchor Books.

Hatfield, Gary C. 1979. "Force (God) in Descartes' Physics." *Studies in History and Philosophy of Science* 10:130–149.

Hedrick, Todd. 2008. "Race, Difference, and Anthropology in Kant's Cosmopolitanism." *Journal of the History of Philosophy* 46:245–268.

Hegel, G. W. F. 1892. *Lectures on the History of Philosophy*. Translated by E. S. Haldane and Frances H. Simson. 3 vols. London: Routledge & Kegan Paul.

———. 1970a. *Hegel on Art, Religion, and the History of Philosophy*. Edited by J. Glenn Gray. New York: Harper Torchbooks.

———. 1970b. *Philosophy of Nature*. Translated by A. V. Miller. Oxford: Clarendon.

———. 1970–71. *Werke*. Edited by Eva Moldenhauer and Karl Markus Michel. 20 vols. Frankfurt: Suhrkamp.

———. 1971. *Philosophy of Mind*. Translated by A. V. Miller. Oxford: Clarendon.

———. 1975a. *Aesthetics*. Translated by T. M. Knox. 2 vols. (with consecutive pagination). Oxford: Oxford University Press.

———. 1975b. *Hegel's Logic*. Translated by William Wallace. Oxford: Clarendon.

———. 1976. *Science of Logic*. Translated by A. V. Miller. New York: Humanities Press.

———. 1977. *Phenomenology of Spirit*. Translated by A. V. Miller. Oxford: Oxford University Press.

———. 1979. *System of Ethical Life*. Translated by H. S. Harris. Albany: SUNY Press.

———. 1983. *Philosophie des Rechts: Die Vorlesung von 1819/20 in einer Nachschrift*. Edited by Dieter Henrich. Frankfurt am Main: Suhrkamp.

———. 1984. *Lectures on the Philosophy of Religion*. Edited by Peter C. Hodgson. 3 vols. Berkeley: University of California Press.

———. 1985. *Introduction to the Lectures on the History of Philosophy*. Translated by T. M. Knox and A. V. Miller. Oxford: Clarendon.

———. 1991. *Elements of the Philosophy of Right*. Edited by Allen W. Wood. Translated by H. B. Nisbett. Cambridge: Cambridge University Press.

Heidegger, Martin. 1959a. *Gelassenheit*. Pfullingen: Neske.

———. 1959b. *An Introduction to Metaphysics*. Translated by Ralph Manheim. New Haven, CT: Yale University Press.

———. 1960. *Der Ursprung des Kunstwerkes*. Stuttgart: Reclam.

———. 1961. *Nietzsche*. 2 vols. Pfullingen: Neske.

———. 1962. *Being and Time*. Translated by John MacQuarrie and Edward Robinson. New York: Harper & Row.

———. 1968. *What Is Called Thinking?* Translated by Fred D. Wieck and J. Glenn Gray. New York: Harper Torchbooks.

———. 1969. *Zur Sache des Denkens.* Tübingen: Niemeyer.

———. 1971a. "The Nature of Language." In Heidegger 1971b, 57–108.

———. 1971b. *On the Way to Language.* Translated by Peter D. Hertz. New York: Harper & Row.

———. 1971c. "The Origin of the Work of Art." In Heidegger 1971e, 17–87.

———. 1971d. "The Way to Language." In Heidegger 1971b, 111–136.

———. 1971e. *Poetry, Language, Thought.* Translated by Albert Hofstadter. New York: Harper & Row.

———. 1975a. "The Anaximander Fragment." In *Early Greek Thinking,* translated by David Farrell Krell and Frank A. Capuzzi, 13–58. New York: Harper & Row.

———. 1975b. *Grundprobleme der Phänomenologie.* Edited by F. W. von Herrmann. Frankfurt: Klostermann.

———. 1977. "The Question Concerning Technology." In *Basic Writings,* edited by David Farrell Krell, 284–317. San Francisco: Harper & Row.

———. 1983. *Die Selbstbehauptung der deutschen Universität / Das Rektorat: 1933/34.* Frankfurt am Main: Klostermann.

———. 1989. *Beiträge zur Philosophie.* Frankfurt am Main: Klostermann.

———. 1996. *Hölderlin's Hymn "The Ister."* Translated by William McNeill and Julia Davis. Bloomington: Indiana University Press.

———. 1998a. "Hegel and the Greeks." In Heidegger 1998e, 323–336.

———. 1998b. "Letter on 'Humanism.'" In Heidegger 1998e, 239–276.

———. 1998c. "On the Essence and Concept of Φύσις in Aristotle's *Physics* B, 1." In Heidegger 1998e, 183–230.

———. 1998d. "On the Essence of Truth." In Heidegger 1998e, 136–154.

———. 1998e. *Pathmarks.* Edited by William McNeill. Cambridge: Cambridge University Press.

———. 1998f. "Plato's Doctrine of Truth." In Heidegger 1998e, 155–181.

———. 2002a. "The Age of the World Picture." In Heidegger 2002d, 57–85.

———. 2002b. "Hegel's Concept of Experience." In Heidegger 2002d, 86–156.

———. 2002c. "Nietzsche's Word: 'God Is Dead.'" In Heidegger 2002d, 157–199.

———. 2002d. *Off the Beaten Track.* Edited and translated by Julian Young and Kenneth Haynes. Cambridge: Cambridge University Press.

Herder, Johann Gottfried von. 2000. *Philosophical Writings.* Edited and translated by Michael N. Forster. Cambridge: Cambridge University Press.

Herman, Arthur. 2001. *How the Scots Invented the Modern World.* New York: Three Rivers Press.

Hintikka, Jaako. 1981. "On the Common Factors of Dialectic." In *Konzepte der Dialektik,* edited by Werner Becker and Wilhelm Essler, 109–110. Frankfurt: Klostermann.

Hobbes, Thomas. 1991. *Leviathan, or the Matter, Forme, & Power of a Common-Wealth Ecclesiastical and Civill.* Edited by Richard Tuck. Cambridge: Cambridge University Press.

Hoffheimer, Michael H. 2005. "Race and Law in Hegel's Philosophy of Religion." In Valls 2005, 194–216.

Hoyningen-Huene, Paul. 1987. "Context of Discovery and Contest of Justification." *Studies in the History and Philosophy of Science* 18:501–515.

Hume, David. 1894. *Enquiry Concerning Human Understanding*. In *Enquiries*, edited by L. A. Selby-Bigge. Oxford: Clarendon.

———. 1896. *A Treatise of Human Nature*. Edited by L. A. Selby-Bigge. Oxford: Clarendon.

Husserl, Edmund. 1960. *Cartesian Meditations*. Translated by Dorion Cairns. The Hague: Martinus Nijhoff.

———. 1970. *Logical Investigations*. Translated by J. N. Findlay. 2 vols. (with consecutive pagination). London: Routledge & Kegan Paul.

Joyce, James. 2000. *Finnegans Wake*. London: Penguin Classics.

Kant, Immanuel. 1902–. *Werke*. 28 vols. Berlin: Berlin Academy.

———. 1967. *Philosophical Correspondence, 1759–99*. Edited and translated by Arnulf Zweig. Chicago: University of Chicago Press.

Kierkegaard, Søren. 1941. *Concluding Unscientific Postscript*. Translated by David F. Swenson. Princeton, NJ: Princeton University Press.

———. 1964. *Repetition: An Essay in Experimental Psychology*. Translated by Walter Lowrie. New York: Harper & Row.

Kirk, G. S., and J. E. Raven. 1960. *The Presocratic Philosophers*. Cambridge: Cambridge University Press.

Kirsch, Adam. 2010. "The Jewish Question: Martin Heidegger." *New York Times Book Review*, April 29.

Knobe, Joshua, and Shaun Nichols, eds. 2008. *Experimental Philosophy*. Oxford: Oxford University Press.

Kockelmans, Joseph. 1984. *On the Truth of Being*. Bloomington: Indiana University Press.

Kolb, David. 1991. *The Critique of Pure Modernity: Hegel, Heidegger, and After*. Chicago: University of Chicago Press.

Kripke, Saul. 1980. *Naming and Necessity*. Cambridge, MA: Harvard University Press, 1980.

Latour, Bruno. 1993. *We Have Never Been Modern*. Translated by Catherine Porter. Cambridge, MA: Harvard University Press.

Lawlor, Leonard. 2002. *Derrida and Husserl: The Basic Problem of Phenomenology*. Bloomington: Indiana University Press.

Leibniz, Gottfried Wilhelm. 1969. *Philosophical Papers and Letters*. Edited by Leroy E. Loemker. 2nd ed. Dordrecht: Reidel.

Leiter, Brian. *Leiter Reports: A Philosophy Blog*. http://leiterreports.typepad.com/blog.

Levin, David Michael, ed. 1993. *Modernity and the Hegemony of Vision*. Berkeley: University of California Press.

Lincoln, Abraham. 1858. "The House Divided Speech." http://showcase.netins.net/web/creative/lincoln/speeches/house.htm.

Lloyd, Genevieve. 1984. *The Man of Reason*. London: Methuen.

Löwith, Karl. 1986. *Mein Leben in Deutschland vor und nach 1933.* Stuttgart: J. B. Metzler.

Lyotard, Jean-François. 1984. *The Postmodern Condition.* Translated by Geoff Bennington and Brian Massumi. Minneapolis: University of Minnesota Press.

———. 1985. *Just Gaming.* Translated by Wlad Godzich. Minneapolis: University of Minnesota Press.

MacIntyre, Alasdair, ed. 1967. *Hegel: A Collection of Critical Essays.* Garden City, NY: Anchor Books.

———. 1984. *After Virtue.* 2nd ed. Notre Dame, IN: University of Notre Dame Press.

Makkreel, Rudolf. 1990. *Imagination and Interpretation in Kant.* Chicago: University of Chicago Press.

Mandt, A. J. 1989. "The Inevitability of Pluralism: Philosophical Practice and Philosophical Excellence." In Cohen and Dascal 1989, 77–101.

Margolis, Joseph. 2005. *Moral Philosophy after 9 /11.* University Park: Penn State University Press.

Marsh, James L. 2000. "How Critical Is Critical Theory?" In *Perspectives on Habermas,* edited by Lewis E. Hahn, 555–568. Peru, IL: Open Court.

Marx, Karl. 1906. *Capital.* Translated by Samuel Morse and Edward Aveling. New York: Modern Library.

———. 1988. "The Communist Manifesto." In *Economic and Philosophic Manuscripts of 1844,* translated by Martin Milligan. Amherst, NY: Prometheus Books.

McCumber, John. 1984. "Hegel's Anarchistic Utopia: The Politics of his *Aesthetics.*" *Southern Journal of Philosophy* 22:203–210.

———. 1988. "Aristotelian Catharsis and the Purgation of Woman." *diacritics* 18(4): 53–67.

———. 1989. *Poetic Interaction.* Chicago: University of Chicago Press.

———. 1993. *The Company of Words: Hegel, Language, and Systematic Philosophy.* Evanston, IL: Northwestern University Press.

———. 1998. "Possibilities of Postmodernity: Foucault and Fackenheim." In *Postmodernism and the Holocaust,* edited by Alan Milchman and Alan Rosenberg, 239–264. Amsterdam: Rodopi.

———. 1999. *Metaphysics and Oppression.* Bloomington: Indiana University Press.

———. 2000a. *Philosophy and Freedom.* Bloomington: Indiana University Press.

———. 2000b. "Writing Down (Up) the Truth: Hegel and Schiller at the End of the *Phenomenology of Spirit.*" In *The Spirit of Poesy: Essays on Jewish and German Literature and Thought in Honor of Géza von Molnár,* edited by Richard Block and Peter Fenves, 47–59. Evanston, IL: Northwestern University Press.

———. 2001. *Time in the Ditch.* Evanston, IL: Northwestern University Press.

———. 2002. "Making Kant Empirical: The Temporal Turn in German Idealism." *Research in Phenomenology* 32:44–59.

———. 2005. *Reshaping Reason.* Bloomington: Indiana University Press.

———. 2011. *Time and Philosophy: A History of Continental Thought.* Durham, UK: Acumen.

McIntyre, Jane. 1990. "Character: A Humean Account." *History of Philosophy Quarterly* 7:193–206.

McTaggart, John Ellis. 1993. "The Unreality of Time." In *The Philosophy of Time*, edited by Robin Le Poidevin and Murray Macbeath, 23–34. Oxford: Oxford University Press.

Meerbote, Ralf. 1982. "Reflections on Beauty." In Cohen and Guyer 1982, 55–86.

Meillassoux, Quentin, Alain Badiou, and Ray Brassier. 2010. *After Finitude: An Essay on the Necessity of Contingency*. London: Continuum.

Meyer, Thomas. 2005. "Denker für Hitler?" *Die Zeit*, July 21.

Mills, Charles. 1997. *The Racial Contract*. Ithaca, NY: Cornell University Press.

———. 1998. *Blackness Visible*. Ithaca, NY: Cornell University Press.

Morrow, Glenn R. 1923. "The Significance of the Doctrine of Sympathy in Hume and Adam Smith." *Philosophical Review* 32:60–78.

Moutsopoulos, Evanghelos A. 1982. "The Idea of False in Proclus." In *The Structure of Being: A Neoplatonic Approach*, edited by R. Baine Harris, 137–139. Albany: SUNY Press.

Mure, G. R. G. 1940. *An Introduction to Hegel*. Oxford: Clarendon.

Murphy, Franklin D. 1976. "My UCLA Chancellorship: An Utterly Candid View." Interview with James V. Mink. Berkeley: The Regents of the University of California.

Nealon, Jeffrey. 2008. *Foucault beyond Foucault: Power and Its Intensification since 1984*. Stanford, CA: Stanford University Press.

Needham, Joseph. 1969. *The Grand Titration: Science and Society in East and West*. Toronto: University of Toronto Press.

Nietzsche, Friedrich. 1986. *Human, All Too Human: A Book for Free Spirits*. Translated by R. J. Hollingdale. Cambridge: Cambridge University Press.

———. 1994. *On the Genealogy of Morality*. Edited by Keith Ansell Pearson. Cambridge: Cambridge University Press.

Nygren, Anders. 1982. *Agape and Eros*. Translated by Philip S. Watson. Chicago: University of Chicago Press.

Okin, Susan Moller. 1979. *Women in Western Political Thought*. Princeton, NJ: Princeton University Press.

Outlaw, Lucius. 1996a. "African Philosophy." In Outlaw 1996d, 51–73.

———. 1996b. "Africology." In Outlaw 1996d, 97–134.

———. 1996c. "Against the Grain of Modernity." In Outlaw 1996d, 135–157.

———. 1996d. *On Race and Philosophy*. London: Routledge.

———. 1996e. "Racial Life-Worlds and Social Theory." In Outlaw 1996d, 159–182.

Pateman, Carole. 1988. *The Sexual Contract*. Stanford, CA: Stanford University Press.

Piercey, Robert. 2009. *The Crisis in Continental Philosophy*. London: Continuum.

Pillow, Kirk. 2000. *Sublime Understanding*. Boston: MIT Press.

———. 2002. "Hegel and Homosexuality." *Philosophy Today* 46:75–91.

Pinkard, Terry. 1988. *Hegel's Dialectic*. Philadelphia: Temple University Press.

———. 2000. *Hegel: A Biography*. Cambridge: Cambridge University Press.

Pippin, Robert B. 1989. *Hegel's Idealism*. Cambridge: Cambridge University Press.

———. 1991. *Modernism as a Philosophical Problem*. London: Blackwell.

———. 1997. *Idealism as Modernism*. Cambridge: Cambridge University Press.

Pöggeler, Otto. 1985. "Den Führer führen: Heidegger und kein Ende." *Philosophische Rundschau* 32:26–67.

———. 1988. "Heideggers politische Selbstverständnis." In *Heidegger und die praktische Philosophie*, edited by Otto Pöggeler and Annemarie Gethmann-Siefert, 17–63. Frankfurt: Suhrkamp.

Popper, Karl. 1965. "What Is Dialectic?" In *Conjectures and Refutations*, 312–335. New York: Basic Books.

———. 2002. *The Logic of Scientific Discovery*. London: Routledge Classics.

Prauss, Gerold. 1983. "Frege's Contribution to the Theory of Knowledge." *Contemporary German Philosophy* 3:27–50.

Quine, W. V. O. 1953a. *From a Logical Point of View*. New York: Harper Torchbooks.

———. 1953b. "Two Dogmas of Empiricism." In Quine 1953a, 20–46.

———. 1959. *Methods of Logic*. 2nd ed. Cambridge, MA: Harvard University Press.

———. 1960. *Word and Object*. Boston: MIT Press.

———. 1969a. *Ontological Relativity and Other Essays*. New York: Columbia University Press.

———. 1969b. "Speaking of Objects." In Quine 1969a, 1–25.

———. 1987. *Quiddities*. Cambridge, MA: Harvard University Press.

———. 1990. *Pursuit of Truth*. Cambridge, MA: Harvard University Press.

Rabinow, Paul, ed. 1984. *The Foucault Reader*. New York: Pantheon.

Reichenbach, Hans. 1938. *Experience and Prediction*. Chicago: University of Chicago Press.

———. 1951. *The Rise of Scientific Philosophy*. Berkeley and Los Angeles: University of California Press.

Reiss, Timothy J. 2005. "Descartes' Silence on Slavery and Race." In Valls 2005, 16–42.

Rockmore, Tom. 1986. *Hegel's Circular Epistemology*. Bloomington: Indiana University Press.

Rockmore, Tom, Joseph Margolis, and Armen T. Marsoobian, eds. 2005. *The Philosophical Challenges of September 11*. London: Wiley-Blackwell.

Rorty, Richard. 1967. *The Linguistic Turn*. Chicago: University of Chicago Press.

———. 1982. "Philosophy in America Today." In *Consequences of Pragmatism*, 211–232. Minneapolis: University of Minnesota Press.

———. 1991. "Is Derrida a Transcendental Philosopher?" In *Essays on Heidegger and Others*, 119–128. Cambridge: Cambridge University Press.

Rousseau, Jean-Jacques. 1987. "Discourse on the Origin of Inequality." In *Basic Political Writings*, translated by Donald Cress, 55–109. Indianapolis: Hackett.

Russell, Bertrand. 1992. *A Critical Exposition of the Philosophy of Leibniz*. London: Routledge.

Ryle, Gilbert. 1978. "Heidegger's *Sein und Zeit*." In *Heidegger and Modern Philosophy*, edited by Michael Murray, 53–64. New Haven, CT: Yale University Press.

Saner, Hans. 1973. *Kant's Political Thought*. Translated by E. B. Ashton. Chicago: University of Chicago Press.

Sappho. 1938. "To a Bride." Translated by Walter Headlam. In *The Oxford Book of Greek Verse in Translation*, edited by T. F. Higham and C. M. Bowra, 206. Oxford: Clarendon.

Sargent, Rose-Mary. 1997. "The Social Construction of Scientific Evidence." *Journal of Constructivist Psychology* 10:75–96.

Sartre, Jean-Paul. 2001. "Existentialism and Humanism." In *Basic Writings*, edited by Stephen Priest, 25–57. London: Routledge.

Schiller, Friedrich. 1982. *On the Aesthetic Education of Man in a Series of Letters*. Translated and edited by Elizabeth M. Willoughby and M. A. Wilkinson [English and German texts facing]. Oxford: Oxford University Press.

Schouls, Peter. 1994. "Human Nature, Reason, and Will." In *Reason, Will, and Sensation: Studies in Descartes' Metaphysics*, edited by John Cottingham, 159–176. Oxford: Oxford University Press.

Schröder, Hannelor. 1997. "Kant's Patriarchal Order." Translated by Rita Gircour. In *Feminist Interpretations of Immanuel Kant*, edited by Robin Schott, 275–296. University Park: Penn State University Press.

Schürmann, Reiner. 1985. "De la philosophie aux États Unis." *Le temps de la réflexion* 6:303–321.

Searle, John. 1983. *Intentionality*. Cambridge: Cambridge University Press.

Shankland, R. S. 1964. "Michelson-Morley Experiment." *American Journal of Physics* 32:16–35.

Shapin, Steven, and Simon Schaffer. 1985. *Leviathan and the Air Pump*. Princeton, NJ: Princeton University Press.

Sheffler, Israel. 1982. *Science and Subjectivity*. Indianapolis: Hackett.

Shermer, Michael. 2010. "When Scientists Sin." *Scientific American* (July). http://www.scientificamerican.com/article.cfm?id=when-scientists-sin.

Sluga, Hans. 1993. *Heidegger's Crisis*. Cambridge, MA: Harvard University Press.

Smith, Adam. 2000. *Theory of Moral Sentiments*. Amherst, NY: Prometheus Books.

Soames, Scott. 2003. *Philosophical Analysis in the Twentieth Century*. 2 vols. Princeton, NJ: Princeton University Press.

Sophocles. 1902. *The Antigone of Sophocles*. Edited by Richard C. Jebb and E. S. Shuckburgh. Cambridge: Cambridge University Press.

Spinoza, Benedict de. 1985. *The Collected Works of Spinoza*. Edited and translated by Edwin Curley. Princeton, NJ: Princeton University Press.

Stanley, Jason. 2010. "The Crisis of Philosophy." *Inside Higher Ed*. http://www.insidehigher ed.com/views/2010/04/05/stanley.

Strawson, P. F. 1979. "Take the B Train." *New York Review of Books*, April 19.

Ströker, Elisabeth. 1993. *Husserl's Transcendental Phenomenology*. Stanford, CA: Stanford University Press.

Tarski, Alfred. 1943–44. "The Semantic Conception of Truth." *Philosophy and Phenomenological Research* 4:341–376.

Taylor, Charles. 1979. *Hegel and Modern Society*. Cambridge: Cambridge University Press.

———. 1994. "The Politics of Recognition." In *Multiculturalism and the Politics of Recognition*, edited by Amy Gutmann, 25–73. Princeton, NJ: Princeton University Press.

Toulmin, Stephen, and Allan Janik. 1973. *Wittgenstein's Vienna*. New York: Simon & Schuster.

Valls, Andrew, ed. 2005. *Race and Racism in Modern Philosophy*. Ithaca, NY: Cornell University Press.

Wallace, David Foster. 1997. "E Unibus Pluram: Television and U.S. Fiction." In *A Supposedly Fun Thing I'll Never Do Again*, 21–82. New York: Little, Brown.

———. 2006. *Infinite Jest*. New York: Little, Brown.

———. n.d. Interview with Larry McCaffery. http://www.dalkeyarchive.com/book/?fa=customcontent&GCOI=15647100621780&extrasfile=A09F8296-B0D0-B086-B6A350F4F59FD1F7.html (retrieved March 27, 2012).

Walton, D. N. 1995. *A Pragmatic Theory of Fallacy*. Tuscaloosa: University of Alabama Press.

Wielenberg, Eric. 2006. "My Turn: I Think, Therefore I Am." *Newsweek*, October 16. http://www.msnbc.msn.com/id/15173080/site/newsweek/.

———. Web page. http://dpuadweb.depauw.edu/ewielenberg_web/.

Wiley, Thomas. 1987. *Back to Kant: The Revival of Kant in German Social and Historical Thought 1869–1924*. Detroit, MI: Wayne State University Press.

Willett, Cynthia. 1995. *Maternal Ethics and Other Slave Moralities*. New York: Routledge.

Williams, Bernard. 2006. *My Sense of the Past: Essays in the History of Philosophy*. Edited by Miles Burnyeat. Princeton, NJ: Princeton University Press.

Williams, Robert R. 1997. *Hegel's Ethics of Recognition*. Berkeley: University of California Press.

Wills, Garry. 2004. "The Day the Enlightenment Went Out." Op-ed, *New York Times*, November 4.

Witt, Charlotte. 1989. *Substance and Essence in Aristotle*. Ithaca, NY: Cornell University Press.

Wittgenstein, Ludwig. 1958. *Philosophical Investigations*. Translated by G. E. M. Anscombe. 3rd ed. New York: Macmillan.

Wolin, Richard. 1990. *The Politics of Being*. New York: Columbia University Press.

Wood, Allen W. 1990. *Hegel's Ethical Thought*. Cambridge: Cambridge University Press.

Young, Iris Marion. 1990a. "Five Faces of Oppression." In Young 1990b, 39–65.

———. 1990b. *Justice and the Politics of Difference*. Princeton, NJ: Princeton University Press.

INDEX